Active Private Equity Real Estate Strategy

The Frank J. Fabozzi Series

Active Private Equity Real Estate Strategy

DAVID J. LYNN, Ph.D.
with
TIM WANG, Ph.D.
MATSON HOLBROOK
BOHDY HEDGCOCK
JEFF ORGANISCIAK
ALISON SAUER
and
YUSHENG HAO

ING Clarion, New York

WILEY
John Wiley & Sons, Inc.

For general information on our other products and services or for technical support, please contact our Customer Care Department within the United States at (800) 762-2974, outside the United States at (317) 572-3993 or fax (317) 572-4002.

Wiley also publishes its books in a variety of electronic formats. Some content that appears in print may not be available in electronic formats. For more information about Wiley products, visit our Web site at www.wiley.com.

Library of Congress Cataloging-in-Publication Data:

Active private equity real estate strategy / David J. Lynn [et al.].
    p. cm.—(The Frank J. Fabozzi series)
    Includes index.
    ISBN 978-0-470-48502-6 (cloth)
    1. Real estate investment—United States.   2. Commercial real estate—United States.
3. Residential real estate—United States.   4. Private equity.   I. Lynn, David J.
    HD255.A58 2009
    332.63′240973–dc22   2009014326

ISBN: 978-0-470-48502-6

Printed in the United States of America

10 9 8 7 6 5 4 3 2 1

Contents

Preface

Active Private Equity Real Estate Strategy is a collection of abridged market analyses, forecasts, and strategy papers from ING Clarion's Research & Investment Strategy (RIS) group. ING Clarion is the U.S. arm of ING Real Estate, a global organization with offices in 22 countries and expertise in the development, financing, and investment management of quality real estate. In the United States, the company has employees in major markets who specialize in assembling and managing portfolios of real estate assets for institutional and individual investors.

We have written this book with a focus on the United States and from the perspective of the active manager of institutional assets, separate accounts, and private investors. Plan sponsors, consultants, broker-dealers, traders, and data providers may also find this book of interest.

This book demonstrates the use of a range of tools available to the private equity real estate investor, including scenario analysis, econometric forecasting, modern portfolio theory, macroeconomic projections, empirical research, and strategy formulation. It is not meant to be a comprehensive approach to strategy formulation for the real estate industry, but instead illustrates a cross section of private equity strategies across the various property types. Technical appendexes are provided for those who wish to delve further into the methodological underpinnings of the work.

We define strategy as *a coherent, structured, and integrative pattern of decisions formulated as a means of investing in markets and assets to achieve above-average financial returns.*

Our approach to strategy embodies three basic steps. The first step is to understand and establish clear goals and objectives. In strategic planning parlance, this is often referred to as the *mission* or *mission statement*. Working at both the corporate headquarters level and the regional business unit level, we formulate goals and objectives that are critical, measurable, fulfill our minimum profit targets, and are achievable.

The second step is to understand the market (both the macroeconomic environment and real estate markets). This is known as the *situation audit*. Changes in the external environment often present new opportunities and new strategies to reach return objectives. We also take into account the firm's capabilities, core strengths, and limitations in order to select the opportunities with the greatest potential. This step, therefore, involves both the external and internal environments. The external environment encompasses two dimensions: the macroeconomic environment and the markets. The macroeconomic environment includes political, economic, social, and technological factors. This is also referred to as a "top-down" approach. "Industry factors," owing to Michael Porter's five forces framework, are often considered.[1] These include barriers to entry, customers, suppliers, products, and competition. The real estate market analysis is fundamental and includes factors such as supply, demand, vacancy, rent levels and growth/decline, comparable properties, and forecasts of many of these factors at the national, regional, and metropolitan statistical area (MSA) levels. This may involve analysis of individual deals and comparable properties. This is often referred to as a "bottom-up" approach. The internal audit (often implicitly integrated but not explicitly explicated in our strategies) may involve factors such as the company culture, core competencies, organizational structure, access to capital, experience, reputation, operational efficiency, market share, relationships, and geographic resource location. Sometimes a strengths, weaknesses, opportunities, and threats (SWOT) analysis is a part of this phase of strategy development.

The third step is strategy formulation. Once a clear picture of the market is in hand, specific strategies, alternatives, and scenarios can be developed. While different firms have different alternatives depending on their particular situations, there are generic strategies in commercial real estate investing which are typically employed when defining strategic alternatives. These generic strategies are core, value-add, and opportunistic investing. The strategies presented in this book span the range. The strategies are expressed in both high-level conceptual terms, as well as pragmatic detailed tactics that can be understood at the functional/business unit level of the organization.

The chapters that make up this book were drafted over a period of 12 months, beginning in summer 2007. In some cases, they reflect an evolution of thinking on subjects, as demanded by the changing macroeconomic and market conditions of a particularly dynamic period.

There are two parts of the book. Part One provides an overall context discussion of real estate markets, forecasts, and recent trends. This section presents our view during that time period on the national and major urban area markets as well as our analysis of each real estate property type (sector).

---

[1]M. E. Porter, "How Competitive Forces Shape Strategy," *Harvard Business Review* 57, no. 2 (March–April 1979): 135–145.

It illustrates techniques of market analysis and forecasting, which set the stage for detailed strategy development later on. Given the highly dynamic period during which these chapters were written, the analysis includes a simulation of the economy in recession and the expected effects on the commercial real estate industry.

Part Two of the book presents specific active strategies in private equity real estate investing around the United States. Each of these studies was developed to identify and analyze real investment opportunities. They focus on multifamily, hotel, land, and industrial investment, along with three niche plays: derivatives, seniors housing, and infrastructure. We also include an example of the application of Modern Portfolio Theory to a hypothetical core real estate portfolio.

DAVID J. LYNN, PH.D.
New York City, New York
December 2008

Disclaimer

This publication is not investment advice or an offer or solicitation for the purchase or sale of any financial instrument. While reasonable care has been taken to ensure that the information contained herein is not untrue or misleading at the time of publication, ING makes no representation that it is accurate or complete. The assumptions used in making forecasts rely on a number of economic and financial variables. These variables are subject to change and may affect the likely outcome of the forecasts. The information contained herein is subject to change without notice. ING and any of its officers or employees may, to the extent permitted by law, have a position or otherwise be interested in any transactions, in any investments (including derivatives) referred to in this publication. ING may provide banking or other services (including acting as adviser, manager, lender, or liquidity provider) for, or solicit banking or other business from, any company referred to in this publication. Neither ING nor any of its officers or employees accepts any liability for any direct or consequential loss arising from any use of this publication or its contents. Copyright and database rights protection exists in this publication and it may not be reproduced, distributed, or published by any person for any purpose without the prior express consent of ING (and further, Wiley). All rights are reserved. Any investments referred to herein may involve significant risk, are not necessarily available in all jurisdictions, may be illiquid, and may not be suitable for all investors. The value of, or income from, any investments referred to herein may fluctuate and/or be affected by changes in exchange rates. Past performance is not indicative of future results. Investors should make their own investment decisions without relying on this publication. Only investors with sufficient knowledge and experience in financial matters to evaluate the merits and risks should consider an investment in any issuer or market discussed herein and other persons should not take any action on the basis of this publication. Additional information is available on request. At the date hereof, the authors, and/or the ING Group may be buying, selling, or holding significant long or short positions; acting as investment and/or commercial bankers; be represented on the board of the issuer; and/or engaging in market making in securities mentioned herein.

Acknowledgments

This book is a product of efforts of the Research & Investment Strategy (RIS) group at ING Clarion. The work was performed for our internal use, clients, trade and academic publications, and for new product and market development. While the authors listed were primarily responsible for the individual chapters, this undertaking was truly a collaborative effort and involved all members of the RIS team including Tim Wang, Ph.D., Matson Holbrook, Bohdy Hedgcock, Jeff Organisciak, Alison Sauer, and Yusheng Hao.

We draw regularly on the significant skills and experience of our colleagues across the firm, including Stephen J. Furnary; Jeffrey Barclay; C. Stephen Cordes; Douglas Bowen; William Krauch; Stephen Latimer; Frank Sullivan, Jr.; Stephen Hansen; Patrick Tully, Jr.; Craig Tagen; James Hendricks; Charles R. Lathem; Bruce G. Morrison; Stephen Spey; Robert Greer; Scott Harris; Jeb Belford; Edward Carey; Dean Rostovsky; David Confer; and Jeffrey Peshut.

We are also indebted to Jeremy Sumpter for his graphics and information research; Hannah Spencer and Sanela Ramovic for their editorial and administrative assistance; Suzanne Franks and the Marketing department for their keen insights; Nathaniel Kiernan and Michelle Gibbons for their thorough review; and the many other professionals at ING Clarion. Any inadvertent errors or omissions contained herein are entirely the fault of the authors.

Finally, we appreciate the cooperation of *Real Estate Issues* and *Commercial Investment Real Estate* in allowing works that were originally published elsewhere to be included in this collection.

About the Authors

David J. Lynn, PhD, MBA, MS, MA, CRE

Dr. David Lynn is an institutional real estate investor, strategist, and portfolio manager with extensive experience in national and international markets. At ING Clarion Partners, he is Managing Director and Head of the Research and Investment Strategy Group. In this capacity, he directs investment strategy for the firm's private equity platform. He is a member of the Investment and Operating Committees, reviewing, recommending, and voting on all investment transactions of the firm. Dr. Lynn serves as an advisor for portfolio management of several of the largest core, value-added and opportunistic funds, including many large separate accounts. He advises on investment strategies (core, value add, opportunistic, niche plays), asset selection, portfolio analytics, market targeting, econometric forecasting, and market entry and exit. He assists the firm's fund and product development initiatives. He directs real estate and economic market forecasts and formulates detailed investment recommendations for 50 major metros and hundreds of associated submarkets. His group provides real-time market intelligence for the U.S. and global markets. He also participates in numerous client presentations and consultations.

He has published widely on the subjects of real estate investment, development, economics, and land use. He is a noted market commentator on national and international real estate investment and is regularly mentioned and quoted in the media. Dr. Lynn has written over 15 articles, one book, and founded an academic journal. He has delivered presentations and papers at national and international professional conferences and meetings.

Dr. Lynn earned his PhD in Financial Economics at the London School of Economics, where he also earned a Master of Science specializing in Finance. His doctoral research focused on financial distress in emerging market countries. He earned an MBA as a Sloan Fellow from the Sloan School of Management, MIT, where he specialized in Finance and Real Estate. He earned a Masters in City and Regional Planning with an emphasis in Real Estate from Cornell University. His thesis research explored the application of strategic planning to the real estate industry. He earned a BA in Architecture from the University of California at Berkeley. He is a Counselor of

Real Estate (CRE), a Certified Portfolio and Investment Manager (CPIM), a Chartered Management Analyst (CMA), a Homer Hoyt Fellow, an ISO 9000 Certified Auditor and a Certified Planner (AICP). He is a member of the American Real Estate Society (ARES), National Council of Real Estate Investment Fiduciaries (NCREIF), National Association for Business Economics (NABE), International Council of Shopping Centers (ICSC), Pension Real Estate Association (PREA), and the Urban Land Institute (ULI) (full member). He serves on the Editorial Board of the Counselors of Real Estate and the Advisory Board of PREA.

Tim Wang, PhD, Head of Macroeconomic Analysis and Strategy
Tim holds an MBA from New York University and a PhD from the University of Georgia. At ING Clarion, Tim concentrates on macroeconomics, investment strategy, market forecasts, asset allocation, and client services.

Matson Holbrook, Senior Associate
Matson holds an MS in Real Estate from New York University and a BS in Cartography and Geographic Information Systems (GIS) from the University of Wisconsin. Matson supports strategy development through market research and publications.

Bohdy Hedgcock, Associate
Bohdy holds a Masters in Urban Planning from the University of Colorado. Bohdy concentrates on both bottom-up and top-down analysis of economic, demographic, and market trends.

Jeff Organisciak, Senior Analyst
Jeff graduated from the University of Pennsylvania with a BA in Economics and Political Science. Jeff works primarily on fundamental U.S. market analysis and forecasting.

Alison Sauer, Analyst
Alison is a graduate of Tufts University where she earned a BS in Mathematics. At ING Clarion, she specializes in U.S. strategy, providing both bottom-up and top-down analyses of market trends.

Yusheng Hao, Analyst
Yusheng specializes in econometric modeling and risk management. He holds an MS in Financial Engineering from Baruch College, City University of New York.

Market Analysis and Forecasts

- "Overview of the U.S. Real Estate Market" analyzes the national and major metro markets, both in terms of macroeconomic fundamentals and real estate market drivers such as supply, demand, rent levels, and vacancies.
- "Forecasting the U.S. Market" projects real estate market fundamentals for major metros around the country. We forecast the NCREIF index based on our proprietary models using data from leading data and information providers.
- "Recession Simulation and Its Effects on Real Estate" analyzes the effects of two different types of economic downturns on property markets: a short and shallow downturn and a severe prolonged recession. This is scenario planning writ large with detailed simulations down to the property sector and metro level.
- "Subprime Fallout: The Impact on Commercial Real Estate" addresses the shock to the economy and investigates ramifications to the commercial real estate industry.
- "Capital Markets: Dramatic Shifts and Opportunities" assesses the current seizure in capital markets and the real and possible effects on commercial real estate. It looks at the challenges of reduced capital and also the potential opportunities created in the process.

- "The Bid-Ask Problem and Game Theory" assesses the dramatic fall in transaction volume since the beginning of the subprime fallout and the yawning gap between sellers and buyers. It utilizes a game-theoretic model to explain how this has occurred and how transactional liquidity may resume.

CHAPTER 1

Overview of the U.S. Real Estate Market

Tim Wang and David Lynn
Spring 2008[1]

A major transition for U.S. commercial real estate occurred in 2007. Triggered by the subprime fallout and credit crisis, the outsized investment returns of the past several years came to an end. With tightening lending and underwriting standards, speculative investments and construction projects are likely to be more limited, resulting in more constrained supply and healthier fundamentals over the long term. Looking forward, we anticipate that 2008 and 2009 will be fraught with challenges as well as opportunities.

OUTLOOK FOR U.S. ECONOMY: NEAR-TERM SLOWDOWN

The U.S. economy is going through a slowdown, if not a recession, as a result of the subprime fallout and residential housing market downturn. Real gross domestic product (GDP) growth declined from 4.9% in the third quarter to 0.6% in the fourth quarter of 2007.[2] Job growth, turning

---

[1] This paper was originally produced in spring 2008. The data, opinions, and forecasts have not been updated for book publication.

[2] U.S. Department of Commerce, Bureau of Economic Analysis—National Economic Accounts, "Gross Domestic Product: Fourth Quarter 2007 (Final)," http://www.bea .gov/newsreleases/national/gdp/2008/gdp407f.htm (accessed March 27, 2008).

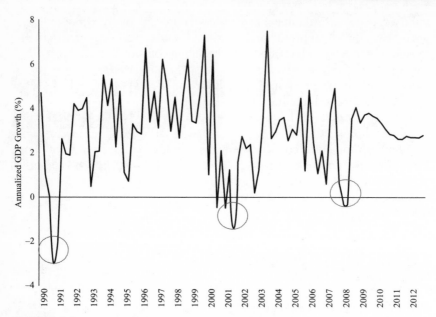

EXHIBIT 1.1   Consumer Spending: Annualized GDP
Source: ING Clarion Research & Investment Strategy and Moody's Economy.com,
as of January 2008.

slightly negative in the first two months of 2008, has been decelerating since
mid-2007 and is likely to be sluggish through year-end. In 2007, 1.1 million
new jobs were created, compared to 2.1 million new jobs created in 2006.[3]
The 2007 year-end unemployment rate rose to 5.0% according to the Bureau of Labor Statistics, the highest level since 2005. While government
and corporate spending remain solid, personal consumption is beginning to
show weakness. Lackluster consumer spending could possibly lead to a mild
recession in early 2008 (Exhibit 1.1).

The credit crunch and housing market downturn are the biggest risks
to U.S. and global economic growth. The largely stalled credit pipeline and
financing activities have severely curtailed investment and M&A projects.
The for-sale housing market continues to soften due to tightening lending

---

[3]U.S. Department of Labor: Bureau of Labor Statistics, "Employment, Hours, and
Earnings from the Current Employment Statistics Survey (National)," http://www
.bls.gov/ces/ (accessed March 21, 2008).

standards, low affordability, and excess supply in many regions. Home prices have fallen approximately 10% year-over-year in most markets, causing negative wealth effects and weakening consumer spending power.[4] Some potential buyers—even those with strong credit—are holding off on purchases, waiting for even bigger discounts. We expect that the housing market will not reach the bottom until 2009.

Recently, crude oil has exceeded $100 per barrel and retail gasoline prices remain elevated at over $3 per gallon, another drag on consumer spending. Although the core consumer price index (CPI) is running at about 2.5% annually, surging energy and commodity prices and the declining value of the U.S. dollar are adding inflationary pressures.[5] A rising inflation rate could lead to higher interest rates thereby decreasing demand for commercial real estate.

U.S. REAL ESTATE: FINDING VALUE IN A CHANGING MARKET

U.S. Real Estate Fundamentals

U.S. commercial real estate fundamentals are generally sound with solid rent growth, albeit at a slower pace than in recent years, and stabilizing vacancy rates in most core markets. Within the next several months, demand for space is expected to soften, along with the slowing U.S. economy, before reaccelerating in 2010–2011. In 2008, vacancy rates have risen moderately. Rent growth is expected to remain positive during the economic slowdown, but will increase at a slower pace.

On the supply side, construction pipeline forecasts across all property types are below their long-term averages (Exhibit 1.2). Higher construction costs and more stringent local entitlement processes have restrained the supply pipelines. Although construction activity has picked up, demand is expected to outpace supply over the next five years, which should bode well for new and existing investments. Profitable opportunities should exist for selected core investments and well-sponsored value-added and development projects.

---

[4]Standard & Poor's, "S&P/Case-Shiller Home Price Indices: Home Price Values— January 2008," http://www2.standardandpoors.com/spf/pdf/index/CS_HomePrice _History_032544.xls (accessed March 25, 2008).

[5]U.S. Department of Labor: Bureau of Labor Statistics, "Consumer Price Index: January 2008," http://www.bls.gov/cpi/ (accessed February 20, 2008).

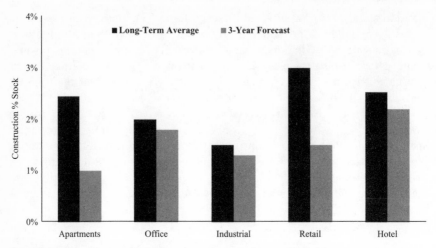

EXHIBIT 1.2   Construction Pipeline Forecasts (as of 2007)
Source: ING Clarion Research & Investment Strategy, TWR, REIS, and Smith Travel as of 2007Q4.

Private real estate investment continues to generate competitive risk-adjusted returns relative to other asset classes. In 2007, the private real estate index (NCREIF Property Index) achieved a strong total return of 15.9% (Exhibit 1.3). Office and hotel properties outperformed other property types. Office markets in the East and West and industrial markets in the West had significant gains. Looking forward, we expect that core real estate investment returns will likely be in the high single digits (between bonds and equities).

EXHIBIT 1.3   Historic Asset Class Performance (% annualized returns)

Asset Class	1 Yr	3 Yr	5 Yr	10 Yr	Std Dev
NCREIF Property Index	15.9	17.5	15.1	12.9	4.4
S&P 500	5.5	8.6	12.8	5.9	17.3
Dow Jones Industrial Average	8.9	9.7	12.2	7.4	14.3
Russell 2000	1.6	6.8	16.3	7.1	18.6
Lehman Government Bond Index	8.7	4.9	4.1	5.7	4.7
T-bill (90 Days)	4.7	4.2	3.0	3.6	1.8

Source: ING Clarion Research & Investment Strategy, NCREIF, NAREIT, and MorningStar as of December 31, 2007.

EXHIBIT 1.4   Bright Spots in the Economic Landscape
Source: ING Clarion Research & Investment Strategy and Moody's Economy.com, 2008.

Regional Outlook

We analyze major markets based on trends and forecasts in population growth, job growth, gross metro product (GMP), fundamentals of local economies, and health of the residential housing markets (Exhibit 1.4).

Despite the gloomy outlook of the U.S. economy in the near term, there are several expanding regions showing above-average growth and relatively healthy fundamentals (Exhibit 1.5). These markets are typically driven by high-tech, biotech, energy, commodities, international trade, housing affordability, and quality of life. Such factors may make these regions especially suitable for value-added and development investment projects.

Multifamily Market Outlook

Multifamily Market Fundamentals   U.S. apartment market fundamentals are sound, supported by favorable demographic trends, a declining for-sale housing market, and a restrained construction pipeline. Members of the

EXHIBIT 1.5   Growth Drivers by Region

Trend	Region	Comments
Expansion	Seattle/Portland	Strong high-tech, biotech, manufacturing, and trade
	San Francisco/San Jose	Strong high-tech, biotech, manufacturing, and trade
	Salt Lake City/Denver	Booming telecom, high-tech, commodity, and energy
	Texas	Booming energy, high-tech, high growth in population/jobs
	Atlanta/Carolinas	High growth in population/jobs
Mixed	So. Cal./Las Vegas/ Phoenix	Negative impact of housing markets on local economies
	Florida	Negative impact of housing markets on local economies
	Boston/NYC/DC	Potential pullback from the financial industry
	Minneapolis/Chicago	Weak population and job growth
Contraction	Detroit/Cleveland	Decline in population/manufacturing jobs

Source: ING Clarion Research & Investment Strategy as of January 2008.

75-million-strong echo boomer[6] cohort are entering the workforce and will constitute the primary demand for apartments as the population of primary renters (age 19–35 years) expands by 3.2 million over the next four years. Because of tightening lending standards, fewer renters will be able to afford homes, helping to boost apartment demand in the near term.

During 2007, the national apartment vacancy rate dropped 20 basis points (bps) to 5.6% according to Reis, Inc.; however, that rate is forecast to edge up to over 6.0% in 2008 and 2009 as job growth slows. Effective rent growth in 2007 was strong at 4.5%, with markets such as New York, San Francisco, San Jose, Stamford, northern New Jersey, and Seattle experiencing the largest rent increases. Looking forward, we expect apartment rent growth to slow to approximately 3–4% annually over the next five years. Transaction volume in 2007 was $99.6 billion according to Real Capital Analytics (RCA), largely driven by the $22 billion Archstone-Smith Trust deal, compared to $91.7 billion in 2006.

---

[6]*Echo boomers,* also known as Generation Y, are the offspring of baby boomers born between 1986–1993.

Shadow Market Impacts   Several markets, especially in Florida where condominium construction and conversion activities far outpaced demand, continue to be challenged with rising vacancy rates and depressed rent growth (Exhibit 1.6). Additionally, in markets where the for-sale housing sector is taking the hardest hit, some vacant, single-family homes are competing with Class A apartments, putting significant downward pressure on rent growth.

Multifamily Sector Outlook   With the lowest cap rate among the four core property types, the apartment sector faces the greatest threat from rising cap rates. Moreover, job growth, the engine of apartment demand, has turned slightly negative for the first two months of 2008. The apartment markets with excess vacant condo or single-family homes will likely suffer the most (Exhibit 1.7).

After cap rate adjustments, new apartment investments in markets that are not suffering from excess shadow vacancy should perform well. Supply-constrained markets such as New York, San Francisco, San Jose, Los Angeles, Seattle, Boston, and northern New Jersey continue to be attractive. Furthermore, stressed assets such as vacant condominiums and selected land sites may offer opportunistic plays. Investment in Class B apartments in core markets can present opportunities, as these properties may attract echo boomers who are graduating from college.

Industrial Market Outlook

Industrial Market Fundamentals   Supply and demand fundamentals of the industrial sector remained balanced through 2007. According to Torto Wheaton Research (TWR), the nationwide industrial vacancy rate was essentially static at 9.4%, but is expected to edge up to the long-term rate of 10% in 2008 and 2009 as the U.S. economy slows. Average rents rose 3.6% in 2007 and are expected to slow to an average annual growth rate of 3.0% over the next five years. On the supply side, industrial development activities are still modest nationwide, constrained by limited suitable building sites near coastal ports and soaring construction costs. In 2007, $48.0 billion of industrial properties were traded according to RCA, compared to $43.6 billion a year ago.

Expanding Global Trade and Strong Exports   So far, the slowing economy has had a minor impact on the nation's demand for warehouse space, which is fueled by expanding global trade. The depreciating U.S. dollar has boosted export growth by more than 12% annually since 2003 (Exhibit 1.8). West Coast warehouse markets such as Southern California, San Francisco, and Seattle experienced low vacancy rates and strong rent growth. In addition,

EXHIBIT 1.6 Condominium Conversion and Shadow Market

Market	2003 Year-End Apt Inventory	2003–2007Q3 Conversion	Inventory Reduction	2007Q3 Apt Inventory	Estimated Shadow Inventory[a]	Percent of Apt Stock	Percent of Housing Stock[b]
Orlando	136,521	31,813	23%	111,458	23,953	21%	2.8%
Ft. Lauderdale	96,099	27,340	28%	71,923	14,279	20%	1.8%
Miami	134,685	28,651	21%	111,289	18,977	17%	1.9%
Tampa	157,708	21,935	14%	142,991	22,572	16%	1.9%
W. Palm Beach	64,829	14,586	22%	53,664	5,567	10%	0.9%
Las Vegas	135,285	15,394	11%	123,843	9,988	8%	1.3%
San Diego	181,796	12,745	7%	175,633	14,031	8%	1.3%
DC Metro	371,344	15,346	4%	370,637	24,079	6%	1.3%
Phoenix	250,239	21,367	9%	243,284	11,904	5%	0.7%

[a]Excess vacant single-family homes, condominiums, and apartments vs. local norm as of 2007Q3. These units are either competing or likely to compete in the local rental market.

[b]Includes single-family homes, condominium, and apartments.

Source: ING Clarion Research & Investment Strategy, REIS, and Witten Advisors, 2007.

EXHIBIT 1.7 SWOT Analysis of Multifamily Market

Strengths	Opportunities
Echo boomers	Stressed assets
Moderate supply pipeline	Development
Weaknesses	**Threats**
Shadow vacancy	Cap rate decompression
Slowing job growth	Improving for-sale affordability

vacancy rates in several R&D flex (San Jose) and manufacturing markets (Chicago and Charlotte) continued to improve.

Industrial Sector Outlook With expanding global trade projected for the next few years, markets in coastal ports and intermodal hubs are expected to continue to benefit. Investments in supply-constrained coastal markets

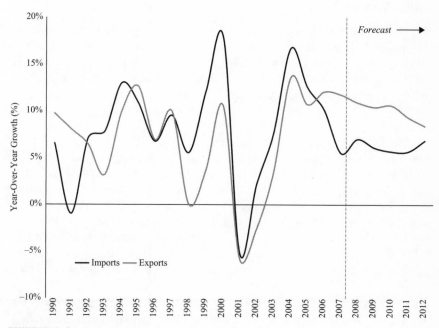

EXHIBIT 1.8 Export Growth
Source: ING Clarion Research & Investment Strategy and Moody's Economy.com as of January 2008.

EXHIBIT 1.9 SWOT Analysis of Industrial Market

Strengths	Opportunities
Expanding global trade	Best port markets/gateways
Surging US exports	R&D/Flex
Weaknesses	**Threats**
Easy to build	Potential supply
Decelerating imports	Recession risk

including Los Angeles, Orange County, Riverside, northern New Jersey, Seattle, and Miami remain attractive. Niche opportunities exist in markets such as Charleston, Houston, Savannah, Oakland, and Austin. R&D flex assets, especially in high-tech and biotech-concentrated markets such as San Jose and San Diego, may offer unique opportunities (Exhibit 1.9).

Office Market Outlook

Office Market Fundamentals   The office sector is expected to face substantial headwinds in 2008 and possibly 2009 before recovering in 2010–2011. In 2007, several central business district (CBD) office markets experienced significant rent growth and declining vacancy rates, and the CBD office subsector achieved a remarkable 24.3% annual total return according to NCREIF. In particular, New York, San Francisco, Los Angeles, San Jose, Seattle, and Austin experienced notable declines in vacancy rates and near double-digit rent growth. Primarily driven by rising vacancy rates in suburban office markets, the 2007 national average vacancy rate edged up 50 bps to 13.1% according to TWR and is expected to spike to over 14.0% in 2008 and 2009 in response to a softer economy. Average office rents rose 9.8% in 2007 and are expected to increase by approximately 2–4% annually over the next five years. On the supply side, the construction pipeline will remain moderate through 2012. Driven by the sale and subsequent retrades of Equity Office assets, total office transaction volume surged to $215.4 billion in 2007 according to RCA, significantly more than the $138.2 billion in 2006.

Slow Growth of Office-Using Jobs   The credit crunch and subprime losses are negatively impacting U.S. office employment, especially in the financial sector. Financial centers such as Manhattan, San Francisco, and Boston may be impacted as several large financial institutions have suffered huge losses. Although office employment growth is decelerating in the near term relative

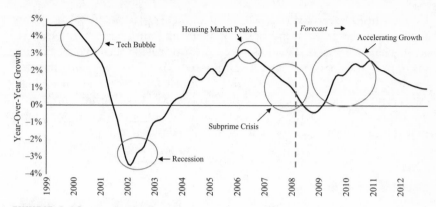

EXHIBIT 1.10 Annual Office Employment Growth
Source: ING Clarion Research & Investment Strategy and Moody's Economy.com as of January 2008.

to 2006, demand for office space is forecast to reaccelerate in 2009–2011 (Exhibit 1.10).

Office Sector Outlook Sensitized by the subprime situation, investors are increasingly seeking safety in high-quality office properties in core markets; however, the office sector has historically been relatively volatile. Selectivity in regard to market, property location, and pricing is increasing in importance. Recent transactions in markets such as Midtown Manhattan showed negative spreads between cap rates and the 10-year Treasury yield. Double-digit rent growth assumptions in underwriting must be carefully evaluated. Better investment opportunities may exist in the top secondary markets (Exhibit 1.11).

Deep, supply-constrained markets, such as New York, San Francisco, Los Angeles, and Washington, DC, still have bright, long-term prospects.

EXHIBIT 1.11 SWOT Analysis of Office Market

Strengths	Opportunities
Low vacancy in CBDs	Best secondary markets
Rent-growth momentum	Value-added/development
Weaknesses	**Threats**
High volatility	Pullback in financials
Slowing job growth	Recession risk

Despite the near-term slowdown, most U.S. corporations (with the exception of financial institutions, home builders, and auto manufacturers) have strong balance sheets. Business services, information technology, finance, insurance, and management consulting are expected to regain robust job growth in 2009–2012. Consequently, knowledge-based and technology-concentrated office markets, including Boston, San Jose, Austin, and Seattle, are expected to continue to benefit. Furthermore, a modest office supply pipeline continues to justify value-added and development projects.

Retail Market Outlook

Retail Market Fundamentals   The retail sector is under pressure due to falling home prices, a slowing job market, and the credit crisis. The residential housing downturn had an immediate impact on big-box retailers with those selling home furnishings, construction materials, and garden equipment experiencing the steepest declines. According to Reis, the national retail vacancy rate edged up 40 bps to 7.5% in 2007 and is expected to rise modestly through 2008 as consumer spending softens. Net absorption fell short of new construction, reflecting the hesitation from retailers and moderating retail sales. Average effective rent growth was only 2.9% in 2007, below the trend in recent years, and is expected to remain below 3.0% over the next three years.

Several West Coast markets, including Los Angeles, Orange County, San Jose, San Francisco, and Seattle, experienced low vacancy rates and strong rent growth in 2007. Overall, strong demographic trends, relatively low interest rates, rising wages, and resilient consumer spending should support the retail sector going forward. Transaction volume totaled $72.1 billion in 2007 according to RCA, compared to $54.8 billion a year ago.

Sluggish Consumer Spending   In 2007, retail sales grew 4.1% according to Moody's Economy.com, the slowest pace since 2002. We expect that 2008 will be a more challenging year for consumer spending (Exhibit 1.12). With a softening economy and fears of an imminent recession, retailers are focusing on same-store profitability and are expected to temper expansion plans over the next 12 months, negatively impacting rent growth. Most recently, major retailers including Macy's, CompUSA, and Sharper Image announced the closing of hundreds of underperforming stores. Malls may experience rising vacancies as consumer spending continues to soften. Even upscale retailers such as Tiffany & Co. and Coach reported disappointing U.S. sales, suggesting pullback on the part of high-end consumers.

EXHIBIT 1.12 U.S. Retail Sales: Personal Disposable Income
Source: ING Clarion Research & Investment Strategy and Moody's Economy.com as of January 2008.

Retail Sector Outlook Despite near-term weakness, the demand for retail space is expected to recover in 2010 and 2011, although the anticipated recovery is largely dependent on the rebound of economic growth and the housing market. Energy prices and inflation could continue to weigh on consumer sentiment. Markets such as New York, Washington, DC, Miami, West Palm Beach, Houston, and several West Coast metros continue to be attractive. Some retail stores may go out of business during 2008, providing value-added opportunities to upgrade tenant quality and mix. Because supply is forecast to lag demand over the next five years, opportunities exist for redevelopment and selective development in high-growth markets (Exhibit 1.13).

Hotel Market Outlook

Hotel Market Fundamentals The U.S. hotel sector has experienced strong growth and is in the middle of its current cycle that began in 2002. Advanced bookings from several large hotel chains suggest solid demand in 2008. According to Smith Travel Research, the 2007 national average occupancy rate stabilized at 63.2%. Revenue per available room (RevPAR) grew by 5.7% in 2007 and is expected to increase approximately 3–4% in 2008–2010 (if the economy can avoid a severe recession). Occupancy rates are expected

EXHIBIT 1.13 SWOT Analysis of Retail Market

Strengths	Opportunities
Growing disposable income	Redevelopment
Long-term leases	Selective development
Weaknesses	**Threats**
Negative wealth effects	Lackluster consumer spending
Slowing job growth	High energy/healthcare costs

to drop modestly in 2008, and RevPAR growth will be achieved mainly through increasing average daily rates (ADR).

On the supply side, the hotel pipeline is still below its long-term average, although construction is projected to increase substantially after 2008. Luxury and Upper Upscale segments are relatively insulated because of high construction costs and more difficult local entitlement processes. Investors continued to show strong interests in hotel assets in 2007 with hotel transaction volume totaling $87.9 billion according to RCA, more than double that of 2006. A particularly notable transaction in 2007 was the $26 billion privatization of the Hilton Hotels by Blackstone.

Declining U.S. Dollar Fueling Hotel Demand   The U.S. dollar has depreciated approximately 35% against major currencies since 2001 and is expected to remain weak for the foreseeable future.[7] As a result, demand from international travelers continues to grow. Meanwhile, domestic travelers, concerned about reduced spending power overseas, are increasingly traveling within the U.S. International gateway cities and vacation destinations, including New York City, Los Angeles, Miami, Orlando, San Francisco, Honolulu, Las Vegas, and Washington, DC, should have high growth potential for business and leisure travel (Exhibit 1.14).

Hotel Sector Outlook   Despite strong momentum, hotel returns could be at risk should a recession occur. The hotel sector is volatile because hotels operate essentially by one-night leases, and hotel demand is highly correlated with GDP growth. Businesses and consumers normally reduce travel during a severe economic downturn. Caution should be observed in core hotel investments over the next six months as the national economic downturn plays out. Nonetheless, a recession could present excellent opportunities

---

[7]Moody's Economy.com, "Weighted Average Exchange Value of U.S. Dollar: Broad Index, for United States," *DataBuffet.com*, http://www.databuffet.com (accessed March 2008).

EXHIBIT 1.14 Overseas Visitors to Selected U.S. Destinations in 2006

Rank	Metro	Market Share	Visitation (000)
1	New York City	28.7%	6,219
2	Los Angeles	11.6%	2,514
3	Orlando	9.2%	1,993
3	San Francisco	9.2%	1,993
5	Miami	9.1%	1,972
6	Oahu/Honolulu	8.0%	1,733
7	Las Vegas	7.6%	1,647
8	Metro DC Area	4.9%	1,062
8	Chicago	4.9%	1,062
10	Boston	4.6%	997

Source: U.S. Department of Commerce, ITA, and Office of Travel and Tourism Industries, 2007.

EXHIBIT 1.15 SWOT Analysis of Hotel Market

Strengths	Opportunities
Strong RevPAR growth	Cap rate compression
High occupancy	Selective development
Weaknesses	**Threats**
Short-term leases	Large supply pipeline
Operating intensive	Recession risk

to buy high-quality hotel assets at reduced prices. Further, the hotel sector still has room for potential cap rate compression if Treasury yields remain relatively low (Exhibit 1.15).

Within the hotel sector, Luxury, Upper Upscale, and Upscale segments are projected to outperform the other segments over the next three years. Strong brand names have created customer loyalty, which facilitates pricing premiums. Business hotels and resorts in selected, supply-constrained markets may perform most favorably. Furthermore, we believe that many projects in the current pipeline will be delayed or canceled, creating opportunities for well-sponsored development projects to move forward. The extended-stay hotel segment is expected to perform well because current supply is significantly lagging demand. During the last recession, occupancy in extended-stay hotels remained relatively stable, suggesting that the segment may experience less volatility through an economic downturn.

CHAPTER 2

Forecasting the U.S. Market

David Lynn
Winter 2007–2008[1]

We utilize an array of proprietary econometric tools for the purpose of forecasting 50 major urban markets and five property types. This chapter discusses the market forecast methodology.

FORECASTING METHODOLOGY

Top-down and bottom-up approaches to forecasting are commonly used in the real estate industry. Macroeconomic (top-down) factors, such as employment growth, gross domestic product (GDP), household formation, and median household income drive both space-using demand and long-term supply. Market construction pipeline data (bottom-up) provides short-term supply information. Current vacancy (bottom-up) is assessed, while future vacancy is derived from forecasted demand, supply, and estimated total market inventory. Current rent (bottom-up) is surveyed, while rent growth is forecast based on forecasted demand and vacancy. Quantitative models built on long-term trends generate baseline results, while adjustments are made to incorporate local knowledge and short-term phenomena.

We conduct rigorous, data-driven analyses, building an analytical framework to support each private market investment decision. On a continuous basis, the team reviews quantitative information on 150 local markets, and uses proprietary models to forecast local fundamentals.

---

[1]This paper was originally produced in winter 2007–2008. The data, opinions, and forecasts have not been updated for book publication.

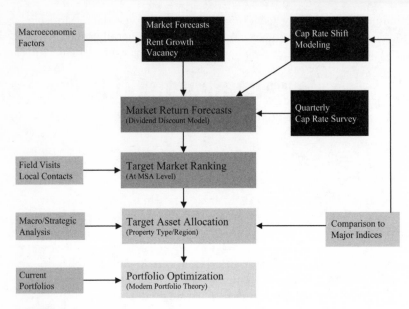

EXHIBIT 2.1   Forecasting Model

Our investment approach incorporates both top-down and bottom-up perspectives as well as detailed portfolio and property evaluations (Exhibit 2.1).

Market Fundamentals Forecast: A Combination of Consensus and Modeling

Our fundamental forecasts are combinations of consensus and modeling results.

Why Consensus?   As a major and active market participant, we are able to access a robust collection of data sources. This offers an opportunity to summarize a timely industry view based on a combination of consensus and survey. With observations and thinking from many market participants, consensus and survey can provide a comprehensive view on markets, and serve to reduce data source bias.

Why Modeling?   Several key variables in real estate economics are linked together to some extent. This enables us to project some variables with econometric models by using consensus and survey data. Modeling can capture long-term relations among variables. Generally, market vacancy is derived from supply and demand forecasts; however, demand forecasts are typically the weakest link because many heterogeneous forces drive space demand, and traditional econometric models generally only capture macro-economic drivers, which also come from imperfect forecasts. As a result, significant adjustments have to be made after vacancy rates are calculated.

Completions: Consensus

Major data providers gather construction pipeline data and estimate completion dates and new space availability. The sources used by these data providers have a broad coverage. Since pipeline data are only good for short-term forecasting, relying solely on pipeline data may cause very lumpy forecasts. Taking this into consideration, the main data providers use modeling processes to forecast long-term completions as well as to smooth the trend. We supplement shorter-term construction data from CoStar with consensus expectations from Torto Wheaton Research (TWR); Reis, Inc.; and Property & Portfolio Research (PPR) to estimate market completions over the next three to five years.

Market Vacancy: Consensus

Using consensus allows us to consider a variety of approaches to estimating market vacancy rates, many of which are beyond the reach of econometric modeling:

- Some are based on quantitative modeling, while others are based on historical experience.
- Some are from a construction perspective, while others are through leasing activities.
- Some are landlords' views, while some are from tenants.
- Some are focused on macroeconomic and demographic trends, while some are according to local events.

Absorption: Calculations

New supply and vacancy rates are based on consensus, while total stock history uses individual data providers for each of the different property sectors. The following calculations are utilized to determine absorption:

$$\text{New supply}_t = \text{Completions}_t - \text{Depletions}_t \pm \text{Conversions}_t$$

$$\text{Total stock}_t - \text{Total stock}_{t-1} + \text{New supply}_t$$

$$\text{Occupied stock}_t = \text{Total stock}_t \times (1 - \text{Vacancy}_t)$$

$$\text{Absorption}_t = \text{Occupied stock}_t - \text{Occupied stock}_{t-1}$$

Rent Growth: Econometric Modeling

Econometric models capture long-term relationships between rent growth and underlying drivers (vacancy, vacancy change, employment, gross metro product [GMP] growth, etc.). We identify several underlying drivers for each property type and apply these same drivers across all markets to achieve consistency. However, because rents respond to drivers differently in each market, we tailor a unique equation for each market with unique coefficients and varying lagging factors. We adjust these 204 equations (50 metros and one national model per sector for four sectors) with each forecasting iteration.

Market Rent Forecast Methodology The demand for property space is primarily derived from employment within specific sectors of the economy. For example, studies of office property use show that more than 80 percent of all office workers come from the Financial Activities and Professional & Business Services sectors of the economy, the latter of which includes accountants, lawyers, consultants, lobbyists, and architects.[2] Using employment forecasts, we project the changes in employment structure likely to occur and derive future demand from these changes.

Given the current stock of office space, together with future employment and current vacancy rates, we forecast total market absorption. Competitive completion minus net absorption produces changes in vacant space. Completions of competitive space over the first forecast year are known from data provider surveys. For future years, we use probability models to predict competitive completions.

---

[2]Moody's Economy.com, "Forecast Catalogs: U.S. Employment, Output & Wages," *DataBuffet.com,* http://www.databuffet.com (accessed December 2007).

Following calculation of the independent variables, we forecast market rent using two econometric models. The first is

Rent growth equation $= \sigma + \beta_1$ Vacancy rate $+ \beta_2$ Change in vacancy rate

where

Vacancy rate $= 1 -$ (Market occupied stock/Market stock)

Market stock $=$ Previous year market stock $+$ Construction

Market occupied stock $=$ Previous year market occupied stock $+$ Absorption

Change in vacancy rate $=$ Vacancy rate $-$ Previous year vacancy rate

$\beta_1, \beta_2, \sigma =$ Calculated constants from regression analysis

"Construction" is forecast from projects in the pipeline provided by CoStar, supplemented with analyst adjustments based upon local market knowledge.

The second econometric model is

$$\text{Market Absorption} = \text{Marginal Absorption per worker}$$
$$\times \text{Office use employment change}$$

"Office use employment change" is forecast from Moody's Economy.com.

Total Return

Total return is a function of the current cap rate, or going-in yield, the forward earnings growth, and the cap rate shift. The current cap rate is a measure of income return, while earnings growth and cap rate shift compete to determine whether the property appreciates or depreciates in value. We conduct a quarterly survey of cap rates in which members of our acquisitions and portfolio management teams offer views on current rates by region and sector.

The following model highlights the calculations used to determine total return. This is, in effect, the real estate version of the Dividend Discount

Model (DDM) which was developed for stock valuation:

$$Total\ Return_t = Income\ Return_t + Value\ Return_t$$

$$= \frac{NOI_t}{Value_{t-1}} + \frac{Value_t}{Value_{t-1}} - 1$$

$$= \frac{NOI_t}{\dfrac{NOI_t}{Cap\ Rate_{t-1}}} + \frac{\dfrac{NOI_{t+1}}{Cap\ Rate_t}}{\dfrac{NOI_t}{Cap\ Rate_{t-1}}} - 1$$

$$= Cap\ Rate_{t-1} + \frac{NOI_{t+1}}{NOI_t} \times \frac{Cap\ Rate_{t-1}}{Cap\ Rate_t} - 1$$

$$Total\ Return_t = Cap\ Rate_{t-1} + \frac{1 + g_{t+1}}{1 + Cap\ Rate\ Shift_t} - 1$$

In which,

$$g_{t+1} = \frac{NOI_{t+1}}{NOI_t} - 1 \qquad Cap\ Rate\ Shift_t = \frac{Cap\ Rate_t}{Cap\ Rate_{t-1}} - 1$$

Market Rankings   Based upon the total returns calculation, we are able to rank markets in each sector by the average total return over three-year and five-year periods. The total return rankings are then used to develop priorities for both acquisitions and portfolio management activities.

CHAPTER 3

Recession Simulation and It's Effects on Real Estate

Tim Wang, Alison Sauer, and David Lynn
Winter 2007–2008[1]

Fears of recession have increased as the subprime fallout and residential housing market downturn push the U.S. economy into slower growth. Even though third quarter real gross domestic product (GDP) growth came in better than expected at 3.9%, fourth quarter growth is expected to be below 1.0%. Currently, only three sectors (Government, Education & Health Services, and Leisure & Hospitality Services) are creating jobs; whereas other sectors are losing jobs, including residential construction, which lost 50,000 jobs over the past two months.[2]

In this chapter, we use employment growth projections (for both normal and recession scenarios) and essentially "shock" the economy by forecasting slower demand while maintaining supply at current projected levels. We examine the major NCREIF geographical regions and illustrate the potential effects on rent growth and vacancy for office, apartment, and warehouse.[3] We then look at the potential effects on growth yields and cap rates.

---

[1]This paper was originally produced in winter 2007–2008. The data, opinions, and forecasts have not been updated for book publication.

[2]David Rosenberg, "All Signals Are Pointing in the Direction of a US Slowdown," *Financial Times*, November 14, 2007.

[3]Retail and hotel sectors are not included in the analysis due to a lack of sufficient data.

Region	Office		Industrial		Apartment	
	Vacancy	Rent	Vacancy	Rent	Vacancy	Rent
East North Central	↗	↓	↗	↘	↗	↔
Mid-Atlantic	↗	↘	↗	↘	↗	↘
Mountain	↑	↘	↑	↘	↑	↘
Northeast	↑	↓	↗	↓	↑	↓
Pacific	↗	↓	↗	↓	↑	↓
Southeast	↗	↘	↑	↓	↗	↘
Southwest	↗	↓	↑	↓	↗	↓
West North Central	↑	↘	↗	↓	↑	↘

↑ Significant Increase	↗ Increase	↔ No Change
↓ Significant Decrease	↘ Decrease	

EXHIBIT 3.1 Differences between the Simulated Recession and Normal Scenario Forecasts for All Property Types
Source: ING Clarion Research & Strategy.

The current ominous economic predictions notwithstanding, we use the previous recession of 2001 as a general guide to the potential behavior of the next recession.

Although varied in magnitude, most property types (office, apartment, industrial, retail, and hotel) we project would be negatively affected in the simulated recession. The general summary of the simulated recession's probable impacts are illustrated in Exhibit 3.1.

- *Office.* In the simulated recession scenario, office vacancy is expected to average 1.7% higher than in the normal scenario forecast while rent growth is expected to be 1.3% below over the five-year forecast.
- *Industrial.* Industrial properties are expected to see a smaller change in vacancy compared to office (1.2% above the normal scenario forecast), but rent growth for industrial properties is expected to be higher than office, averaging 2.5% below throughout the forecast period.
- *Apartment.* Apartment vacancy rates are expected to average 1.3% above the normal scenario forecast, and rent growth is projected to average 1.0% per year below.

The impact of a recession tends to vary across markets and regions. The previous recession affected the Northeast and Pacific regions the most. Similarly, the simulated recession scenario forecasts reveal that the Northeast and Pacific regions would also be most severely affected if a recession were to occur in 2008. The Northeast region is considered a high-beta market, which experiences higher growth during a strong economy and lower growth during a slow economy. The Pacific region is projected to experience the strongest growth during the normal scenario forecast and therefore would encounter a significant drop due to a downturn in the economy. However, even with a recession, this region is expected to see the strongest growth of the eight regions.

Minimal impact would likely occur in the Southeast and Mid-Atlantic regions. The Southeast is already forecast to experience slower growth in the normal scenario and therefore a recession would not have as significant of an impact. The Mid-Atlantic (which includes Washington, DC) is considered a low–beta market due to a large concentration of government jobs and, therefore, a recession's impact would not be as significant.

Property market fundamentals tend to lag recessions. In the last recession, it took two years before property market fundamentals reached their lowest levels.

IMPACT OF THE LAST RECESSION (2001) ON COMMERCIAL PROPERTY MARKETS

In general, negative growth in the economy reduces demand for commercial property across the board, with a full impact of a downturn usually lagging by about a year or two. In the previous recession, it took two years before fundamentals in the property markets reached their worst levels (Exhibit 3.2). A decline in property demand generally leads to an increase in vacancy rates, which then leads to a decline in rents. However, a recession's impacts differ across property types and markets.

Office

The office sector is highly sensitive to changes in the economy and exhibits a high correlation with GDP growth. In the past, recessions have negatively impacted the financial activities sector, which comprises a considerable portion of office-using employment. At the national level, office absorption has been positive in all but two (2001 and 2002) of the last 20 years. During those two years, demand for office space was −3.1% and −0.4% of stock, respectively. Average rent growth declined to −7.7% in 2002 and −4.6% in 2003. This significant decline can be attributed to two main events: (1) high unsustainable rent levels reached during the tech bubble; and (2) the 9/11

EXHIBIT 3.2 Fundamentals of U.S. Property Markets during the 2001 Recession

Year	Apartment				Office				Industrial			
	Abs % Stock	Const % Stock	Vac Rate	Rent Growth	Abs % Stock	Const % Stock	Vac Rate	Rent Growth	Abs % Stock	Const % Stock	Vac Rate	Rent Growth
2000	2.7%	2.0%	3.0%	8.6%	3.6%	3.0%	8.6%	3.4%	2.7%	2.2%	6.7%	13.5%
2001	−0.1%	1.7%	4.8%	3.2%	−3.1%	2.7%	14.1%	1.8%	−1.3%	2.1%	10.0%	3.3%
2002	−0.1%	1.5%	6.3%	1.0%	−0.4%	2.2%	16.5%	−7.7%	−0.1%	1.3%	11.2%	−4.1%
2003	0.4%	1.4%	6.9%	1.3%	0.7%	1.3%	16.8%	−4.6%	0.3%	0.9%	11.7%	−4.3%
2004	0.4%	1.1%	6.8%	2.2%	2.3%	1.1%	15.4%	0.9%	1.6%	1.1%	11.1%	−0.7%
2005	0.3%	1.0%	5.7%	2.6%	2.7%	1.2%	13.6%	1.5%	2.4%	1.3%	9.9%	5.4%

Source: Moody's Economy.com, Reis, Inc.; Torto Wheaton Research (TWR); and ING Clarion Research & Investment Strategy.

terrorist attack on the financial district in New York City, causing many office occupiers to delay their office space decisions.

Industrial

Similarly, though not as pronounced, the industrial sector is closely linked with the performance of the economy. A recession severely disrupts imports and exports, reducing demand for warehouse space. During the last recession, industrial absorption as a percentage of stock was −1.3% in 2001 and −0.1% in 2002. However, the impact on rent growth had a lag of 6 to 12 months. Rent growth was at a record high prior to the last recession before dropping to −4.1% in 2002 and −4.3% in 2003. Industrial vacancy rates started to decline again in 2004 when demand increased to 0.3% of stock.

Apartment The apartment sector was also severely affected during the last recession, in part because it had much farther to fall. Prior to the previous recession, apartment availability rates were at a record low of 3.0% and rent levels were lifted to new highs by stock wealth. Net absorption was negative in 2001 and 2002 before recovering in 2003 to 0.4% of stock. Between 2000 and 2002, rents dropped by 7.6% and vacancy rates jumped by 3.3%.

Retail Remarkably, the retail sector has not reported a single year of negative absorption over the past 17 years, thanks to resilient consumer spending and less expensive goods from overseas. U.S. consumers continued spending during the last recession, helping the economy through difficult times. Nevertheless, during a recessionary period, retail rent growth tends to slow substantially but stay positive. Following this trend, rent growth slowed to 1.2% and 1.1% in 2001 and 2002, respectively, before recovering to 2.4% growth in 2003, while net absorption decreased to 0.9% and 1.5% of stock in 2001 and 2002.

Hotel Hotels have essentially one-night leases and more operating components—and are typically hit the hardest as businesses and consumers cut expenses by reducing travel activities. During the last recession, the average occupancy rate dropped by 5.6% from 2001 to 2002 and net absorption was −3.4% of stock. Revenue per available room (RevPAR) declined by 7.0% and 2.7% in 2001 and 2002, respectively, before starting to recover in late 2002. After a flat 2003, the average RevPAR rebounded robustly to roughly 8.0% annually between 2004 and 2006 and net absorption was strong at 4.0% and 2.8% of stock in 2004 and 2005, respectively.

METHODOLOGY

The recession scenario was created to model the effects on demand, vacancy, and rent growth, and the recession economy is simulated by using employment predictions for a severe recession scenario.

Using these predicted economic conditions, we project the demand for commercial properties starting in the first quarter of 2008, while using the supply forecasted for the normal scenario. Negative growth in the economy decreases demand for commercial properties. By leaving supply unchanged and decreasing demand, markets respond with increasing vacancy rates, thereby leading to a decline in rent growth.

The simulation is performed both at the national and regional levels for three property types: office, apartment, and industrial. The United States is divided into eight regions following NCREIF regional definitions as seen in Exhibit 3.3. As the foregoing results will illustrate, regions and property types behave differently when faced with an economic downturn.

EXHIBIT 3.3   NCREIF Regional Definitions
Source: NCREIF.
Note: U.S. economy had negative GDP growth in Q3 2000, Q1 2001, and Q3 2001.

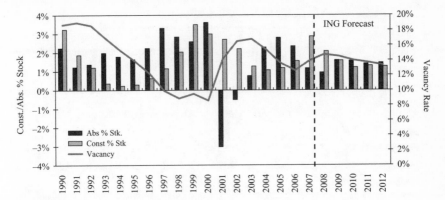

EXHIBIT 3.4 National Office Supply and Demand Trends for the Normal Scenario Forecast
Source: ING Clarion Research & Investment Strategy, TWR, and Moody's Economy.com, 2007.

Office

National Normal Scenario Forecast Despite layoffs in the financial sector around the country, the office property sector is expected to continue to be strong with construction and absorption within historic levels. Vacancy, while still not back to the low of 8.6% attained in 2000, is expected to decline throughout the five-year forecast. Ending 2012 at 13.3%, the vacancy rate is forecast to average 14.0% annually during the next five years, below the long-term average (Exhibit 3.4). Rent is expected to stay positive going forward, growing an average of 2.9% annually throughout the next five years.

National Simulated Recession Scenario Forecast Vacancy reached a historic low in 2000 before the economy was hit by the last recession. Since then it has not returned to those levels. The recession beginning in 2008 would lead to vacancy averaging 15.9% over five years, peaking in 2009 and decreasing thereafter. Absorption, which is expected to be below the long-term average at 1.2% of stock, is forecast to be negative in 2008 before turning positive again and surpassing construction levels in 2010 (Exhibit 3.5). Rent growth is expected to slow but stay positive over the next five years, averaging 2.0% annually (Exhibit 3.6).

Regional Comparisons In general, vacancy rates in this recession scenario jump due to decreased demand. On average across the eight regions, vacancy rates in the office sector would be 1.7% higher and rent growth would be

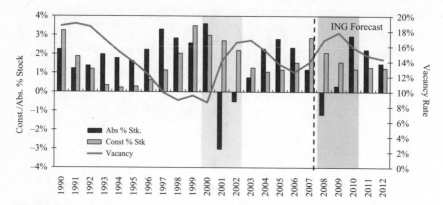

EXHIBIT 3.5 National Office Supply and Demand Trends for the Recession
Scenario Forecast
Source: ING Clarion Research & Investment Strategy, TWR, and Moody's
Economy.com, 2007.

1.3% lower than in the normal scenario. If a recession were to occur in
2008, the East North Central region would have the worst outcome with
rent growth dropping to −2.6% per year. Rents in the Pacific and Mid-
Atlantic regions would drop, but rents would still top other regions at 1.2%
and 1.4% per year, respectively (Exhibits 3.7 and 3.8).

The impact of the recession would be limited in the Southeast because
normal scenario projections already capture slower growth in that region.
Vacancy rates are expected to have mild growth and rents are projected to
have minimal change in the simulated recession scenario forecast compared
to the normal scenario forecast.

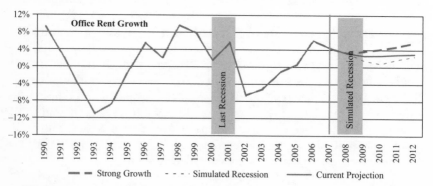

EXHIBIT 3.6 National Office Rent Growth
Source: ING Clarion Research & Investment Strategy, TWR, and Moody's
Economy.com, 2007.

Region	Average Annual Industrial Vacancy Rate—5-Year Forecast		
	Current Economy	Simulated Downturn Economy	Changes
East North Central	18.1%	19.7%	↗
Mid-Atlantic	12.4%	13.7%	↗
Mountain	14.5%	16.2%	↑
Northeast	10.8%	12.7%	↑
Pacific	12.9%	14.2%	↗
Southeast	16.3%	17.8%	↗
Southwest	18.5%	20.1%	↗
West North Central	17.3%	19.8%	↑

↑ Significant Increase   ↗ Increase

EXHIBIT 3.7   Office Vacancy Rates in Both the Normal and Simulated
Recession Scenarios
Source: ING Clarion Research & Strategy.

Industrial

National Normal Scenario Forecast   Levels of construction for industrial
properties were very strong in the years leading up to the previous recession.
New construction was being delivered above historic averages (at over 2.0%
of stock annually from 1997 to 2001), leaving a glut of space to become

Region	Average Annual Office Rent Growth—5-Year Forecast		
	Current Economy	Simulated Downturn Economy	Changes
East North Central	−1.3%	−2.6%	↑
Mid-Atlantic	2.1%	1.2%	↙
Mountain	2.3%	1.1%	↙
Northeast	3.4%	1.4%	↓
Pacific	3.6%	1.2%	↓
Southeast	1.8%	1.2%	↙
Southwest	1.1%	−0.4%	↓
West North Central	0.8%	0.3%	↙

↑ Significant Decrease   ↙ Decrease

EXHIBIT 3.8   Office Rent Growth in Both the Normal and Simulated
Recession Scenarios
Source: ING Clarion Research & Strategy.

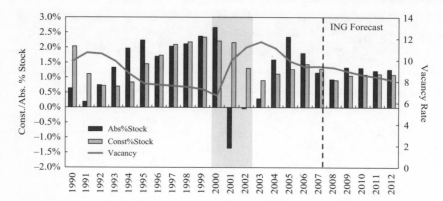

EXHIBIT 3.9   National Industrial Supply and Demand Trends for the Normal Forecast
Source: ING Clarion Research & Investment Strategy, TWR, and Moody's Economy .com, 2007.

vacant in the last downturn. Currently, however, construction levels are not nearly as high as they had been in the early part of the decade and are expected to average below historic levels at 1.1% of stock over the next five years. Demand is expected to exceed supply at 1.2% of stock during the same time, leading to decreasing vacancy rates (averaging 8.8%) through the forecast (Exhibit 3.9). Rent growth is forecast to be strong, increasing by an average of 3.9% annually.

National Simulated Recession Scenario Forecast   The industrial vacancy rate ended 2006 at 9.4%, 2.7% above the vacancy rate seen in 2000. Applying the severe recession economic conditions to the normal scenario causes absorption to drop (averaging 1.0% of stock) and vacancy to rise (averaging 10.0%) through 2012. As vacancy rises, hitting its peak in 2009, rent growth is forecast to decrease but recover thereafter, averaging 1.4% annual growth over the next five years (Exhibits 3.10 and 3.11).

Regional Comparisons   Across the eight regions listed in the following exhibit, the annual vacancy rate is expected to be greater by 1.6% in the simulated recession scenario forecast than in the normal scenario forecast (Exhibit 3.12). Rent growth is forecast to average 2.1% below the normal scenario forecast (Exhibit 3.13).

The Pacific and Mid-Atlantic regions are forecast to be minimally affected by the onset of a recession with vacancy averaging 0.8% above the normal economic forecast in both regions. Rent is expected to drop in the Pacific region but it will still top all other regions at 2.3% per year. A

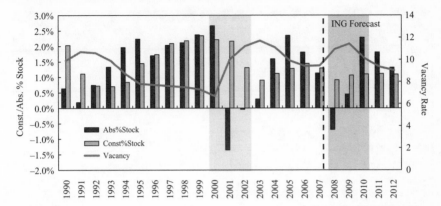

EXHIBIT 3.10 National Industrial Supply and Demand Trends for the Recession Scenario Forecast
Source: ING Clarion Research & Investment Strategy, TWR, and Moody's Economy .com, 2007.

recession's impacts will also be minimal in the East North Central region due to slower growth in the normal scenario projection. The Southwest industrial market, however, is expected to be impacted the most by a recession. Vacancy would average 3.3% higher under the recession scenario and rent growth would average 3.4% lower.

Apartment

National Normal Scenario Forecast The apartment sector was slow to recover after the previous recession but the current outlook is good as demand

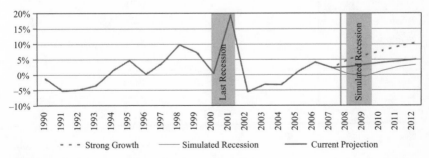

EXHIBIT 3.11 National Warehouse Rent Growth
Source: ING Clarion Research & Investment Strategy, TWR, and Moody's Economy .com, 2007.

Region	Average Annual Industrial Vacancy Rate—5-Year Forecast		
	Current Economy	Simulated Downturn Economy	Changes
East North Central	11.4%	12.2%	↗
Mid-Atlantic	10.4%	11.2%	↗
Mountain	9.0%	11.2%	↑
Northeast	10.1%	11.3%	↗
Pacific	5.3%	6.6%	↗
Southeast	9.1%	11.0%	↑
Southwest	8.7%	12.0%	↑
West North Central	8.2%	9.7%	↗

↑ Significant Increase   ↗ Increase

EXHIBIT 3.12   Industrial Vacancy Rates in Both the Normal and Simulated
Recession Scenarios
Source: ING Clarion Research & Strategy.

is forecast to be level with supply. Due to this, vacancy is projected to be
flat, averaging 5.7% through 2012, similar to historic levels (Exhibit 3.14).
Rent growth is forecast to average 2.9% annually over the next five years,
below the national long-term average.

Region	Average Annual Industrial Rent Growth—5-Year Forecast		
	Current Economy	Simulated Downturn Economy	Changes
East North Central	−0.1%	−1.1%	↙
Mid-Atlantic	2.3%	1.8%	↙
Mountain	3.2%	1.3%	↙
Northeast	1.0%	−1.7%	↓
Pacific	4.6%	2.3%	↓
Southeast	2.5%	0.0%	↓
Southwest	2.3%	−1.1%	↓
West North Central	1.5%	−1.1%	↓

↓ Significant Decrease   ↙ Decrease

EXHIBIT 3.13   Industrial Rent Growth in Both the Normal and Simulated
Recession Scenarios
Source: ING Clarion Research & Strategy.

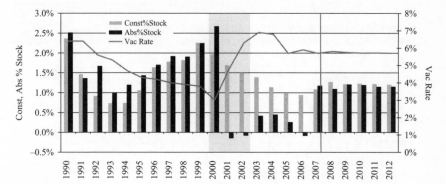

EXHIBIT 3.14 National Apartment Supply and Demand Trends for the
Normal Forecast
Source: ING Clarion Research & Investment Strategy; Reis, Inc.; and Moody's
Economy.com, 2007.

National Simulated Recession Scenario Forecast The apartment sector
is expected to end 2007 with a 5.7% vacancy rate. Using severe recession economic figures, vacancy is expected to be level with the past five
years averaging 6.3% annually through 2012. Over the next five years,
construction (1.2% of stock) is projected to slightly outweigh absorption
(1.1% of stock) (Exhibit 3.15). Even in the simulated recession scenario, rent
growth is forecast to stay positive through 2012, growing at 2.7% per year
(Exhibit 3.16).

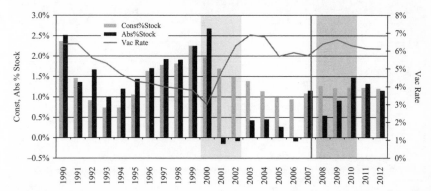

EXHIBIT 3.15 National Apartment Supply and Demand Trends for the
Recession Scenario Forecast
Source: ING Clarion Research & Investment Strategy; Reis, Inc.; and Moody's
Economy.com, 2007.

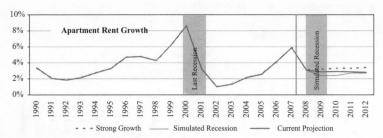

EXHIBIT 3.16 National Apartment Rent Growth
Source: ING Clarion Research & Investment Strategy; Reis, Inc.; and
Moody's Economy.com, 2007.

Regional Comparisons The apartment market is expected to have the
smallest change of the three major sectors between the normal scenario forecast and the simulated recession scenario forecast. On average, vacancy rates
would be 1.3% higher and rent growth would be 0.9% lower per annum in a
recession scenario forecast than in the normal economy forecast. The Northeast region would be impacted the most, with vacancy rates jumping above
the long-term averages and rent growth dropping significantly. The recession
would impact the Mid-Atlantic the least. Although the difference between
the normal scenario forecast and the simulated recession scenario forecast
is big in the Pacific region, vacancy rates are low and rent growth is high
compared to the other regions in both forecasts (Exhibits 3.17 and 3.18).

| | Average Annual Apartment Vacancy Rate—5-Year Forecast | | |
Region	Current Economy	Simulated Downturn Economy	Changes
East North Central	7.0%	7.4%	↗
Mid-Atlantic	6.2%	6.9%	↗
Mountain	6.8%	8.2%	↑
Northeast	4.9%	7.4%	↑
Pacific	3.6%	5.0%	↑
Southeast	6.5%	7.6%	↗
Southwest	6.8%	8.1%	↗
West North Central	5.2%	7.0%	↑

↑ Significant Increase   ↗ Increase

EXHIBIT 3.17 Apartment Vacancy Rates in Both the Normal and Simulated
Recession Scenarios
Source: ING Clarion Research & Strategy.

Region	Average Annual Apartment Rent Growth—5-Year Forecast		
	Current Economy	Simulated Downturn Economy	Changes
East North Central	1.0%	1.0%	↔
Mid-Atlantic	2.7%	2.5%	↙
Mountain	1.6%	0.9%	↙
Northeast	1.8%	–0.5%	↓
Pacific	3.9%	2.2%	↓
Southeast	2.4%	2.1%	↙
Southwest	3.6%	2.2%	↓
West North Central	1.9%	1.1%	↙

↓ Significant Decrease   ↙ Decrease   ↔ No Change

EXHIBIT 3.18   Apartment Rent Growth in Both the Normal and Simulated Recession Scenarios
Source: ING Clarion Research & Strategy.

CAP RATES AND TOTAL RETURNS

During past recessions, the Fed has aggressively cut interest rates. As a result, yields of 10-year T-notes dropped substantially, which typically makes commercial real estate relatively more attractive than other asset classes. We expect the same pattern to occur in the simulated recession. If a recession occurs in 2008, cap rates for Class A properties in primary markets for the next three years are projected[4] (Exhibit 3.19).

EXHIBIT 3.19   Forecasted Cap Rates Under a Recession Scenario

	Yields and Cap Rate Spreads Over 10-Year T-Note			
	2007Q3	2008E	2009E	2010E
10-Y T-Note	4.25%	3.50%	3.75%	4.50%
Apartment	4.75% (50 bps)	5.25% (175 bps)	5.25% (150 bps)	5.25% (75 bps)
Industrial	6.00% (175 bps)	6.50% (300 bps)	6.50% (275 bps)	6.50% (200 bps)
Office	5.17% (92 bps)	5.75% (225 bps)	5.75% (200 bps)	5.75% (125 bps)
Retail	5.30% (105 bps)	5.75% (225 bps)	5.75% (200 bps)	5.75% (125 bps)

Source: ING Clarion Research & Investment Strategy.

---

[4]Cap rate decompression for non-Class-A properties in secondary and tertiary markets is expected to be greater.

EXHIBIT 3.20 Forecasted Total Returns Under Both Normal and Recession
Scenarios

	Normal Scenario					Recession Scenario			
	2007	2008	2009	2010	3-Y Avg	2008	2009	2010	3-Y Avg
Apartment	12.06%	5.94%	6.46%	7.21%	6.54%	5.40%	6.02%	6.75%	6.06%
Industrial	16.42%	8.63%	7.81%	6.87%	7.77%	7.72%	5.43%	4.92%	6.02%
Office	21.46%	10.49%	9.26%	8.14%	9.29%	8.78%	6.85%	3.34%	6.32%
Retail	11.97%	6.93%	6.88%	7.35%	7.05%	6.49%	6.79%	7.11%	6.80%

Source: ING Clarion Research & Investment Strategy.

Cap rate spreads over 10-year T-notes are expected to widen by about
125 basis points (bps) from the current levels during the recession and then
gradually fall in 2009 and 2010. Based on the forecasted cap rates and rent
growth, the total returns for the four core property sectors are projected in
Exhibit 3.20.

The office sector is forecast to suffer the most, with a 297 bps decline
in three-year average total returns. Three-year average total returns for industrial and apartment are forecast to drop by 175 and 48 bps, respectively.
Retail is expected to weather the recession the best, with a decrease of only
25 bps forecast for three-year average total returns.

The forecast total returns for the recession scenario are not significantly
lower than those of the normal scenario. One key reason is that the economic
slowdown and widening credit spreads have already been taken into account
for our forecast for the normal scenario. Another reason is that cap rates are
forecast to widen only approximately 50 bps while the yield of the 10-year
T-note is likely to fall by 75 bps.

CHAPTER 4

Subprime Fallout

The Impact on Commercial Real Estate

Tim Wang and David Lynn
Summer 2007[1]

The U.S. subprime mortgage fallout has sent shockwaves throughout the world's financial system, causing volatility in the capital markets. Investors are concerned that an increasing liquidity crisis could deleteriously impact the overall economy. In this chapter, we assess the impact of the subprime crisis on U.S. commercial real estate investment as viewed during the weeks following the onset of the credit crunch in August 2007.

HOW DID WE GET TO THIS POINT?

Subprime Fallout

The phenomenal expansion of the U.S. housing market beginning in the late 1990s was fueled by 40-year-low mortgage rates, the participation of speculators in some markets, and buyers of second homes, particularly by Baby Boomers. Rapid capital appreciation of this buoyant national housing market caused many borrowers to be priced out of the market. Some financial institutions responded by offering creative financing such as no documentation of income, adjustable mortgages with lower teaser rates, no

---

[1]This paper was originally produced in summer 2007. The data, opinions, and forecasts have not been updated for book publication.

down payment, zero interest for the first year(s), and interest-only loans with negative amortization.

Subprime mortgages now total $1.2 trillion, or 12.8% of total outstanding mortgage debts, according to *Inside Mortgage Finance*. These subprime instruments have made borrowers vulnerable not only to rising interest rates but also to falling home prices. After the Federal Reserve (the Fed) began tightening interest rates in June 2004, the delinquency rate of subprime mortgages increased, doubling to 6.23% by mid-2005.

The distribution of subprime mortgage originations has tended to be nonuniform with high concentrations in a handful of markets listed below (Exhibit 4.1). As expected these markets are characterized by a high degree of speculative transactions.

A surge in housing prices resulted in a glut of inventory and a slowdown in sales, beginning in late 2005. To compound the problem, adjustable-rate mortgages (ARM) underwritten two to three years earlier started to reset in 2006 and 2007. An estimated $500 billion in adjustable-rate mortgages, 80% of which are subprime, will reset in the second half of 2007 and 2008. As a consequence of these resets, subprime borrowers face significantly higher monthly payments, which many borrowers cannot afford to pay.

EXHIBIT 4.1   Metro Areas with the Highest Percentage of Subprime Loans

Top 10	Subprime Loans as a Percent of Total Outstanding Residential Mortgages	
1	Rural (no-metro area)	26.8%
2	McAllen-Edinburg-Mission, TX	26.0%
3	Memphis, TN	24.0%
4	Sharon, PA	23.1%
5	Miami, FL	23.0%
6	Richmond-Petersburg, VA	22.3%
7	Brownsville-Harlingen-San Benito, TX	21.6%
8	Merced, CA	21.6%
9	Sumter, SC	20.7%
10	Bakersfield, CA	20.2%
Major Metro Areas		
37	Houston, TX	13.9%
144	Los Angeles–Long Beach, CA	12.4%
159	Chicago, IL	12.0%
167	Philadelphia, PA	11.8%
198	New York, NY	10.6%

Source: ING Clarion Research & Strategy and First American LoanPerformance, March 2007.

Stalled Credit Pipeline

The subprime market has been dominated by independent mortgage companies specializing in subprime mortgages. These companies typically make loans to subprime borrowers and then sell the high-yield subprime loans to Wall Street investment banks. The investment banks repackage pools of loans and mortgages into structured credit products such as asset-backed securities (ABS), residential mortgage-backed securities (RMBS), and collateralized debt obligations (CDO).

Structured credit products are designed for different investors with varying risk appetites. Pension funds and insurance companies typically buy the high investment-grade tranches of structured products. Conversely, hedge funds and other opportunistic investors prefer the low investment-grade and nonrated equity tranches. Under normal default rates, this high-risk/high-return strategy has the potential to yield an annual return of more than 20%.

Not surprisingly, these high-risk investments were the first to take losses when subprime delinquency rates skyrocketed during the past several months. The Mortgage Bankers Association recently reported that the percentage of subprime loans that were 30 or more days past due climbed to 13.8% in the first quarter of 2007.[2] Several hedge funds took huge losses and filed for bankruptcy protection. Fearing further losses, many investors have stopped investing in subprime-related securities. Without demand for structured products, credit markets are left with a significant amount of debt in the pipeline. Consequently, some subprime lenders have been forced out of business.

NEAR-TERM IMPACT ON THE COMMERCIAL REAL ESTATE MARKET

Will This Push the United State into a Recession?

The current situation is not only a liquidity squeeze but also a confidence crisis. The daily news of foreclosures and hedge fund losses is creating negative sentiment and wider fears that credit is drying up. Although a recession is possible, we do not anticipate such a scenario for the following reasons.

With the exception of the residential housing market, the overall U.S. economy remains strong. Real gross domestic product (GDP) growth was

---

[2]Mortgage Bankers Association, "Delinquencies Decrease in Latest MBA National Delinquency Survey," press release, June 14, 2007. http://www.mbaa.org/NewsandMedia/PressCenter/55132.htm (accessed March 27, 2009).

3.4% during the second quarter of 2007. Unemployment stands at a low 4.6%, reflecting a very tight labor market. The weaker dollar has served to drive growth in exports. Corporate profits are near all-time historic highs, productivity growth is strong at over 2.0% per annum, and P/E (price-earnings) ratios are relatively low (unlike the late 1990s). While the housing sector has slumped, a surging commercial real estate sector in many regional markets has softened the economic blow by shifting employment and investment from the residential sector.

Although credit markets are in temporary disarray, credit fundamentals have not changed. The current default rates of most debt, including corporate bonds, consumer credit, and commercial mortgage-backed securities (CMBS), have not exhibited any meaningful uptick yet. In fact, defaults for commercial mortgages are near an all-time low. For the moment, the subprime crisis seems to be contained in the residential mortgage industry and their investors. In a sense, commercial lending learned its hard lessons in the early 1990s. After the virtual collapse of commercial real estate lending, underwriting standards were raised, transparency increased, and procedures were implemented that are still in place today, keeping the industry healthy. While debt-equity ratios have risen, especially over the last several years, the strong underlying fundamentals of commercial real estate, including income growth and capital appreciation, have justified greater leverage in most cases.

Moreover, consumer spending is strong. Real household incomes have risen 6.0% this year, well above inflation. Speaking of inflation, it is much tamer this year than in the last two, in part due to reduced demand for a wide variety of commodities used in housing production. While the housing sector has been one of the twin locomotives (consumer spending being the main one) pulling the United States out of the last recession, the corporate sector has now more than enough momentum to continue the expansion, albeit at a more subdued rate of growth.

Finally, the Fed has shown to be responsive to the current situation. In case of a full-blown financial crisis or collapse in consumer spending, we expect the Fed to adjust monetary policy by swiftly cutting interest rates. On August 10, 2007, the Fed increased liquidity in the credit market through the direct purchase of $38 billion of MBS.[3] This unprecedented move is strongly suggestive of the Fed's willingness and readiness to restore market confidence. The Fed publicly indicated that it would continue to provide liquidity to the market as it is needed.

---

[3] Al Yoon, "Banks Push MBS on Fed for Liquidity Boost," Thomson Reuters, August 10, 2007.

Widening Spreads

It is clear that credit markets have been repricing in response to investor demand for more favorable terms on corporate bonds and loans. Credit spreads are widening for all levels of debts, including CMBS. The current spreads for AAA-, AA-, A-, and BBB-rated debt are 70, 150, 200, and 400 bps respectively, marking a 45 to 325 bps increase since mid-February 2007.[4]

While this shift is disadvantageous to leveraged buyers, all-cash and low-leveraged buyers will be better positioned to dictate competitive pricing. Over the past two years, leveraged buyouts (LBOs), such as the $39 billion EOP (Equity Office Properties) transaction, have injected a tremendous amount of liquidity into the commercial real estate market. Higher borrowing costs and lackluster demand for such risky debt will no doubt complicate LBO transactions of commercial real estate assets. Consequently, in the near term, large portfolio deals will take longer to execute and capital flows into commercial real estate will occur at a slower pace.

For new commercial real estate transactions, the demand for a higher risk premium is simultaneously putting upward pressure on cap rates and downward pressure on pricing. In particular, the apartment sector, which enjoys very low cap rates, will likely be negatively impacted by increasing borrowing costs. Whether cap rates will rise accordingly remains to be seen; property valuation in markets that are priced to perfection will be under pressure.

Impact on Demand

The fundamentals of the U.S. commercial real estate market remain generally sound, with improving vacancy rates and healthy rent growth in most markets. With the exception of Orange County, where subprime lenders were concentrated, the office sector has not yet suffered the negative impacts of the subprime fallout. As lenders continue to tighten underwriting standards, it is likely that fewer renters will become homeowners. With many more households expected to be renting in the near future, the apartment sector will benefit. The industrial sector (especially assets in coastal core markets) will remain healthy as long as consumer spending does not level off. In the retail sector, markets such as Florida, Southern California, Phoenix, and Las Vegas, where housing corrections have been far more severe than the rest of the country, may face the greatest risk. Big-box discount chains and home furnishing store tenants are suffering the most.

---

[4]Data are provided by Property & Portfolio Research, August 2007.

What's Next?

The Fed's August 2007 survey reported that most commercial banks have tightened lending standards for nontraditional mortgages, including subprime. The new underwriting standards are reminiscent of the aggressive lending reform during the commercial real estate credit crunch of 1990–1991. While the stricter underwriting standards will reduce future residential mortgage defaults, they will certainly delay the recovery of the U.S. housing market. Nevertheless, over the long-run, more stringent standards are good for the housing industry and the U.S. economy.

The repackaged subprime securities have been purchased by numerous investors and as such, ownership and exposure remain unclear. As additional adjustable mortgages reset over the next 18 months, the current subprime unease and the volatility of the financial market are expected to continue, possibly worsening before improving. Hedge funds, investment banks, and insurance companies may well report additional losses over the next several months.

The current subprime fallout is still largely contained within the mortgage investment industry by hedge funds and some financial institutions. It is still too early to determine whether the subprime fallout will spread to other credit areas during the next 6 to 12 months. We are closely monitoring the delinquencies of Alt-A mortgages, prime HELOC (home equity line of credit) loans, and prime ARMs, as well as key economic metrics including employment reports and retail sales. Nonetheless, there are encouraging signs that some opportunistic investors are buying distressed debts, believing that investors are overreacting and that the debt markets will recover some of the losses.

Although debt financing is more expensive, interest rates today are still very low by historic standards. For example, the current yield of the 10-year Treasury note is about 4.7% in comparison to the 30-year average of 7.7%.[5] With the U.S. economy just emerging from a period of historically low interest rates, debt market repricing is a normal, expected adjustment. With a growing amount of capital on the sidelines, investors should recognize the sound fundamentals and return to the market shortly.

---

[5]U.S. Department of Treasury, Office of Debt Management, "Daily Treasury Yield Curve Rates," http://www.ustreas.gov/offices/domestic-finance/debt-management/interest-rate/yield.shtml (accessed June 2007).

CHAPTER 5

Capital Markets

Dramatic Shifts and Opportunities

David Lynn and Tim Wang
Spring 2008[1]

As the subprime mortgage fallout continues to rattle global financial systems, we revisit the topic and evaluate the state of the market. Although widening credit spreads, tightened underwriting criteria, cap rate decompression, declining transaction volumes, and shrinking commercial mortgage-backed securities (CMBS) and securitization markets are all results of the current crisis, commercial real estate continues to be an attractive asset class for institutional investors. This chapter discusses the dramatic shifts in the capital markets as well as strategic investment opportunities.

WIDENING CREDIT SPREADS

Rising subprime delinquencies have led to a stalled credit pipeline and a dramatic widening of credit spreads of all non-Treasury debt including CMBS (Exhibit 5.1). Investors are increasingly seeking safety in U.S. Treasuries, and the yield of the 10-year T-note has dropped to below 3.7%.[2] Concerned about a possible severe economic downturn, the Federal Reserve has

---

[1] This paper was originally produced in spring 2008. The data, opinions, and forecasts have not been updated for book publication.

[2] U.S. Department of Treasury, Office of Debt Management, "Daily Treasury Yield Curve Rates," http://www.ustreas.gov/offices/domestic-finance/debt-management/interest-rate/yield.shtml (accessed March 2008).

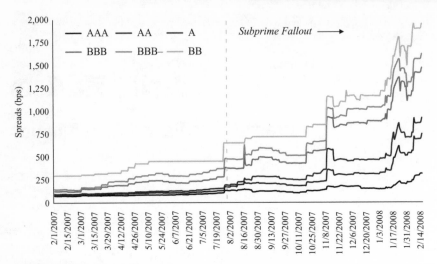

EXHIBIT 5.1   CMBS Spreads (bps) to 10-Year Treasury (newly issued CMBS)
Source: ING Clarion Capital.

cut the target federal funds rate by 300 bps to 2.25%, with additional cuts possible over the next few months.[3]

TIGHTENED UNDERWRITING CRITERIA

Sensitized by the subprime fallout, investors' perception of risk has elevated considerably. Widening credit spreads and tightened lending standards require more equity, lower loan-to-values (LTVs), and higher debt service coverage ratios for new investments. Higher risk premia have simultaneously put upward pressure on cap rates and downward pressure on asset pricing. Cap rate decompression will of course negatively impact total investment returns in the near term.

Cap Rate Decompression

During the last quarter of 2007, cap rates for Class A assets in core markets rose by approximately 10–40 bps according to NCREIF. Going into 2008, we expect that credit market turmoil will continue to negatively influence

---

[3]Federal Reserve Board, Open Market Operations, "Intended Federal Funds Rate," http://www.federalreserve.gov/fomc/fundsrate.htm (accessed March 18, 2008).

EXHIBIT 5.2 Expected Rise in Cap Rates (cap rates are for institutional-quality assets)

	Cap Rates and Cap Rate Changes		
	2007Q4	2008E	Cap Rate Change (bps)
Apartment	5.15%	5.45–5.75%	30–60
Industrial	6.00%	6.30–6.60%	30–60
Office	5.32%	5.62–5.92%	30–60
Retail	6.00%	6.30–6.60%	30–60

Source: ING Clarion Research & Investment Strategy and NCREIF.

commercial real estate investments. The credit crisis has proven to be longer and more severe than initially expected and, with no clear solution in sight, could drag on for several months. Debt financing will remain relatively more expensive and cap rates could continue to rise accordingly. Capital inflow into commercial real estate will slow down substantially in the near future as highly leveraged buyers are forced to the sidelines. With less competition, all-cash and low-leverage institutional investors are better positioned to influence pricing. Many poorly sponsored construction projects could be delayed or even canceled. Overall, we expect cap rates for core properties in primary markets to rise modestly by 30–60 bps for new transactions in 2008 (Exhibit 5.2). In this period of expected low transaction volume, it may take several months for buyers and sellers to reach new "equilibrium pricing."

DECLINING TRANSACTION VOLUMES

According to Real Capital Analytics (RCA), transaction volumes set new records for all property types in 2007, with the total amount surging to $523.0 billion compared to $366.5 billion in 2006 (Exhibit 5.3). A significant component of the higher volume was the privatizations of Equity Office Properties ($39 billion), Hilton Hotels ($26 billion), and Archstone-Smith Trust ($22 billion).

The subprime fallout and credit market volatility are reducing the number of buyers, particularly highly leveraged ones. At the same time, some owners are choosing to hold properties through the downturn rather than to sell at reduced prices. Transaction volumes in the second half of 2007 were down approximately 18% from the first half of the year. We expect this downtrend to continue at least through 2008.

EXHIBIT 5.3   Record Transaction Volumes in 2007

	Transaction Volumes (in USD billions)				
	Apartment	Industrial	Office	Retail	Hotel
2001	20.5	13.6	32.1	11.7	0.3
2002	22.7	11.6	41.3	26.8	0.3
2003	30.3	14.5	46.8	30.1	1.3
2004	51.0	21.0	74.4	58.5	16.1
2005	88.8	36.9	104.1	50.9	29.5
2006	91.7	43.6	138.2	54.8	38.2
2007	99.6	48.0	215.4	72.1	87.9

Source: ING Clarion Research & Investment Strategy and Real Capital Analytics, 2008.

SHRINKING CMBS AND SECURITIZATION MARKETS

New CMBS issuance in the United States totaled $235.8 billion in 2007, a 10% increase over 2006; however, the issuance volume has fallen off sharply since September 2007.[4] The CMBS market is currently in disarray with wide bid-ask spreads and extremely low liquidity. Triggered by the credit crunch, worldwide securitization, including asset-backed securities (ABS), mortgage-backed securities (MBS), CMBS, and collateralized debt obligations (CDOs), has declined sharply (Exhibit 5.4). This dramatic shift in the capital markets presents opportunities for pension funds, insurance companies, commercial banks, and syndicates to lend capital directly to high-quality investment projects at more attractive spreads. Balance sheet lending is expected to regain popularity.

INCREASED REAL ESTATE ALLOCATION

Despite the recent market turmoil, commercial real estate continues to be an attractive asset class, especially for institutions because of its diversification benefits, high current cash flow component, and hedge against inflation. The recent volatility in equity markets, falling U.S. Treasury yields, and rising credit risks could make private real estate investment more attractive.

---

[4]Commercial Mortgage Alert, "Market Monitor: US CMBS Monthly Issuance," March 14, 2008, p. 15.

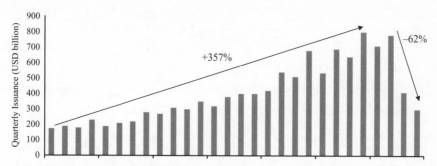

EXHIBIT 5.4 Worldwide Securitization (ABS, MBS, CMBS, CDOs) Issuance
Source: ING Clarion Research & Investment Strategy and Commercial Mortgage
Alert, 2007.

According to Kingsley Associates' 2008 Plan Sponsor Survey, pension
funds are increasing target allocations in real estate. New capital flows to
real estate are projected to be $76 billion in 2008, a 65% increase from 2007
(Exhibit 5.5).[5] Whether this materializes remains to be seen. Opportunistic
and value-added strategies continue to gain a larger share of new capital.

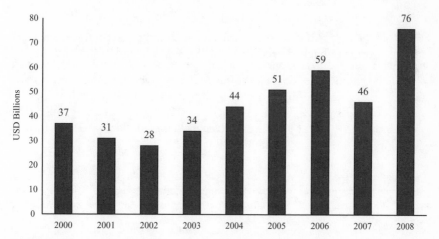

EXHIBIT 5.5 Pension Funds Projected New Capital to Real Estate
Source: ING Clarion Research & Investment Strategy, Kingsley Associates, and IREI,
2008.

---

[5]Larry Gray, "Investors Ramp Up Allocations, Favor High-Yield Strategies: The
Annual Plan Sponsor Survey," *Institutional Real Estate Letter* 20, no. 4 (April 2008).

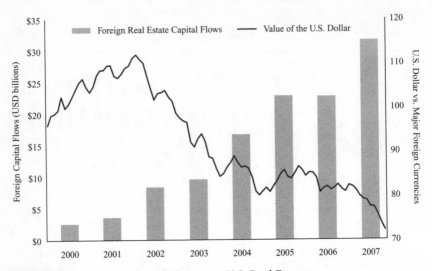

EXHIBIT 5.6   Foreign Capital Flows into U.S. Real Estate
Source: ING Clarion Research & Investment Strategy and Real Capital Analytics, 2007.

Allocation to foreign real estate is also expected to soar, thanks to higher returns in some markets.

The U.S. dollar has declined approximately 35% against major foreign currencies since 2001.[6] One of the effects of this is that U.S. real estate assets have become less expensive for foreign buyers to purchase. In fact, according to RCA, foreign capital flows into U.S. commercial real estate have increased by more than 11 times since 2000, totaling approximately $33 billion in 2007 (Exhibit 5.6). With a weakening dollar, we expect foreign capital inflow to remain strong in 2008.

---

[6]Moody's Economy.com, "Weighted Average Exchange Value of U.S. Dollar: Broad Index, for United States," *DataBuffet.com,* http://www.databuffet.com (accessed March 2008).

CHAPTER 6

The Bid-Ask Problem and Game Theory

Jeff Organisciak, Tim Wang, and David Lynn
Fall 2008[1]

A large bid-ask spread between buyers and sellers of commercial real estate has been widely reported. Evidence of this spread can be seen in the drastic reduction of transaction volume in the commercial real estate market. This chapter attempts to explain the ongoing situation of low transaction volume in commercial real estate due to the bid-ask differential. It 'employs a game-theoretic approach to explain recent market conditions and how transaction liquidity may resume.

EVIDENCE OF A BID-ASK SPREAD

Commercial real estate transaction volume decreased drastically over the first half of 2008. After peaking in the second quarter of 2007 at over $140 billion, transaction volume for the second quarter of 2008 was only $38 billion, a decline of 73% (Exhibit 6.1). Transaction volume is a measure of market liquidity, and this severe decline in volume implies a large reduction in the liquidity of commercial real estate assets.

Liquidity varies over time and is typically driven by the number of potential buyers, and changes in cash flows and debt capacity.[2] Many

---

[1]This paper was originally produced in fall 2008. The data, opinions, and forecasts have not been updated for book publication.

[2]Andrei Shleifer and Robert W. Vishny, "Liquidation Values and Debt Capacity: A Market Equilibrium Approach," *Journal of Finance* 47, no. 4 (1992): 1343–1366.

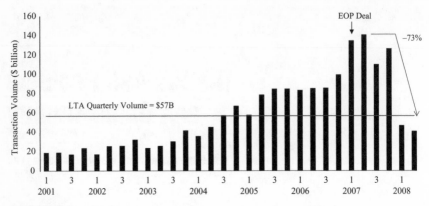

EXHIBIT 6.1 Total Commercial Real Estate Transaction Volume,
2001Q1–2008Q2
Source: ING Clarion Research & Investment Strategy and Real Capital Analytics,
2008.

highly leveraged buyers entered the commercial real estate market over the
past few years due to low interest rates and easily available debt financing.
The broadening of the set of real estate buyers had the effect of simultaneously increasing asset prices and liquidity. Recent credit market turmoil
removed many of these highly leveraged buyers from the commercial real
estate market and consequently liquidity has decreased.

In a rising economy, capital flows into real estate are high and expectations of future cash flows are optimistic. These factors increase property
valuations and the overall health of the real estate industry. When the industry is healthy, market participants are likely to be in a position to acquire additional assets, which has the effect of expanding market liquidity.
Expanded liquidity further increases competition for assets, tightening the
bid-ask spread. Slowing economic growth in many markets is currently forcing real estate market players to readjust expectations, leading to uncertain
pricing and lower liquidity.

The combination of fewer buyers and differing expectations has triggered a period of market adjustment where pricing is uncertain. For example, while general sentiment would indicate that commercial real estate prices are declining, the NCREIF Transactions-Based Index showed
an increase of 2.1% in the first quarter of 2008, after declining for the
previous two quarters. The market pricing adjustment is manifested in
negotiations as a widening "bid-ask spread" between buyers and sellers.

Henry Pollakowski, a senior economist at MIT Center for Real Estate observes that "the gap represents a historically sharp disconnect between supply and demand."[3]

Evidence of a bid-ask spread can be seen clearly in the actions of individual buyers and sellers. Potential buyers have been influenced by negative market sentiment and expectations of lower future capital values and are subsequently bidding low for assets. On the other side, most sellers are not feeling great pressure to sell and, therefore, are not lowering asking prices. Owners of quality buildings do not want to sell their assets for less than their perceived value. Instead, sellers are opting to pull their properties from the market and continue to reap the cash flows from the rent roll. The income-producing feature of commercial real estate makes delaying a sale an attractive option. Indeed, for well-leased buildings with sustainable capital structures, there is very little incentive to sell. The cumulative effect of these buyer-seller interactions is shown in Exhibit 6.2, as the ratio of closed-deal volume to offered-deal volume has fallen well below 1.0 over the first two quarters of 2008.

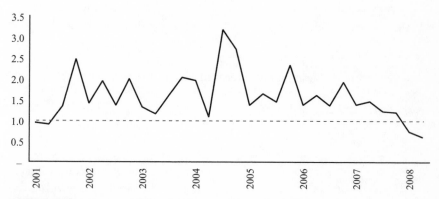

EXHIBIT 6.2 Average Ratio of Property Closings to Offerings (four core property types)
Source: ING Clarion Research & Investment Strategy and Real Capital Analytics, 2008.

---

[3]Comment on "MIT Commercial Property Price Index Turns Higher," *Center for Real Estate: MIT News Blog,* May 6, 2008, http://web.mit.edu/newsoffice/2008/real-estate-0506.html.

GAME THEORETIC EXPLANATION
OF THE BID-ASK SPREAD

Game theory attempts to explain behavior in strategic situations, where the success of an individual's action depends on the choices of others. When applied to bargaining situations, game theory is known as bargaining theory. A bargaining situation is defined as "an exchange situation where a pair of individuals (or organizations) can engage in mutually beneficial trade, but have conflicting interests over the terms of the trade."[4] Here we apply the game theoretic framework to the current bargaining situations in the commercial real estate market to help explain the widening bid-ask spread.

Bargaining situations are modeled as non-cooperative sequential move games, based on the alternating-offers model (Exhibit 6.3). In this model, a buyer B and a seller S, bargain over the price p, at which a property is traded. Each player has his own valuation of the property. The seller has a holding value V_s, for continued ownership of the asset. The buyer has an investment value V_b, which represents the discounted cash flow valuation of owning the asset. The seller's expected profit (also known as the reservation price) is the transaction price minus the holding value $(P - V_s)$, and the buyer's expected profit is the investment value minus the transaction price $(V_b - P)$.

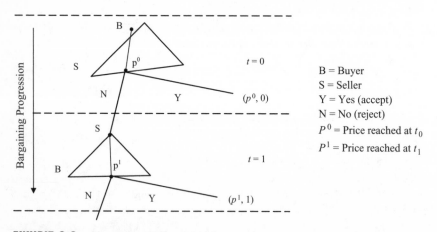

EXHIBIT 6.3   Alternating-Offers Model
Source: M. J. Osborne & A. Rubinstein, *Bargaining and Markets* (1990), reprinted with permission from Emerald Press.

---

[4]Abhinay Muthoo, *Bargaining Theory with Applications* (Cambridge: Cambridge University Press, 1999), 1.

Bargaining begins with the buyer making an offer p^0, to the seller at time $t = 0$. The seller can accept Y, or reject N, and make a counter offer. If the seller accepts, then the agreement reached is $(p^0, 0)$ meaning that an agreement was reached at price p^0 in period $t = 0$. If the seller rejects and makes a counter offer, then the game moves into period $t = 1$ and the buyer can either accept or make a counter offer. This process of alternating offers continues until an agreement is reached. If no agreement is ever reached, then each player receives the disagreement outcome d, which is the utility from not reaching an agreement.[5] The model makes three main assumptions about player preferences: (1) bargaining failure is the worst outcome; (2) profit is desirable; and (3) time is valuable.[6]

The real estate market is made up of buyers and sellers with heterogeneous expectations and a range of property valuations. When in the market, if a buyer's reservation price is higher than a seller's reservation price, a trade will occur. Exhibit 6.4 illustrates the distribution of reservation prices, where the overlap is interpreted as the transaction zone. As general expectations become more positive, reservation prices shift up (seller's market in Exhibit 6.4) which narrows the bid-ask spread, and increases liquidity and market pricing. When expectations become negative (buyer's market), buyers reservation prices shift down, which widens the bid-ask spread and decreases liquidity and market pricing. As these ranges move apart, the bid-ask spread widens and transaction volume drops.

While not a perfect description of the negotiation process in commercial real estate markets, the model captures many of the key components and is

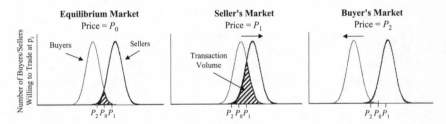

EXHIBIT 6.4 Reservation Price Distributions
Source: ING Clarion Research & Investment Strategy and Fisher, Gatzlaff, Geltner, and Haurin, 2003.

---

[5]Ibid., 36.

[6]Martin J. Osborne and Ariel Rubinstein, *Bargaining and Markets* (New York: Academic Press, 1990), 33.

a relevant abstraction. We present three plausible explanations of widening bid-ask spreads below.

Imperfect Information

Imperfect information refers to the fact that one party in a negotiation may not know the counterparty's valuation of the asset in question. The uncertainty of market participants of the proper valuations for commercial real estate assets is causing a *delay in the bargaining process*. The widening bid-ask spread is a result of this delay, caused by a negotiation strategy employed under imperfect information.

Under imperfect information, each party uses offers and counter offers to learn information about the counterparty's valuation as well as to signal whether they are in a strong bargaining position.[7] This strategic delay in bargaining is extending negotiations, which is partly responsible for the current slowdown in transaction volume.

Consider a situation where a seller's valuation is common knowledge and the buyer's valuation can be either high or low. A seller makes the first offer by listing a price for the asset, or by communicating pricing expectations through market sources. The choice of the seller's first offer depends on the expectation of the buyer's valuation. If the buyer has a high valuation, as would be the case in a market with positive expectations (Seller's Market in Exhibit 6.4) then the seller would ask a high price. If it turns out that the seller's expectation was incorrect and the buyer actually had a low valuation, the buyer would reject this offer and make a low counter offer. This counter offer would typically be made after a strategic delay by the buyer in order to communicate that he is in a stronger bargaining position.[8]

If the buyer has a low valuation (a market with negative expectations: Buyer's Market in Exhibit 6.4), then the seller cannot afford to ask high because it is probable that the buyer will reject and the delay between offers will be more costly. Therefore, in this market, the seller will ask a low price, and the buyer will accept.[9]

In the current environment, market expectations are shifting from positive to negative, and sellers are unsure of potential buyers' valuations. This

---

[7]Ibid., 92.

[8]Anat R. Admati and Motty Perry, "Strategic Delay in Bargaining," *Review of Economic Studies* 54 (1987): 345–364.

[9]Ibid.

uncertainty makes the sellers' best strategy difficult to determine. Many sellers are still maintaining high price expectations, and therefore as buyers' price expectations decrease negotiations often result in rejected offers and strategic delay, in other words a widening bid-ask spread.

Inside Options

In a negotiation, the seller has what is known as an *inside option*, the option to retain ownership of the asset. This option allows the seller to continue collecting whatever utility he receives by owning the asset. In commercial real estate, this option is especially valuable because leased assets produce a steady cash flow. The inside option increases a seller's bargaining power, and in today's environment many are using this strategy to their advantage. While commercial real estate market fundamentals are weakening, they are still sufficiently strong in most markets to justify stable cash flows.

A seller's increased bargaining power has a significant impact on the equilibrium price. He will require a higher selling price as compensation for giving up the future cash flow. The seller is always guaranteed to receive at least the property's cash flow by rejecting any offer below his desired price. The seller's payoff is described as

$$\int_0^{t\Delta} g_s \exp(-r_s s)ds + p_s \exp(-r_s\, t\Delta)$$

where the first term is the net present value of the seller's future cash flows (at discount rate, $\exp(-r_s\Delta)$), and the second term is the net present value of the price at which an agreement is reached. To reach an agreement, the buyer must offer at least the net present value of the seller's future cash flows, and then bargain over the remaining disagreement in price.[10]

The strength of the inside option is a unique feature of bargaining in commercial real estate. Residential real estate generally does not produce income. Consequently, single-family sellers are left with an inside option to either continue living in the home or to rent the home. The relative weakness of the single-family sellers' inside option may help to explain the faster pricing adjustment in the for-sale housing market. A single-family

---

[10]Muthoo, *Bargaining Theory with Applications*, 139.

seller's bargaining power is lower, and as a result he is likely to accept a lower price.

Outside Options

The option to cease negotiation with the current counterparty and find another counterparty to bargain with is known as an *outside option*. If a buyer or seller feels that he can increase his payoff by bargaining with a different counterparty in the future, then this option is valuable.

The value of the outside option depends on the degree of competition in the property market. Competition affects the length and costs of the search for a new counterparty. As markets become more competitive it is easier to find a new counterparty, which makes search costs lower. Lower search costs effectively increase the value of the outside option. Under this circumstance, the sellers' strategy is to ask for higher prices, because they have a better chance of getting the desired price from one of the many other buyers. The buyers, on the other hand, can make relatively lower bids (than in a less competitive market), because they have a better chance of getting their desired price accepted by some other seller.[11] This competition keeps the sellers' prices from being too high and buyers' bids from being too low, causing low volatility of prices.

Outside options do not shift the curves in Exhibit 6.4, but make them wider or narrower depending on the level of market competition (Exhibit 6.5). In more competitive markets, the bid-ask spread is relatively narrow, and many transactions occur around the market price. As markets become less competitive, the range of potential price agreements expands. Buyers and sellers may choose to continue bargaining with the current counterparty, even if the outcome is not ideal, because the cost of finding a better trading partner outweighs the potential benefit. As a result, an increasing number of negotiations are characterized by wide bid-ask spreads, and price agreements are more evenly distributed around the theoretical market price. This could also explain the volatility of asset prices in markets with low liquidity.

In competitive markets with strong fundamentals the outside option is more valuable, as an asset with an equal or higher cash flow may be purchased rather easily at a similar price. In the current environment, an asset with strong cash flow may be hard to replicate, and therefore may

---

[11]S. Maekawa, Bargaining Model in the Property Market with Outside Option, unpublished manuscript, Korea Real Estate Analyst Association, 2008.

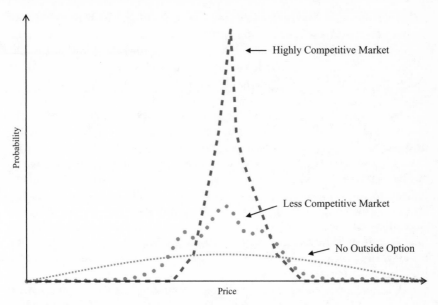

EXHIBIT 6.5 Transaction Price Volatility by Degree of Competition
Source: ING Clarion Research & Investment Strategy.

command a premium, making the outside option less valuable. This describes the phenomenon of the "flight to quality" in slowing economic times.

HOW WILL LIQUIDITY RETURN?

Bargaining costs drive bargaining outcomes. The costs of delay in bargaining affect the time preferences of each player. A player's payoff decreases as time goes on, so he is motivated to make an agreement sooner, rather than later. Relative bargaining costs determine the strength of a player's position. If Player A's bargaining cost is lower than Player B's, then Player A is in a strong bargaining position. Under perfect information, the player with the lower bargaining costs accrues a disproportionate amount of economic "rents."[12]

In commercial real estate, bargaining costs are often described in colloquial parlance as "motivation" for buyers or sellers. A seller is said to

---

[12]Osborne and Rubinstein, *Bargaining and Markets.* 93.

be highly motivated or even distressed, when there is a high carrying cost driving the need to sell. The result of these transactions is for the buyer to reap much of the benefit of the transaction in the form of a low sale price. In these cases, the buyer is able to reach an outcome at a price lower than the fundamental value of the asset, because of the high bargaining costs of the seller.

The primary bargaining costs for sellers are property carrying costs, debt coverage, and if the asset is held in a fund, redemption requirements. Some of these costs are constant and fixed, but others are variable. A property financed with a short-term loan may have low debt coverage in the near term, but faces the risk of increasing debt costs in the future. A recent example is the sale of New York City's General Motors Building by Macklowe Properties. Refinancing the property was not possible due to higher debt costs. Accordingly, Macklowe's bargaining costs were well known to be high, and this put potential buyers in a very strong bargaining position. The resulting trade was favorable for the buyer, as evidenced by a significant discount to previous market pricing.

A similar problem currently confronts the retail REIT General Growth Properties. As shown in Exhibit 6.6, a large amount of debt is scheduled to mature in the near term, likely at higher costs. To alleviate this problem, company management is attempting to raise equity by establishing private joint ventures on certain assets. Because their bargaining costs are well known to be high, they may be forced to accept lower bids from potential partners.

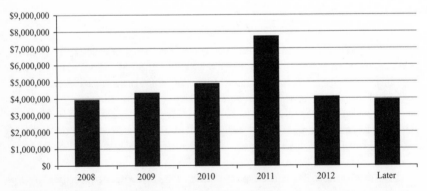

EXHIBIT 6.6 Annual Debt Maturities of General Growth Properties
Source: ING Clarion Research & Investment Strategy, General Growth Properties Annual Report, Form 10-K, December 31, 2007, 49.

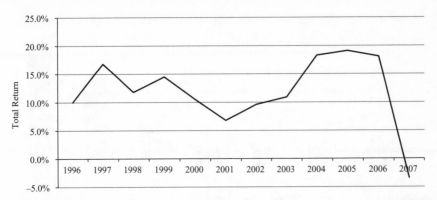

EXHIBIT 6.7 IPD-UK Total Return Index, 1996–2007
Source: ING Clarion Research & Investment Strategy and Investment Property Databank.

Redemption requirements increase a seller's bargaining costs as redemptions are requested and the fund needs to liquidate assets to pay investors. The wave of distressed sales in the UK office market during the third quarter of 2007 was driven by a large number of redemption requirements on the open-end funds holding those properties. The effect of the rash of redemptions was to simultaneously raise the bargaining costs of a large number of sellers, which put buyers into an extremely strong bargaining position. The resulting impact on prices can be seen in the sharp decline in the IPD UK Total Return Index over that time (Exhibit 6.7). Buyers were able to use their strong bargaining positions to command very low pricing.

While bargaining costs for buyers may not be as apparent, they still play an important role in the bargaining process. The main bargaining cost for buyers is the opportunity cost of capital invested in real estate funds, sometimes referred to as "treasury drag." When money invested into a real estate fund is not used to purchase real estate, it costs the fund the spread between real estate returns and the present allocation. More money has been raised in real estate equity funds than ever before; Real Capital Analytics forecasts that over $300 billion will be raised in 2008 alone (Exhibit 6.8). As the investment period for these funds moves toward expiration, the opportunity cost of buyers will continue to increase.

In the current environment, reliable comparable sales information is not always available because transaction volume declined so quickly. Negotiations are taking longer while each party attempts to understand the bargaining strength of the counterparty, attempting to maximize the

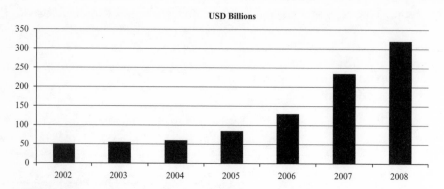

EXHIBIT 6.8   Real Estate Equity Fundraising,[a] 2002–2008 (forecast, targeted equity raised by high-yield real estate funds)
Source: ING Clarion Research & Investment Strategy, IREI/Kinsley Investor Survey, 2008; reprinted with permission from Pricewaterhouse Coopers LLP; *Korpacz Real Estate Investor Survey,*® second quarter 2008.

payoff. As the bargaining costs of sellers increase, bargaining outcomes will be reached more quickly. In the near term, buyers will demand distressed prices, and some transactions driven by sellers with high bargaining costs will be priced at levels below fundamental values. When transactions occur, pricing outcomes in the current environment will be revealed and new price expectations will be established.

As more time passes, the growing volume of capital waiting for investment will likely have to be deployed as buyers' bargaining costs rise. This will level the relative bargaining costs of buyers and sellers, and could support market clearing pricing, potentially obviating truly distressed pricing. These expectations will probably drive future price negotiations as prices continue to adjust. As this cycle repeats, we expect new equilibrium prices will be established that should provide increased pricing transparency and further influence price adjustment and transaction liquidity.

CONCLUSION

The bid-ask spread is largely influenced by pricing uncertainty and differing expectations. In today's thinly traded market, pricing tends to be more volatile or nonexistent, which further increases pricing uncertainty. The bid-ask spread will likely remain wide in the short term as buyers and sellers are divided in their expectations about future property pricing, and the pace of negotiations continues to be tepid.

Nonetheless, there are and will be motivated sellers with high carrying costs, who will be forced to accept low bids. As more such transactions repeat in the marketplace, additional sellers will adjust their pricing expectations downward. This will move the market toward a new pricing equilibrium over the next twelve to eighteen months. The new pricing equilibrium will reflect the new risk and return expectations.

Two

Active Strategies

- "Residential Land Investment" examines the dramatic fall of residential land and housing prices around the country. It maps the geography of distress and develops a number of strategies to exploit this opportunity while considering attendant risks.
- "The U.S. Hotel Market and Strategy" surveys the current hotel market and forecasts returns for metros around the country and also by hotel segment, concluding that urban luxury hotels are better-positioned relative to other niches.
- "Global Gateway Industrial Market Investment" makes a strong case for investing in globally integrated industrial markets. These markets have experienced higher growth, and many are beginning to become supply constrained.
- "The Opportunity in Senior Housing" suggests that this niche could be opportune given surging demographic trends in both the silent generation and baby boomers. It maps geographic areas of opportunity and outlines several investment strategies.
- "Active Portfolio Management Using Modern Portfolio Theory" examines historic and forecast returns and volatilities in major property sectors and metro areas. That analysis is then used to illustrate the potential for increasing returns in a hypothetical core real estate fund by rebalancing the mix of assets and markets.
- "Derivatives in Private Equity Real Estate" discusses the potential for real estate derivatives as a tool for hedging downside risk, for certain long strategies, and to gain coverage of markets and sectors faster

and with lower transaction costs. While still nascent, we anticipate eventual growth and widespread use of these tools in commercial real estate.

- "Opportunities in Infrastructure Investment" explores certain potential opportunities with private sector investment in this expanding sector.

CHAPTER 7

Residential Land Investment

Bohdy Hedgcock and David Lynn
Summer 2008[1]

Distress in the housing market is presenting increasing opportunities to acquire land intended for future residential development at a discount. The general approach is simple: Take control of land at reduced prices due to the current market distress and resell the land at a higher price when the market returns. Adding value by increasing the permitted intensity of development allows for increased potential returns.

Given the amount and variety of land available, a thorough understanding of market fundamentals is essential to identifying target markets. The focus should be on areas with strong long-term growth prospects (employment, income, and population), attractive quality of life amenities, and a political/regulatory environment that strikes a balance between predictability in the entitlement process and some element of supply constraints. Opportunities to move beyond the traditional single-family subdivision to include a mix of housing types and uses offer potentially higher returns.

In selecting markets, our analysis identifies three related approaches, targeting a range of metro markets.

- *Distressed land markets.* These markets have seen significant declines in home prices, presenting opportunities to purchase land at a steep discount to peak prices. The target markets exhibit a combination of price declines with strong, long-term expectations for job and population growth.

---

[1]This paper was originally produced in summer 2008. The data, opinions, and forecasts have not been updated for book publication.

- *High-growth land markets.* These markets are primarily distinguished by relatively affordable housing coupled with strong prospects for job and population growth over time. While the absolute numbers of employment and population in high growth markets may be lower than in many larger markets, the rate of growth in these markets is higher, indicating momentum, desirability, and potential. Price declines are not as steep as in the distressed markets. While development on the urban edge is more likely in these markets, infill opportunities also provide attractive opportunities. Development in more suburban locations should be readily served by necessary infrastructure and located within the path of growth.
- *Infill land markets.* Supply constraints, both physical and political, limit opportunities for land development in many global gateway cities and mature metros. Nonetheless, where vacant or underutilized land can be identified, these markets offer potential for strong returns based on a combination of dependable demand and high or accelerating housing prices. Projects may be more complicated, including a mix of uses, higher density development, and a more challenging entitlement process.

There is overlap across these strategies. Actual investment decisions must consider an even larger variety of factors that explore the unique aspects of individual properties as well as the market and submarket fundamentals.

THE MARKET

The single-family housing market represents an untapped opportunity for institutional investment. Despite the size of the market and its historic returns, the diversified ownership pattern severely limits the ability of investors to participate in the housing market.

Even with recent declines in the market, housing remains the second largest asset class in the United States, just under the fixed income market

EXHIBIT 7.1 Housing Correlation

	Housing	Bonds	Stocks	REITs
Housing	X			
Bonds	−0.169	X		
Stocks	−0.390	0.052	X	
REITs	−0.074	0.177	0.153	X

Source: Chicago Mercantile Exchange, 2007.

and larger than the equities market. Relative to other real estate sectors, the single-family housing market is far larger; more than four times the market value of all commercial real estate and dwarfing the public equity (REIT) market. The housing market also offers historically attractive returns, relative stability, and diversification (Exhibit 7.1) from other markets.

Because the market's value is held largely by individual households and small operating companies, however, there have typically been relatively limited opportunities for the institutional investor to participate in the single-family housing market. The most common approach relies on equity investment in publicly traded homebuilding companies. The development of derivatives and futures markets related to single-family home prices suggests a likely future opportunity, but the small scale of that market and concerns related to derivatives trading in the current economic environment limits the potential. More direct participation—partnering with homebuilders or land developers to hold land and potentially bring projects through the entitlement and development process—has historically been limited.

Distress in the Housing Market

The housing market began showing signs of weakness in some markets as early as 2004. Production began declining in all regions in 2005, and prices started to decline in most markets and nationally in 2006. Distress related to subprime mortgages has intensified the fall. With foreclosures rising, particularly for subprime loans, lenders have instituted stricter underwriting standards, reducing the pool of potential buyers (Exhibit 7.2). With demand reduced and supply still high, home prices began falling in many markets. Some potential buyers—even those with strong credit—are waiting

EXHIBIT 7.2 Q4 2007 Foreclosure Statistics

Loan Type	Percent of Outstanding Loans (Q4 07)	Percent of Foreclosures Started (Q4 07)	Quarterly Change in Foreclosure Starts (basis points)
Prime Fixed	65%	18%	0
Prime ARM	15%	20%	4
Subprime Fixed	6%	12%	14
Subprime ARM	7%	42%	57
FHA & VA	7%	8%	−4

Source: ING Clarion Research & Investment Strategy and Mortgage Bankers Association National Delinquency Survey, March 2008.

on the sidelines, holding out for even bigger discounts. The distressed housing market is expected to continue to be a drag on economic growth through 2009.

A variety of indicators confirm that the current U.S. housing market is struggling with high inventories of new and existing homes, reduced mortgage financing availability, and weak homebuyer confidence.

- *Sales volume.* Sales of new one-family houses in January 2008 were down by 34% over the previous year, while sales of existing one-family homes were down by 23% over the same period. The current inventory of homes on the market represents about a 10-month supply based on the current sales rate.[2]
- *Production.* New home starts in 2007 totaled 1.355 million housing units, the fewest since 1993, and down 25% from the previous year. A three-decade peak for new starts of 2.29 million units was reached in January 2006. In past housing downturns, production declined for between three and five years before increasing again. While the oversupply problem is receding as homebuilders pull back on deliveries, data suggests that a continued slowdown, on par with those of previous housing downturns, is required to bring supply back in line with the long-term demand trend. Witten Advisors estimates an oversupply of both owner-occupied and rental units totaling more than 1,000,000 units as of Q3 2007 (Exhibits 7.3 and 7.4).[3]
- *Prices.* Home prices in an aggregate index of 20 metropolitan areas fell 7.7% in the 12 months through December 2007, according to the S&P/Case-Shiller Index. Only three markets—Seattle, Portland, and Charlotte—recorded gains in home prices over 2007. Miami, Phoenix, and Las Vegas saw the largest declines over the same period.[4] Another measure of home prices, reported by the National Association of Realtors, reports the national median home price declined by 1.8% in 2007. According to that measure, Sacramento, Detroit, and New Orleans saw

---

[2]U.S. Department of Commerce, "U.S. Census Bureau News Joint Release U.S. Department of Housing and Urban Development," http://www.census.gov (accessed February 27, 2008).

[3]U.S. Census Bureau, "New Residential Construction Index," and Witten Advisors, "Q3 2007 Market Reports."

[4]Standard & Poor's, "S&P/Case-Schiller Home Price Index: U.S. National Home Price Values," http://www2.standardandpoors.com/spf/pdf/index/CS_HomePrice_History_022603.xls (accessed February 26, 2007).

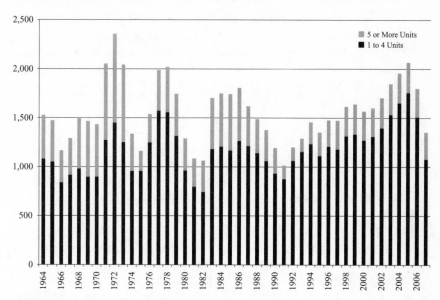

EXHIBIT 7.3 U.S. Annual Housing Starts
Source: ING Clarion Research & Investment Strategy and U.S. Census Bureau, 2008.

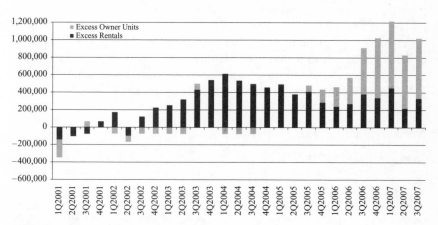

EXHIBIT 7.4 U.S. Excess Housing Units
Excess housing supply is derived from vacancy surveys of housing units and estimates the over- and undersupply based on the spread from historic vacancy rates in owner-occupied and rental units (Witten Advisors, U.S. Market Report, Q3 2007).

Source: ING Clarion Research & Investment Strategy and Witten Advisors, 2007 Q4.

the largest decreases of major metro areas over the year; Salt Lake City, San Antonio, and Charlotte saw the biggest gains.[5]

- *Mortgage lending and foreclosure.* Data from the Mortgage Bankers Association (MBA) reports that 2.04% of all loans outstanding at the end of the fourth quarter are in the foreclosure process, up 35 basis points (bps) from the previous quarter and 87 bps from the prior year. In addition, 5.8% of all loans were in default, up 23 bps from the third quarter of 2007, and up 85 bps from the previous year (Exhibit 7.2). The delinquency rate is the highest in the MBA survey since 1985, while the rate of foreclosure starts and the percentage of loans in the process of foreclosure are at all-time highs. The foreclosure rate will likely continue to climb as adjustable-rate mortgages reset to higher rates.[6]

Saddled with debt and working from a business model that relies on a steady flow of cash from sales and associated mortgage businesses, the homebuilders are aggressively decreasing their inventories. For example, D.R. Horton has been auctioning off properties. Hovnanian completed a "Deal of the Century" promotion in September, slashing prices on unsold homes by up to 30%. Pulte Homes offered to pay buyers' mortgages and taxes for six months. Lennar Corp. put homes up for auction on the Internet. Ryland Group offered buyers a free finished basement and a plasma television in one promotion.[7]

Homebuilders have also begun selling off excess land acquired for future development. Hovnanian notes in its most recent annual report that the company has reduced its total land position by 47% from the peak in April 2006, and that they expect that number to come down even further in 2008.[8] D.R. Horton reduced its land and lot supply by 29% in Fiscal 2007, and by

[5]National Association of Realtors, "Metropolitan Area Prices," Fourth Quarter, 2007, http://www.realtor.org/research/research/metroprice (accessed February 24, 2008).

[6]Mortgage Bankers Association, "Delinquencies and Foreclosures Increase in Latest MBA Surveyt," http://www.mortgagebankers.org/NewsandMedia/PressCenter/60619.htm (accessed March 6, 2008).

[7]Bob Ivry, "Homebuilders Liquidate Assets in Desperation Sales," *Bloomberg.com*, October 5, 2007, http://www.bloomberg.com/apps/news?pid=20601109&refer=home&sid=aUiIJ0tcL_OQ.

[8]Hovnanian Enterprises, Inc., "Hovnanian Enterprises Reports Fiscal 2007 Results," *Trading Markets.com*, http://www.tradingmarkets.com/.site/news/Stock%20News/926151/ (accessed December 18, 2007).

46% from its March 2006 peak.[9] In November 2007, Lennar Corp. sold an 80% stake in 11,000 properties in eight states to Morgan Stanley Real Estate. The price represented a 60% discount from the valuation just two months prior.[10] The five biggest homebuilders by revenue—Lennar, D.R. Horton, Pulte, Centex, and KB Home—wrote off a combined $3.3 billion in the third quarter on land they own and will not build on or options to buy land they are choosing not to exercise. Exhibit 7.5 illustrates the number of lots controlled by many of the largest U.S. homebuilders and the change from 2005 to 2007.[11]

All of these examples illustrate the lengths that homebuilders are going to as they struggle to maintain cash flow and move land off of their balance sheets. As the housing slump continues, we expect more and more sellers will start cutting prices. In addition, having moved their least desirable properties

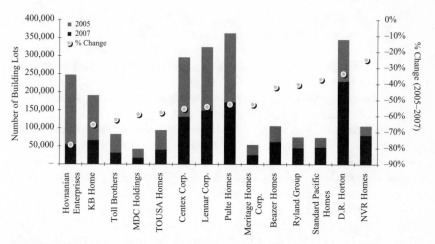

EXHIBIT 7.5 Percent Change in Number of Building Lots, 2005–2007
Source: ING Clarion Research & Investment Strategy, National Association of Homebuilders, *Mortgage Banking*, July 2008.

[9]D.R. Horton, *2007 Annual Report*, p. 3, http://www.drhorton.com/corp/RedirectDisclaimer.do?irRedirect=finAnnualReportDef (accessed March 14, 2008).

[10]Michael Corkery, "How Hot Land Sales Offset a Housing Glut in Phoenix," *Wall Street Journal*, December 10, 2007, p. B1.

[11]National Association of Homebuilders, compiled from annual reports of public companies, as reported in Kenneth S. Lewis, "Down the Road," *Mortgage Banking*, July 2008, 62.

first, prime properties may become increasingly available if homebuilders continue to struggle. We believe that buyers with the financial strength to wait out the slump will be well-positioned for gains when the housing market recovers.

Opportunities in the Housing Market

Despite the current distress, we believe the long-term picture for the housing market is strong. Interest rates remain at historically low levels, recent declines have helped to address affordability gaps between prices and incomes, and solid supply and demand fundamentals suggest both short- and long-term opportunities in the market. Writing in his quarterly report, Peter Linneman of the Wharton School observes:

> [T]he problem will not be too much housing, but rather acute short-ages in many markets, as homebuilders will lag in terms of pro-duction. Never forget that the U.S. population continues to grow, homes are still being burned and torn down, and building restrictions are becoming ever more difficult. These factors will increase the demand for housing relative to supply for the next decade.[12]

Growing Demand A growing population will continue to demand additional housing stock in the long run. The U.S. population is projected to expand by nearly 30% between 2000 and 2030, adding more than 80 million people. Growth will likely be focused primarily in the West and the South, with those regions expected to grow by 45.8% and 42.9%, respectively. The top 10 states in terms of total growth are expected to absorb 74% of the national population increase. Only two states (North Dakota and West Virginia) and the District of Columbia are projected to lose population over the period (Exhibits 7.6–7.7).

"Toward a New Metropolis: The Opportunity to Rebuild America," a study by the Brookings Institution, uses U.S. Census population projections to estimate the amount of new development necessary to accommodate future growth.[13] That study estimates that by 2030 the nation will need about 427 billion square feet of built space. About 82 billion square feet of that total will be from the replacement of existing space and 131 billion will

---

[12]Peter Linneman, *The Linneman Letter*, 7, no. 4 (Winter 2007).

[13]Arthur C. Nelson, "Toward a New Metropolis: The Opportunity to Rebuild America," Brookings Institute, December 2004, http://www.brookings.edu/reports/2004/12metropolitanpolicy_nelson.aspx.

EXHIBIT 7.6 Top and Bottom States by Absolute and Percentage Population Growth, 2000–2030

Rank	State	Change in Total Population (2000–2030) Number	State	Change in Total Population (2000–2030) Percentage
	United States	82,162,529	United States	29.20%
1	Florida	12,703,391	Nevada	114.30%
2	California	12,573,213	Arizona	108.80%
3	Texas	12,465,924	Florida	79.50%
4	Arizona	5,581,765	Texas	59.80%
5	North Carolina	4,178,426	Utah	56.10%
6	Georgia	3,831,385	Idaho	52.20%
7	Virginia	2,746,504	North Carolina	51.90%
8	Washington	2,730,680	Georgia	46.80%
9	Nevada	2,283,845	Washington	46.30%
10	Maryland	1,725,765	Oregon	41.30%
42	Maine	136,174	Nebraska	6.40%
43	Nebraska	109,984	South Dakota	6.00%
44	Rhode Island	104,622	Wyoming	5.90%
45	Vermont	103,000	Pennsylvania	4.00%
46	South Dakota	45,618	New York	2.60%
47	Wyoming	29,197	Ohio	1.70%
48	Iowa	28,848	Iowa	1.00%
49	North Dakota	−35,634	West Virginia	−4.90%
50	West Virginia	−88,385	North Dakota	−5.50%
51	District of Columbia	−138,645	District of Columbia	−24.20%

Source: Brookings Institute; ING Clarion Research & Investment Strategy and U.S. Census, 2004.

be newly constructed space. Thus, 50% of that 427 billion will have to be constructed between now and 2030.

According to the Brookings study, the vast majority of that new space will be for housing. In 2000, the nation had 116 million residential units. About 155 million units will be needed to accommodate the increased population in 2030. Thus about 39 million units will be needed to accommodate the new population (plus an additional 20 million units to replace obsolete existing housing). Therefore, approximately 38% of all residential units that will exist in the United States in 2030 will be built after 2000. The Northeast will see the fewest number of new housing units, while the South and the

EXHIBIT 7.7   Residential Development Change, Ranked by the Percent of Housing Units in 2030 Built Since 2000

MSA	Units 2000	Units 2030	New Units Needed 2030[a]	% Units Built After 2000	% New Units 2030
Las Vegas	656	1,343	810	123.50%	60.30%
Austin	496	983	580	116.90%	59.00%
Phoenix	1,331	2,417	1,336	100.40%	55.30%
West Palm Beach	556	980	529	95.10%	54.00%
Orlando	684	1,204	649	94.90%	53.90%
Raleigh-Durham	496	838	435	87.70%	51.90%
Dallas-Fort Worth	2,031	3,344	1,695	83.50%	50.70%
Salt Lake City	456	748	378	82.90%	50.50%
Sacramento	715	1,161	580	81.10%	50.00%
Charlotte	616	991	491	79.70%	49.50%

[a] "New Units Needed" is a composite number taking into account the number of growth-related units necessary to house population increase, plus an additional number to acknowledge the loss of existing units over time.
Source: Brookings Institute; ING Clarion Research & Investment Strategy, Brookings Institution, and U.S. Census, 2004.

West will see the greatest change. The South will add nearly 26 million new units by 2030, or about 43% of the units currently in place. Two-thirds of the housing units in the West in 2030 will be built after 2000.

Population growth is expected to be increasingly focused in urban areas. Worldwide, more people are now living in cities and towns than in rural locations for the first time in recorded history. The United Nations reports:

> The twentieth century witnessed the rapid urbanization of the world's population. The global proportion of urban population increased from a mere 13 per cent in 1900 to 29 per cent in 1950 and, according to the 2005 Revision of World Urbanization Prospects, reached 49 per cent in 2005. Since the world is projected to continue to urbanize, 60 per cent of the global population is expected to live in cities by 2030. The rising numbers of urban dwellers give the best indication of the scale of these unprecedented trends: the urban population increased from 220 million in 1900 to 732 million in 1950, and is estimated to have reached 3.2 billion in 2005, thus more than quadrupling since 1950. According to the latest

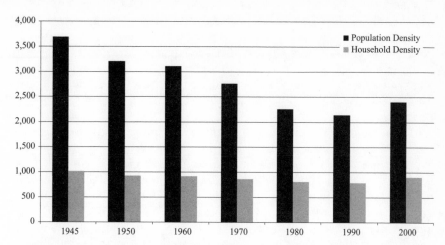

EXHIBIT 7.8 Population and Household Density in the United States (per square mile)
Source: ING Clarion Research & Investment Strategy and Demographia.com, 2005.

United Nations population projections, 4.9 billion people are expected to be urban dwellers in 2030.[14]

In the United States, more than three-quarters of the population now live in urban areas, with the trend toward urbanization expected to continue. While that fact would suggest that land absorption would slow, as more and more of the population gathers in denser environments, development patterns suggest that Americans are actually using more and more land per capita. Between 1945 and 2000, urbanized population in the United States grew by 157% but the urbanized land area grew by 294%, resulting in urban land density dropping from 3,700 persons per square mile to 2,400[15] (Exhibit 7.8). These findings are consistent with both a decreasing average household size and an increasing average home size. As fewer people live in each housing unit, but the size of units increases, additional area is needed on a per capita basis.

---

[14]United Nations Department of Economic and Social Affairs, Population Division, "World Urbanization Prospects: The 2005 Revisions," http://www.un.org/esa/population/publications/WUP2005/2005wup.htm.

[15]Estimated from U.S. Census Bureau & Department of Agriculture Economic Research Service data, 2006.

Combining these findings allows for an estimation of the amount of land needed for future housing demand. Assuming that all population growth between 2000 and 2030 occurs in urban areas at the 2000 density of 2,400 people per square mile, an additional 43,285 square miles of land will be needed to accommodate the projected 39 million new housing units. This represents a nearly 50% increase in urban land area over the forecast period.

This demand for land will undoubtedly be mitigated to some extent by the increasing interest nationwide for denser development in urban areas, as evidenced by the uptick in both population and household density between 1990 and 2000. A combination of demographic, economic, and political factors is likely to continue this trend. Concerns about the various impacts of lower-density "sprawl" development, in particular, are encouraging a more dense urban development pattern, with a mix of uses and a variety of housing options as an alternative to the traditional single-family subdivision.

Limited Supply   While the demand for land will continue to grow as the population expands, the supply of buildable land is actually shrinking, placing additional upward pressures on the price of land in the long-run. These supply constraints come in a variety of forms, including the following.

Growth Controls   An increasing number of communities are moving beyond traditional land use regulations to more explicitly address the pace, quantity, location, and character of new development. These efforts are typically based on concerns related to the impacts of new development on both environmental and fiscal resources, and are particularly aimed at limiting sprawling development patterns. From urban growth boundaries to affordable housing mandates, these regulatory approaches to mitigating the impacts of new development also impact the amount of land available for development. In some cases, these limitations are balanced by increased potential density within urban areas, increasing the attractiveness of infill development.

In addition to limits on the amount of land available for development, the increasingly rigorous development review process adds costs to the development process, in the form of both time delays and direct expenses. According to an Urban Land Institute (ULI) study, "Developers face stricter scrutiny regarding the impact of development on the community and the environment. Local governments are holding developers to increasingly high standards regarding environmental impacts, community design, and amenities through their land use regulations and approval process. Impacts on the environment, traffic, tax base, schools, parks, and other public facilities must be mitigated."[16]

Types of growth management provisions can include:

- Urban growth boundaries or other limitations on the extent of new development, designed to encourage new construction in areas already served by infrastructure, while discouraging projects on the urban edge.
- Linking zoning and subdivision approvals to the availability of infrastructure such as water, sewer or roadway capacity, or other public facilities, such as parks, schools, or transit services.
- Fees or taxes that require payments to help offset the increased impacts of new development.
- Limits on the number of housing units or square feet of space that can be built, either as a total amount or on an annual basis.
- Increased scrutiny of building and site design, including design review requirements.
- Requirements that demand new development to include or subsidize affordable housing.

One study of the impact of land use regulation on housing prices found that:

> *Metropolitan areas with more extensive regulation can have up to 45 percent fewer starts and price elasticities that are more than 20 percent lower than those in less-regulated markets. One implication of regulations that lengthen the development process is that short- and long-run effects of demand shocks will vary relative to conditions in markets without such delays. We [also] find other differences by type of regulation: development or impact fees have relatively little impact on new construction, but regulations that lengthen the development process or otherwise constrain new development have larger and more significant effects.*[17]

As previously mentioned, these growth management restrictions may be coupled with enhanced opportunities for increased density and mixed-use

---

[16]Richard B. Peiser and Anne B. Frej, *Professional Real Estate Development: The ULI Guide to the Business* 2nd ed. (Washington, DC: Urban Land Institute, 2004), 58.
[17]Reprinted from *Regional and Urban Economics* 30, no. 6, Christopher J. Mayer and C. Tsuriel Somerville, "Land Use Regulation and New Construction," 1–23, Copyright (2000), with permission from Elsevier.

development at key nodes (downtowns, transit nodes, etc.), improving the opportunities for an infill approach and potentially offsetting increased costs. This is increasingly true in both supply-constrained and high-growth markets. As such, attention to local and regional planning initiatives is essential for any project with an entitlement element.

Infrastructure Limits   The rapid expansion of metro areas, particularly in fast-growing newer cities, is taxing our infrastructure systems to the point that new development can be frustrated. The lack of adequate roadways, transit systems, and basic services such as water and sewer systems can delay new development or increase the costs of development substantially as the financial burden is shifted to the developer.

Water and Natural Resource Limits   A variety of environmental limitations (and an increasing attention to them on the part of local governments and the general public) is removing more land from potential development. Coastal zones, wetlands, stream and river corridors, steep slopes, and wildlife habitats are all increasingly protected from development. Public support for open space acquisition programs and the designation of parks and recreation areas are also competing for vacant lands. In some areas—especially western states—the combination of federal and state-owned lands accounts for as much as 70% of the total land supply. A growing number of communities have established standards requiring or incentivizing "green" building for commercial properties, typically in the form of a requirement to meet some level of LEED or similar certification.[18] That regulatory approach has not been applied to single-family homes at this point but there is a possibility of increased regulation in the future.

The Impact on Residential Land Prices

A recent academic study looking at changes in residential land prices over the past 20 years provides some insights into the combined impacts of the shrinking land supply and the increasing emphasis on land use regulation. The study found that land constitutes an increasingly large percentage of total housing prices:

> *The value of residential land accounted for about 50 percent of the total market value of housing [in 2004], up from 32 percent in*

---

[18]LEED—Leadership in Energy and Environmental Design, a program of the U.S. Green Building Council that offers third-party certification as a means to benchmark the design, construction, and operation of green buildings.

1984. An implication of our results is that housing is much more land intensive than it used to be, meaning that the future course of home prices—the average rate of appreciation and volatility—is likely to be determined even more by demand factors than was the case even ten or twenty years ago.[19]

The basic premise of the study assumes that housing value can be understood as a bundle of physical structure and location. These components serve distinct functions and are priced quite differently. Data combined from several sources was used to estimate changes in the value and price of residential land for 46 large metro areas from 1984 to 2004. Over the 20-year period, nearly every large U.S. city experienced a significant increase in the average share of home value attributed to the market value of residential land. For example, while residential land represented less than a quarter of average home value in 19 of the 46 U.S. metro areas studied 20 years ago, only one city (Oklahoma City) meets that criteria currently. It follows from the increase in average land values that nearly every large U.S. city has also seen a significant decrease in the elasticity of supply of housing.

Where land is abundant (both physically and free from regulatory constraints) and thus, inexpensive, the construction cost of housing represents a more significant portion of house value. New homes on readily available high-quality land can be built relatively easily and cheaply. Where land is scarcer, and therefore expensive, the land price represents a higher portion of the overall price, and drives down the elasticity of supply for new housing. Data from the Davis and Palumbo study demonstrates that while a number of large U.S. cities were operating under conditions similar to the first scenario as early as the early 1990s, "by the late 1990s and early 2000s, the evidence indicates that land had become significantly more scarce just about all around the country."[20] Land accounted for an average of 32% of the total housing cost across the markets in 1984, but nearly 51% in 2004 (Exhibit 7.9).

The rate of increase in the percentage of land values was not even across markets, however, nor did it necessarily follow expected patterns. As could be predicted, the increase in land prices from 1998 to 2004 was generally highest along the East and West coasts, where residential land was arguably already in shortest supply. More surprising, however, is the

---

[19]Reprinted from *Journal of Urban Economics* 63, no. 1, Morris A. Davis and Michael G. Palumbo, "The Price of Residential Land in Large U.S. Cities," 352–384, Copyright (2008), with permission from Elsevier.

[20]Ibid., 354.

EXHIBIT 7.9 Components of Home Value by Region, 2004

Region	Home Value ($000)	Structure Value $0	Land Value ($000)	Land's % Share of Value (1984)	Land's % Share of Value (2004)	% Change in Land's Share (1984–2004)
Midwest	$192	$119	$73	11%	36%	25%
Southeast	$187	$108	$79	27%	42%	15%
Southwest	$179	$106	$73	35%	38%	3%
East Coast	$376	$131	$245	38%	64%	26%
West Coast	$568	$128	$440	55%	74%	19%
Full Sample	$307	$120	$187	32%	51%	19%

Source: Morris A. Davis and Michael G. Palumbo, "The Price of Residential Land in Large U.S. Cities," *Journal of Urban Economics* 63, no. 1 (2008): 362.

significant increase in land prices as a component of home value in a number of Midwest cities—including Cleveland, Kansas City, Milwaukee, and Minneapolis—where in 1998 land was relatively inexpensive. In a handful of cities, all typified by a lack of supply constraints, the land component as a percentage of overall cost actually decreased: San Antonio, Oklahoma City, Phoenix, Dallas, and Fort Worth.[21] Exhibit 7.10 includes a summary of changes by region. Note that in every region the percentage increase in land value was the leading factor in the increase in overall home value increase.

These data suggest "residential land has become significantly more scarce in large cities all over the United States, in the sense that new housing construction evidently has occurred in places that are poor substitutes for the existing stock of residential land, driving up the average price and value of the existing stock."[22] That scarcity is a result of both physical and political constraints.

In addition, the study demonstrates that, since 1984, most large U.S. cities have experienced at least one pronounced price-cycle in which residential land lost value for an extended period of time. That decline usually followed several years of particularly rapid appreciation. "In real terms, land prices have generally taken several years to go from peak to trough, and the subsequent recovery from these price declines has generally occurred at a more gradual pace."[23]

---

[21]Note that this does not necessarily mean that actual land prices decreased; only that the relative component of land in the total housing cost decreased.

[22]Ibid., 356.

[23]Ibid., 367.

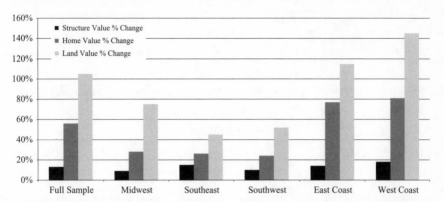

EXHIBIT 7.10 Percent Change in Home, Structure, and Land Value by Region, 1998–2004
Source: ING Clarion Research & Investment Strategy and Morris A. Davis and Michael G. Palumbo, "The Price of Residential Land in Large U.S. Cities," *Journal of Urban Economics* 63, no. 1 (2008): 361.

Exhibit 7.11 charts the index of real land prices across nine cities in the southwestern United States that experienced a peak near early 1985. "The indexes are normalized so that their value in 1985:Q1 is 100, and separate indexes are shown for the median city in each quarter after 1985:Q1 and for the cities representing the 20th and 80th percentiles of the distribution. The median city in this group (Houston) saw its land price index fall 50%, cumulatively, in real terms, over the five years ended in 1989. Although real land prices in Houston began rising gradually in 1990, the estimates imply that the index did not fully return to its early-1985 level until 1999—15 years later. Denver's experience is reflected. There, real land prices fell, cumulatively, by 60% from 1985 through 1991; however, the recovery in that city was much sharper, and by the mid-1990s, Denver's index of real land prices had returned to its 1985 level. By 1999 (the last year shown on Exhibit 7.11), the index of real land prices was two-and-a-half times as high as it had been 15 years earlier. By contrast, San Antonio saw a remarkably large drop in real land prices, and by 1999 the level of the index in that city had recovered only about halfway."[24]

The performance of individual markets within the Southwest region is not discussed in the study. However, a review of the data suggests that the three markets where land prices recovered most quickly (Denver, New Orleans, and Salt Lake City) can all be characterized as more supply-constrained, either by physical or political limits, than the remaining

---

[24]Ibid., 365.

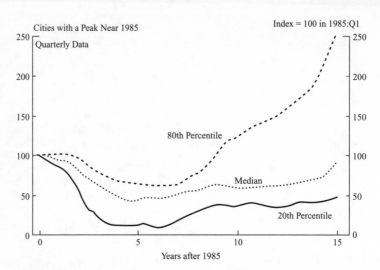

EXHIBIT 7.11   Real Residential Land Prices in Southwest Metro
Areas after 1985
Source: Reprinted from *Journal of Urban Economics* 63, no. 1, Morris A.
Davis and Michael G. Palumbo, "The Price of Residential Land in Large U.S.
Cities," 365, Copyright (2008), with permission from Elsevier.

cities (Phoenix, Houston, Dallas, Fort Worth, San Antonio, and Oklahoma
City). A more detailed review of the underlying supply, demand, and economic fundamentals of each city during this period would be needed to more
fully understand the varying performances.

The study finds similar results when looking at the remaining 37 cities
outside the Southwest. Fifteen of the metro areas experienced, at some point
since 1986, a cumulative net three-year decline in real land prices of 16%
or more. The median city in this group (Tampa) took a full 10 years for
the real land price index to return to the level at its previous peak. Another
15 metros experienced a milder decline of about 10% beginning around
1990, with the recovery to the previous peak occurring in four or five years.
A set of seven Midwest cities experienced a smooth upward march in real
land prices, rather than the volatility that characterized the other markets.[25]

In a separate analysis, illustrated in Exhibit 7.12, we reviewed national figures on historic prices for finished lots in order to model the expected change in prices going forward. The analysis established a correlation

---

[25]Ibid., 365–367.

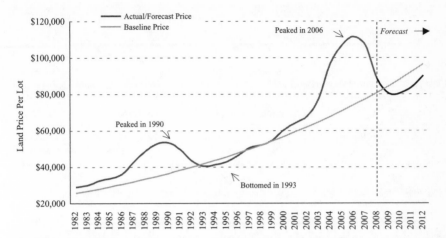

EXHIBIT 7.12 Forecast Average Land Prices (finished lots)
Baseline price is calculated using 1998 land price and 4.5% long-term land appreciation rate.

Source: ING Clarion Research & Investment Strategy, Credit Suisse, and Economy. com.

between change in new home prices and change in finished lot prices and then used forecast changes in new home prices to estimate the corresponding change in land values. In the previous downturn, prices peaked in 1990 and then declined for three years before reaching the bottom. It took until 1999 for prices to surpass the previous peak. The rate of appreciation in values that began in 2002 was much steeper than in the previous boom, suggesting that the decline will be steeper, as well. Our model suggests that average land prices could decline by approximately 30% from the peak reached in 2006, bringing prices back in line with the long-term historic appreciation in land values of 4.5%. We expect the market to hit that point in late-2008 or 2009 on the national level (Exhibit 7.12). Land prices in certain markets, including South Florida, Las Vegas, and Phoenix are expected to experience more severe corrections, as housing prices had appreciated significantly more than the national averages since 1999.

The relationship between home prices and the land prices is intuitive but deserves further analysis. The following simple model shown in Exhibit 7.13 illustrates how a reduction in the average sales price of a home impacts the value of underlying land, calculated as a residual value. In this example, the 20% reduction in home price results in a 50% reduction in the calculated land value. Actual pricing will vary based on local market conditions and investor expectations.

EXHIBIT 7.13   Impact of Hypothetical Change in Home Prices on Residual Land Value

	2005	2008
Average Home Sales Price	$500,000	$400,000
Less Cost to Build	$250,000	$250,000
Less 20% Required Profit on Building Costs	$50,000	$50,000
Land Value (Residual)	$200,000	$100,000

Source: ING Clarion Research & Investment Strategy, 2008.

Three versions of a more sophisticated pro forma typical to a land deal are provided in Appendix A and summarized in Exhibit 7.14. In this example, the initial analysis (Scenario I) suggests a 12.1% profit (Total Revenues less Total Costs). Scenario II reduces the expected home sales prices by 20% but keeps the land cost the same, resulting in a loss of −14.06%. In Scenario III, we illustrate the required reduction in land price

EXHIBIT 7.14   Summary of Pro Forma Analysis[a]

	Scenario I	Scenario II	Scenario III
Home Prices			
Plan 1 (45 units)	305,000	244,000	244,000
Plan 2 (45 units)	320,000	256,000	256,000
Plan 3 (45 units)	335,000	268,000	268,000
Total Revenue	44,258,400	35,514,720	35,514,720
Costs			
Land Value at Sale	6,600,000	6,600,000	840,722
Other Costs[b]	32,303,314	33,906,950	30,376,717
Total Costs	38,903,314	40,506,950	31,217,439
Total Profit	5,355,086	−4,992,230	4,297,281
Profit	12.10%	−14.06%	12.10%

[a]See also Appendix A.
[b]Note that "Other Costs" change somewhat in Scenarios II and III due to assumptions in the model based on land costs and/or revenue projections. The increase in costs in Scenario II is primarily due to increased interest costs as reduced revenues limit the ability to pay down debt at the same rate as in Scenario I.
Source: ING Clarion Research & Investment Strategy, 2008.

necessary to return the same 12.1% profit from Scenario I despite the 20% reduction in home prices. In this example, land costs must be reduced by 87% to maintain the original profit margin.

These findings suggest that the current downturn in the housing market will have a negative impact on land values in most metros, but the extent of impact will vary. Those areas that have shown slow but steady increases in values may be relatively insulated from the impacts, though the long-term growth prospects for those areas also limit the potential for future returns. In the more dynamic markets we can expect to see declines lasting over a period of several years, with the depth of the decline and the strength of the recovery varying considerably. In distinguishing between the performances of individual markets, a variety of factors should be considered, including the underlying supply and demand fundamentals.

THE ENTITLEMENT PROCESS

Overview

The process of taking raw land through the development process to create a residential community is lengthy, complicated, and risky. The timeline from the initial purchase of land through the construction of homes can take many, many years. The process will vary considerably by community and based on the specific characteristics of the property and the proposed development, but will generally include the five basic phases shown in Exhibit 7.15. The focus of this analysis is on Phase 3 (Entitlements). Phase 4 (Construction) is optional depending on the site and investment platform.

Market Analysis and Site Selection   Because of the inherent risks in the land development play, a thorough strategic analysis of supply and demand drivers across markets and product types is essential, along with a detailed financial feasibility analysis.

Acquisition   Any purchase should include a three-stage contract offering a free-look period, a period during which earnest money is forfeitable, and a closing. Extending the initial period through options allows the purchaser to control the land while minimizing capital outlays and risk. The option provides a mechanism to control the land but does not obligate the buyer to complete the sale unless certain conditions are met. Conditioning the sale upon entitlement approvals and financing and tying the sales price to the actual number of units entitled offer additional means to mitigate risk.

EXHIBIT 7.15
Development Process
Source: ING Clarion Research & Strategy.

Entitlements The process of adding value to a site by increasing the permitted density or intensity of uses through rezoning or subdivision. This process typically occurs in two stages: (1) an initial approval (zoning and subdivision) that sets the general parameters for the range of uses, density, and infrastructure improvements, and (2) a second approval, in the form of building permits that allow for the construction of individual buildings.

Construction Construction occurs in two stages: first the development of lots and on-site infrastructure and then construction of buildings. Both stages of construction are optional, depending on the specific land development strategy.

Disposition Sale of the property, either as a single parcel or as subdivided lots, with or without entitlements and infrastructure construction.

Roles in the Land Development Process

While some larger homebuilders may see a development through from initial land acquisition through construction of individual units, different players typically take different roles in the process, spreading the commitment and the risk. Exhibit 7.16 summarizes those players and their typical role in the development process. Expected minimum returns will vary considerably by investor and deal. This section focuses on the role and strategies associated with the land speculator, predeveloper, and land developer.

Here are more in-depth descriptions:

- *Land Speculator: buy and hold for future land sale.* This concept involves simply buying and holding large tracts of land for future sale (wholesale or in smaller pieces) to other speculators or developers. Because land holdings are considered a liability, homebuilders do not typically like to keep them on the books. For publicly traded companies this is a particular problem. The expected return for this strategy can vary significantly and reflects the large holding period with minimal cash flow.
- *Predeveloper: entitle land and sell lots.* Taking the strategy one step further involves taking the land through the entitlement process in order to facilitate more intense development than permitted under the existing standards. This stage would likely require environmental analysis, planning and architectural studies, and the various steps required for approval by the local (and potentially state and federal) authorities.

EXHIBIT 7.16 Types of Land Investors

	Types of Land Investors			
	Land Speculator	Predeveloper	Land Developer	Builder/ End User
Major Function	Holds the property waiting for growth to approach	Analyzes market and plans development; clears all regulatory hurdles	Installs utilities; completes subdividing program	Builds structures for sale, rent, or own use; may employ general contractor
Typical Financing	Non-institutional	May attract institutional investment on selective basis	May be able to obtain construction loans and long-term real estate investors	May be able to obtain construction loans and long-term real estate investors
Typically Sells To	Predeveloper	Land developer or end user	Other (smaller) builders or end users	Other (smaller) builders or end users
Typical Length of Tenure:	8–10 years	2–5 years	1+ years	Indeterminate
Minimum Expected Return:	30%	30%	20%	Varies

Source: ING Clarion Research & Investment Strategy and Peiser & Frej. *Professional Real Estate Development: The ULI Guide to the Business* (Washington, DC: ULI-The Urban Land Institute, 2004): 61.

This strategy requires significant time and resources, particularly in slow-growth communities, but also offers the greatest potential return on equity.

- *Land Developer: entitle, develop infrastructure, and sell lots.* This strategy involves moving beyond development approval to actually constructing infrastructure improvements such as roads and utilities. Because such facilities are often required prior to selling pieces of an approved project, this approach allows us to sell off smaller pieces once completed. The costs for these elements can be substantial, and the time required for construction can be considerable, as well. Exit options would be increased as parcels could be sold in smaller pieces.

Entitlement Returns

Data on the return for securing entitlements is limited, but it is generally accepted as one of the most potentially profitable steps in the land development process. These returns reflect the significant risks inherent in that political process. The increase in value varies significantly by location, reflecting the entitlement risk. Land prices in communities with more onerous regulatory schemes and longer review times reflect a wider range between the cost of entitled versus unentitled land, often reflected in a "multiple"; that is, the difference in value between unentitled versus entitled land. For example, the National Association of Realtors reports a multiple of 7× in Hawaii and 5× in California, both notoriously highly regulated states. The difference in value in more developer friendly states like Florida, Texas, and Tennessee, in contrast, are only around 2× (Exhibit 7.17).

Negotiating the maze of entitlements—federal, state, and local, and going beyond zoning to often include a variety of environmental regulations—is daunting. As such, many developers choose to enter into the land play only after at least some element of the project entitlements has been secured.

The Entitlement Process

Local land use regulations play an important role in determining the feasibility and financial success of land development opportunities. Given the general assumption that properties acquired as part of a land development

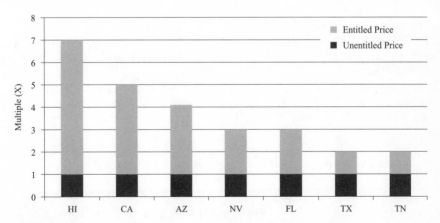

EXHIBIT 7.17 Spread in Land Costs by State/Entitlement Status
Source: ING Clarion Research & Strategy, National Association of Realtors, and Hearthstone Group, 2006.

strategy will be zoned for minimal development (often agricultural or very low density residential), the opportunity to increase value lies largely in revising the zoning on the property to allow for more intense development. As land use regulations become increasingly complex, this process can be both lengthy and risky. The potential rewards reflect that risk and are the most attractive of any step in the development process.

Regulations   There are three general types of local land use regulations that must be considered in any development project.

Master Plans   Also called *comprehensive plans* or *general plans*, these documents lay out desired development patterns, generally looking out 15 years or more. The plans are adopted by a City Council or other elected or appointed governmental body based on input from the community. While the contents will vary by locale, the master plan typically includes both policy statements and a land use map that together indicate the preferred pattern of future development. The map divides the planning area into districts, differentiated by their preferred use, intensity/density, and character of future development. These districts define areas where development is encouraged and other areas where development is discouraged or prohibited. Within the development areas, the plan may distinguish between areas for low-, medium-, and high-density residential development, along with commercial, industrial, public facilities, and mixed-use districts. Within each land use district, target ranges for density are common. The master plan may also address the location and timing of infrastructure improvements, recreational facilities, and other elements that impact the feasibility of future development. Depending on state and local law, the master plan may be advisory (voluntary compliance) or regulatory (mandatory compliance). Communities vary based on the timeline for updating master plans. At one extreme, some jurisdictions only permit changes to the land use map once every several years. At the other end of the spectrum, others permit changes concurrent with zoning and subdivision review. In the former case, the timeline for moving a property from one master plan designation to another can obviously take many years.

Zoning   Zoning regulations implement the master plan policies and map. Zoning standards use another menu of districts, often (but not always) similar to the land use categories discussed previously. These district standards more directly regulate the permitted uses, density, and character of future development in each area of a community. Limitations on building location (setbacks), bulk, height, and parking are common. In addition, zoning increasingly addresses issues such as landscaping, lighting, signage, and building and site design. Development must be consistent with these standards to receive required permits, or must receive waivers or variances from the standards through a discretionary review process before a local board or commission. Changes to zoning that are consistent with the general plan may proceed relatively easily, but changes that are inconsistent—seeking residential development in an area designated for agriculture, or high density development in an area designated for low-density—can be very contentious and difficult. Depending on the community, changes in zoning may be considered at the same time as master plan and subdivision review, or may be required to proceed separately.

Subdivision Subdivision regulations provide the procedures and standards for dividing a large parcel of land into smaller parcels for sale and development. As with zoning, subdivision regulation is a land use control used to carry out a community's master plan by defining requirements for new development. Specific considerations typically include lot size and layout, circulation and street patterns, the availability of public services, and infrastructure requirements. The impact of subdivision regulations is more permanent than zoning, which can be more readily amended. Once land is divided into lots and streets are laid out, development patterns are largely set.

The result of a subdivision review is the approval of a plat—a map documenting the division of a piece of property into lots and blocks, along with streets, easements, and other lands intended to be dedicated to public use. The plat facilitates the future development and sale of the property and also helps to ensure that each parcel of land sold for development has sufficient size, shape, utilities, and access to function for its intended purpose. The review may also document dedications or exactions to be provided by the developer to the local jurisdiction, such as transportation improvements, open space set-asides, or other concessions agreed upon between the parties.

In addition to the above regulations, federal, state, and local environmental regulations may also impact the ability to develop a property. These regulations can include limitations on development involving or adjacent to wetlands, stream or riparian corridors, wildlife habitats, and steep slopes. A separate review for consistency with construction codes (building, electric, etc.) is considered prior to the issuance of building permits, the second stage of the regulatory review process.

Review Process The process of negotiating these various regulations varies considerably by community and the specifics of the property in question. Despite these variations, a few key steps are common.

Preapplication   Many jurisdictions encourage, and some require, an informal consultation with the planning staff or representatives of an approval body such as the planning commission prior to official application for a subdivision. The preapplication step is intended to introduce the project, identify key concerns, and establish the roadmap for the development review process.

Application   Most jurisdictions have at least a two-stage subdivision process requiring review of a tentative or preliminary plan and a final plan. Each will require a separate application with supporting documents, which will vary by community. The preliminary plan typically includes a map or drawing of a proposed subdivision, laying out the location and width of proposed streets, lots, blocks, easements, infrastructure, and environmentally sensitive features such as floodplains. Increasingly, communities are also requiring general information on the character of the development, including conceptual architecture and landscaping plans. The final plan will include the previous information with additional detail.

Preliminary Plan   An initial review by local government bodies, typically a planning commission or planning board, but with referral to other agencies, including local fire and police officials and utility providers. The formal review is held at a public hearing, providing an opportunity for the public to comment on the proposal. Because of the public nature of the approval process, it is essential for the developer to be proactive in securing support for the project. This may include holding community meetings at the initial stages of the project design to solicit input and educate the public on the plan. Approval of the preliminary plan establishes the general parameters and conditions for the site development. Rezoning, if necessary, is typically considered concurrent with the subdivision review but may require a separate hearing process.

Final Plan   The final plan is reviewed through a similar public hearing process, but final approval authority typically lies with the elected body of the community such as city council. Approval of the final plan allows for recording of a plat, legally documenting the subdivision of land and requiring future development to proceed consistent with that approval. Often the final plan is reviewed at the same time as the detailed construction plans for buildings.

The overall subdivision process may take anywhere from several months to many years, with the developer facing potential delays at every stage. The process of negotiating these various regulations varies considerably by community and the specifics of the property in question. The ULI offers the following simple tips for negotiating the entitlement process:[26]

- Be prepared to work with the community to resolve concerns and challenges to the project.
- Take time to understand the local political climate.
- Prepare for the local regulatory process and public hearings.
- Use qualified and experienced consultants, lawyers, and architects to give your project added credibility.
- Anticipate and do not underestimate delays in the approval process.

INVESTMENT RISKS

As discussed previously, the risks in any land play are significant. While no strategy can eliminate risk or guarantee returns, mitigation strategies are essential to limit equity, market, and entitlement risks.

Limiting Equity Exposure

Limiting out-of-pocket expenses by using options to leverage as much land as possible with as little money as possible is essential to success in the typical land play. The approach involves obtaining options on a property (usually subject to entitlement approvals) and then flipping the land to a new buyer—typically a large homebuilder—when the market returns or entitlements are secured. Current market conditions find more and more homebuilders looking to move land off their own books, including entitled lots. Opportunities exist to purchase properties at a discount with an expectation that a builder will take the land back at a premium down the road.

Long-Term Hold and Limited Cash Flow

The turnaround time on land investments can be lengthy. In order to capture the largest return, this strategy typically involves controlling property within the path of growth and entitling it for additional development capacity. There is typically little cash flow from the property during that waiting period. Focusing on more infill locations where infrastructure is readily

---

[26]Peiser and Frej, *Professional Real Estate Development: The ULI Guide to the Business*, 2nd ed., p. 22.

available, or looking for land that has already been entitled offer ways to potentially speed up the process, but may also reduce total returns.

Entitlement Risk

Fast-growing areas and global gateway cities are primary targets for land development strategies, but concerns about the impacts of additional growth have led to increasingly complex and rigorous development review processes in these communities, offering increased entitlement risk. The approvals process is often longer, more complex, and more expensive than other areas. Detailed designs, studies, and analyses costing millions and taking years may have to be undertaken. There is more political opposition. Many land parcels lie near sensitive or protected open space or natural habitat. Because these areas have become disproportionately affluent compared to the rest of the country, citizens are savvier and have the knowledge and money to fight long, expensive entitlement battles.

A thorough understanding of local planning and land use regulations and a proactive public involvement effort can help to smooth the process. Community plans increasingly call for "smart growth" developments that include a mix of uses and housing types, especially in supply-constrained markets that are struggling with a diminishing land supply and housing affordability. Incorporating "smart growth" elements in a proposal can help to smooth the review process with local officials, though the general public is not always on board with these more intensive development patterns. Local partners—described next—can also be invaluable in helping to secure approvals.

Lack of Local Knowledge Can Be Detrimental

The statement that all real estate is local is especially true in the context of a land play. Sourcing deals and negotiating the entitlement process demands local partners who know both the place and the players. Local operators and consultants with good-standing relationships with sellers, buyers, and the players in the entitlement process (city planning staff, local officials) are important partners to the successful project.

Continuing Housing Declines

Most experts expect the housing market to begin a rebound in early 2009, but a review of past housing declines shows that it has taken around three years for home prices to fully recover. Pursuing entitlements during the slowdown is a good strategy—the process may be quicker and smoother, as the pipeline is less clogged, local governments are more concerned with current revenues than future impacts, and the general public may not be as opposed to development proposals. But the risk remains that even entitled land will not be in demand if the market continues to suffer. Infill property in prime markets will always be the first to recover and should be given priority over land on the fringes.

In evaluating markets, several key metrics should be monitored to suggest when an individual market may be turning, including the pace of housing starts, the pace of home sales, home prices, and overall housing inventory. In general, look for a flattening of the trends that could indicate the beginning of an upswing in the market.

TARGET MARKET SELECTION AND RANKING

Residential development will be most successful in markets that have strong or well-developing economic and demographic fundamentals. Regardless of strategy, healthy fundamentals are intrinsic to successful development. Consequently, target market selection involves identifying those markets that demonstrate future strength and potential in terms of a variety of demographic and market fundamentals. The criteria considered should include historic and forecast employment, population, household and income growth, along with home prices, home starts, home sales, home affordability, and a supply-constraint index.[27] These criteria identify larger,

---

[27]The limited ability to deliver new product in supply-constrained markets helps to support high values. Supply constraints are generally categorized as physical (natural features) or regulatory (zoning or other legal and political limitations). In areas that are desirable but where supply constraints keep the rate of new construction low, prices tend to rise. In areas in which constraints on construction are fewer, the demand for housing will be more evident in the rate of new construction.

The level of supply constraint in a particular market can be estimated by comparing the rate of home price appreciation to the rate of new construction, in this case, on a 10-year basis, from 1997– 2007 (percent of total price appreciation/percent increase in total stock). For example, San Francisco, a prototypical supply-constrained market, saw an increase in housing prices of 178% over the period compared to an increase of 8.6% in new stock, resulting in an index value of 20.6. Dallas, a metro noted for a lack of supply constraints, on the other hand, saw an increase of 29% in prices compared to an increase of 33% in new stock, resulting in an index value of 0.87. The markets with a higher index number are considered more

slower-growth markets and smaller, higher-growth markets: both categories inherently enjoy healthy demand for residential product.

While much of the focus in discussions about land investment are focused on distressed markets, we believe that opportunities are available based upon three different investment strategies; specific metro markets can then be targeted based upon the strategy selected. Rankings within each strategy were developed by weighting the various metrics differently.

There is overlap across these strategies. Actual investment decisions must consider an even larger variety of factors that explore the unique aspects of individual properties as well as the market and submarket fundamentals.

Distressed Land Markets

These markets have seen significant declines in home prices, presenting opportunities to purchase land at a steep discount to peak prices. The target markets exhibit a combination of price declines with strong long-term expectations for job and population growth. Based on market conditions at the time of this analysis, metro areas such as Phoenix, Las Vegas, and many of the Florida and California markets rank highly in this category over both a three-year and a five-year period.

High-Growth Markets

These markets are primarily distinguished by relatively affordable housing coupled with strong prospects for job and population growth over time. While the absolute numbers of employment and population in high growth markets may be lower than in many larger markets, the rate of growth in these markets is higher, indicating momentum, desirability, and potential. Price declines are not as steep as in the distressed markets. While development on the urban edge is more likely in these markets, infill opportunities also provide attractive opportunities. Development in more suburban locations should be readily served by necessary infrastructure and located within the path of growth. Based on market conditions at the time of this analysis, the Texas markets (Austin, Houston, Dallas, San Antonio, and Fort Worth) and North Carolina markets (Charlotte and Raleigh-Durham) all rank highly in this category in the three-year forecast. Interestingly, some distressed markets, such as Las Vegas and Phoenix,

---

supply-constrained, with demand for housing evidenced by price increases rather than supply increases.

also rank highly in the five-year outlook, based on strong long-term growth forecasts.

Infill Markets

Supply constraints, both physical and political, limit opportunities for land development in many global gateway cities and mature metros. Nonetheless, where vacant or underutilized land can be identified, these markets offer potential for strong returns based on a combination of dependable demand and high or accelerating housing prices. Projects may be more complicated, including a mix of uses, higher density development, and a more challenging entitlement process. Based on market conditions at the time of this analysis, metros such as Los Angeles, Washington, DC, Seattle, and San Francisco rank highly in this category.

CHAPTER 8

The U.S. Hotel Market and Strategy

Tim Wang, Matson Holbrook, and David Lynn
Spring 2008[1]

The U.S. hotel market is in the beginning stages of a cyclical slow-down as supply has recently begun to outpace demand. The overall lodging industry is expected to experience softness in 2008 and 2009 before recovering in 2010. Acquisition opportunities may arise as hotel assets' pricing declines. Based on our latest forecast, the Luxury and Upper Upscale segments, driven by better supply-and - demand fundamentals and strength in international gateway cities, should outperform the five other chain scale segments as well as the four core property sectors.

BACKGROUND

Investment Background

Hotel investment is considered to be both a real estate business as well as an operating business. Generally characterized as a noncore asset class, the hotel sector exhibits relatively greater volatility than other property types (Exhibit 8.1). This is due primarily to the extremely short effective lease terms as hotel rooms are essentially leased on a daily basis. Historically, hotel revenues have been largely correlated with gross domestic product (GDP)

---

[1]This paper was originally produced in spring 2008. The data, opinions, and forecasts have not been updated for book publication.

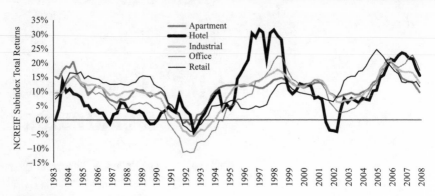

EXHIBIT 8.1 Hotel Returns
Source: ING Clarion Research & Investment Strategy, NCREIF, 2008.
Note: Hotel returns are four 12-month trailing total returns.

growth, and are therefore quite sensitive to fluctuations in the economy (Exhibit 8.2).

With a consistent record of transparency and improved fundamentals, hotels are becoming an increasingly attractive asset class for institutional investors. The number of hotel assets in the NCREIF Property Index (NPI) has been steadily increasing from six in 1982 to 1989, in the third quarter of

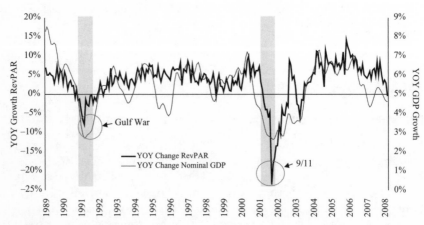

EXHIBIT 8.2 Hotel Revenue: Moves Closely with the U.S. Economy[a]
[a]Shaded area indicates recessions.
Source: ING Clarion Research & Investment Strategy, Smith Travel Research, and Moody's Economy.com, 2008.

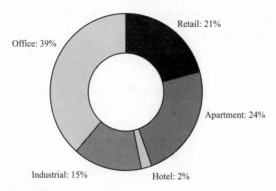

EXHIBIT 8.3 NCREIF Property Index Property
Type Allocation
Source: ING Clarion Research & Investment Strategy
and NCREIF, March 2008.

2007. However, the hotel sector is still substantially underweighted in the
NPI with only $5.8 billion, or 1.8%, in market value as of March 31, 2008
(Exhibit 8.3). Therefore, hotel assets included in the NPI are a very small
portion of the hotel investment universe, and the NPI hotel subindex may
not be representative of hotel industry returns.

Concerned about a possible severe economic downturn, some institutions apparently have recently decided to reduce their exposures to this
particular sector. As of the first quarter of 2008, there are 76 hotel assets
in the NPI, reflecting a decrease of 10 properties during the first quarter of
2008. The average market value per hotel asset in the NPI is only $76.9 mil-
lion, implying that most of these properties are probably in the middle range
of the chain scale. It is worth noting that the hotel sector is the only sector
that experienced a reduction of assets within the NPI during the first quarter
of 2008.

Nonetheless, hotels can be used to enhance investment returns and reduce portfolio risk. First, hotels can potentially generate attractive returns
during cyclical upturns. The hotel sector has been a top performing property type, averaging 20% annual total returns in the 2005–2007 period
(slightly ahead of the office sector). Therefore, overweighting hotels in an
upturn market can greatly enhance total returns and position portfolios to
outperform the NPI. Second, hotels should be a component of a diversified
real estate portfolio as they exhibit low correlations to other property types
(Exhibit 8.4).

For investors who can tolerate the higher volatility of the hotel sector, the investment strategy should clearly define not only the expected

EXHIBIT 8.4 Total Returns: Correlations w/ Other
Property Types

	Apartment	Hotel	Industrial	Office	Retail
Apartment	1				
Hotel	0.52	1			
Industrial	0.86	0.61	1		
Office	0.84	0.67	0.96	1	
Retail	0.62	0.12	0.65	0.60	1

Source: ING Clarion Research & Investment Strategy and
NCREIF, 2007.

returns, but also the means by which they will be achieved. The potential risk
exposure that will be incurred over the investment period should also be considered. Most importantly, the exit strategy must be well thought out and
planned.

Hotel Industry Overview

There are four main drivers for hotel room demand: business travelers,
meetings, conventions, and leisure travelers. The demand for each category
is affected by the health of the economy. The group meeting business is
most closely tied to the economy because it is dominated by sales incentive
meetings, new product introductions, and training. Business and convention
travel demand tends to lag the economy by 6 to 12 months because of the
advance booking nature of this segment. Leisure travel patterns are driven by
household incomes, wealth effects, travel costs, and demographic structure.
With the exception of the wealthy individual traveler, all three sources of
demand tend to fall off sharply in economic downturns and typically recover
only after corporate profits have rebounded. Demand by wealthy individual
travelers will decline, but likely to a much milder degree.

Domestic passenger arrivals and overseas visitors are good indicators of
domestic and international demand. Exhibit 8.5 identifies top hotel markets
by the largest number of domestic passenger arrivals and overseas visitors.

In aggregate, new supply for hotel rooms is the result of hotel market
fundamentals, replacement costs, and capital market conditions. As shown
in Exhibit 8.6, historical hotel supply responds rather slowly to changes in
demand. When demand hits a bottom, supply will trend down four to five
years later. While new construction is by far the most significant component
of supply change, room closings, either due to obsolescence or a conversion

EXHIBIT 8.5 Top Hotel Markets with the Highest Passenger Demand
Source: ING Clarion Research & Investment Strategy and Bureau of Transportation
Statistics, 2007.

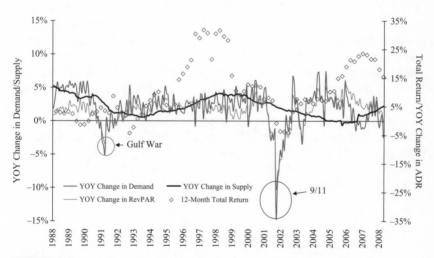

EXHIBIT 8.6 Total Return and Changes in Supply, Demand, and RevPAR
of Hotels
Source: ING Clarion Research & Investment Strategy NCREIF, Smith
Travel Research, and Lodging Econometrics, Portsmouth, NH 03801,
March 2008.

to an alternative real estate use, play a part in arriving at an accurate inventory count. For example, the United States experienced a net decline in room supply in 2005–2006. This is partly due to hotel rooms being converted to condos in markets such as New York City.

On the other hand, revenue per available room (RevPAR) growth is highly correlated with changes in hotel room demand. Furthermore, hotel total returns tend to surge after a period of three to four years when demand outpaces supply (1992–1995 and 2004–2007). In the current hotel cycle, supply growth surpassed demand growth in the fall of 2007, and this divergence has continued since then. As of March 2008, annual demand growth is negative 2.4% while annual supply growth is positive 2.3%. It is evident that demand and supply dynamics have turned decisively negative in the near term.

Asset Types

The modern lodging industry has become more specialized, offering an array of products that target specific segments of customers. For example, limited service hotels were created to cater to business and leisure customers who do not need meeting, banquet, or dining facilities. Extended-stay hotels were developed to serve customers who need longer-term accommodations and prefer a more residential atmosphere. Exhibit 8.7 lists common classifications for hotels in the United States.

The hotel market is commonly categorized into seven different segments (or chain scales), each with its own risk and return characteristics. Each segment also has its own operational characteristics that directly affect the performance of the underlying real estate. Luxury and Upper Upscale segments account for only 2% and 12% of the total hotel supply, respectively (Exhibit 8.8). In particular, Luxury is the fastest growing segment (by percentage) within the hotel sector. Appendix B has a full list of hotel brands under each chain scale segment.

Branding

More so than with other real estate assets, branding is important for hotel investments, especially business-oriented hotels. Business travelers often select a hotel based upon the rewards offered by the brand's frequent stay program. Brands offer consistency of service and product, and strong branding creates customer loyalty that facilitates pricing premiums. Resort guests are typically less influenced by branding; however, nonbranded resorts do

EXHIBIT 8.7 Hotel Classifications

Classification Mode	Description	
Service Level	Full Service	A hotel that includes services provided to its guests outside of lodging (i.e., food and beverage, retail, and restaurant).
	Limited Service	A hotel that offers lodging services only.
Location	Urban	Urbanized areas in metropolitan areas of 150,000 and up. Population size can vary dependent on market orientation.
	Suburban	Suburbs of urbanized areas. Distance from center city varies based on population and market orientation.
	Airport	Properties in close proximity of international airports that primarily serve demand emanating from airport traffic. Distance from airports varies.
	Interstate	Properties in close proximity of major interstate highways whose primary source of business is through interstate travel. Interstate properties located in suburban areas have the suburban classification.
	Resort	Properties located in resort areas where the primary source of business is from leisure destination travel.
	Small Metro/Town	Metropolitan small-town areas with less than 150,000 people. Size can vary dependent on market orientation. Suburban locations do not exist in proximity to these areas.
Property Type	Hotel/Motel	A standard hotel or motel operation.
	All-Suite	Properties that offer only suite room accommodations. Suite rooms will be the only type of room offered at properties that fall in the All-Suite category.
	Conference	Lodging properties that place major focus on conference operations. Properties must meet guidelines of the International Association of Conference Centers.
	Convention	Lodging properties that place major focus on convention operations. These properties offer or are located near convention facilities.

EXHIBIT 8.7 (*Continued*)

Classification Mode	Description	
Chain Scale	Luxury	Classified by the hotel average daily rates
	Upper Upscale	
	Upscale	
	Mid-Price	
	Economy	
	Independents	Stand-alone hotel

Source: Real Capital Analytics and Smith Travel Research, 2008.

have a challenge in overcoming lack of knowledge. This is especially true for nonluxury resorts. Exhibit 8.9 displays the largest brands, in terms of unit distribution, as well as the various segments of each brand, as applicable.

Technology and Staffing Innovation

Beyond supply and demand, several other factors including marketing, product positioning, customer service levels, and cost management directly affect a hotel asset's operating cash flow. The wide use of high technology

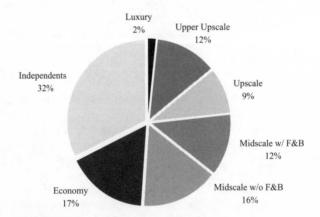

EXHIBIT 8.8 Supply of U.S. Hotel Rooms by Segment
4,507,164 Total Rooms
Source: ING Clarion Research & Investment Strategy and Smith Travel Research, as of March 2008.

EXHIBIT 8.9   Largest Hotel Brands

Choice (Clarion, Comfort Inn, Comfort Suites, Quality, Sleep Inn)
Fairmont Raffles
Four Seasons
InterContinental (Crowne Plaza, InterContinental, Hotel Indigo, Holiday Inn,
   Holiday Inn Express, Staybridge Suites)
Hilton (Embassy Suites, Hampton Inn, Hilton, Hilton Garden Inn, Homewood
   Suites, Waldorf Collection)
Hyatt (Grand Hyatt, Hyatt Place,[a] Park Hyatt)
Mandarin Oriental
Marriott (Courtyard, Fairfield Inn, JW Marriott, Marriott, Renaissance, Residence
   Inn, Marriott Vacation Club, Ritz-Carlton)
Starwood (aloft,[a] element,[a] Le Meridian, Luxury Collection, St. Regis, Sheraton,
   Westin, W)
[a]This is a new brand.

Source: ING Clarion, 2007.

significantly boosts Internet bookings, speeds up the front desk check-in process, and enhances the in-room experience for guests. Furthermore, as a result of the severe demand drop related to 9/11, the lodging industry went through a period of aggressive cost cutting. The lodging industry has adopted improved staffing models by using business intelligence systems to better forecast demand and plan employee schedules more efficiently. Consequently, profitability has been on the rise with profit margins increasing to 20.3% in 2007 and 19.9% in 2006, up from 18.4% in 2005.

U.S. HOTEL MARKET OUTLOOK

Fundamental Trends

ADR Drives Revenue Growth   Despite the economic slowdown, the U.S. hotel market is performing better than expected. Coastal markets and business destinations experienced strong average daily rate (ADR) growth mainly through increases in room rates and fees. Business travel remains robust although leisure travel has started to weaken. During the first quarter of 2008, ADR and RevPAR grew year-over-year by 4.7% and 1.9%, respectively. However, the average occupancy rate has been on the decline since fall 2007. During the first quarter of 2008, average occupancy fell by 2.7% compared to the first quarter of 2007. For the rest of 2008 and 2009, RevPAR is expected to face downward pressure due to weakened demand, increased supply, negative consumer sentiment, and surging gasoline prices. Despite the decline in occupancy, hotel managers continue to be aggressive in raising room rates and other fees. We expect this trend to continue especially for the high-end segments for which travelers are less price-sensitive.

Hotel Demand Is Moderating in Response to a Slowing Economy The U.S. economy is going through a sharp downturn as the effects of the credit crunch and weakening housing market continue to ripple across the nation. In the first quarter of 2008, GDP expanded by only 0.9%.[2] At the same time, U.S. consumers are facing significant challenges: job losses, higher energy and food prices, and declining home values. Additionally, consumer spending has weakened, and consumer confidence has dropped to a 28-year low.[3]

Demand for hotel rooms is largely correlated with economic growth. Typically, hotel demand lags GDP growth by about two quarters. Since November 2007, demand growth has been declining. As of March 2008, hotel demand growth had decreased 2.4% compared to the same period a year ago. The average occupancy rate also weakened, dropping approximately 2.7% year-over-year. Reflecting these figures, the NCREIF hotel total return was only 1.35% during the first quarter of 2008, slightly above the apartment sector.

Hotel Supply Is in a Cyclical Upturn Fueled by exceptional returns, hotel supply, which hit a bottom in 2006, is on a cyclical upturn. Approximately 123,000 and 160,000 new hotel rooms (without casinos) are projected to hit the U.S. market in 2008 and 2009, respectively. These new supplies represent 2.7% and 3.4% of existing U.S. hotel room inventory, above the long-term average of 2.5%.

Among the seven chain scale segments, Upscale and Midscale without food and beverage (F&B) are projected to have the largest supply increases in 2008–2009 (Exhibit 8.10). Several metros including Phoenix, Las Vegas, San Antonio, Houston, New York, and Washington, DC, showed substantial increases in supply pipelines over the past two quarters.

---

[2]U.S. Department of Commerce: Bureau of Economic Analysis—National Economic Accounts, "Gross Domestic Product: First Quarter 2008 (Preliminary)," http://www.bea.gov/newsreleases/national/gdp/gdpnewsrelease.htm (accessed May 29, 2008).

[3]Reuters/University of Michigan, "Confidence Sinks: Surging Prices & Shrinking Incomes," *Reuters/University of Michigan Surveys of Consumers,* May 2008, https://customers.reuters.com/wetfetch/index.aspx?CID=02701&doc=PR200805.pdf&base=/community/university/default.aspx.

EXHIBIT 8.10 Large Number of New Hotel Rooms Will Enter the Market

	2008		2009		2010	
Segment	New Rooms	% of Stock	New Rooms	% of Stock	New Rooms	% of Stock
Luxury	3,850	4.7%	2,915	3.4%	2,960	3.2%
Upper Upscale	13,224	2.4%	11,563	2.0%	11,086	1.9%
Upscale	28,256	6.7%	46,009	10.3%	21,821	4.2%
Midscale w/ F&B	9,098	1.5%	11,282	1.8%	5,372	0.8%
Midscale w/o F&B	44,401	5.9%	55,447	7.0%	23,037	2.6%
Economy	10,989	1.4%	16,687	2.1%	3,660	0.4%
Independent	13,348	1.0%	16,010	1.2%	45,278	3.2%
US	123,166	2.7%	159,913	3.4%	113,214	2.3%

Source: ING Clarion Research & Strategy, Lodging Econometrics, Portsmouth, NH 03801, March 2008.

Impact of the Credit Crunch The credit crunch has had only a minimal impact on hotel construction (Exhibit 8.11). Year-over-year construction starts increased 35% to 176,172 rooms in 2007, compared to 130,132 rooms in 2006. Historically, the first quarter has always been the slowest construction start quarter of the year. However, the first quarter of 2008 saw construction starts at an unsurpassed level of 51,864 rooms, the highest total of all quarters recorded this decade.

Many of the new construction projects are likely to have obtained loan approvals before the credit crunch. As lenders continue to tighten lending standards, we expect some forthcoming hotel construction projects, especially in suburban locations, to have difficulty obtaining loans. Indeed, compared to the fourth quarter of 2007, three chain scale segments—Midscale w/ F&B, Midscale w/o F&B, and Economy—had some cancellations in planned projects. Surprisingly, most Luxury and Upper Upscale pipeline

EXHIBIT 8.11 Construction Starts Are Accelerating

	2005	2006	2007	2008 Q1
New construction starts (projects)	840	1,000	1,450	420
Projected new rooms (000s)	106	130	176	52

Source: ING Clarion Research & Strategy, Lodging Econometrics, Portsmouth, NH 03801, March 2008.

projects continue to move forward, perhaps reflecting strong institutional sponsorships.

Impact of Rising Energy Prices   Crude oil prices are currently hovering around $130 per barrel, and some analysts even predict that the price could possibly reach $145 by the end of 2008. Retail gasoline prices have also increased, ballooning by more than 40% over the past two years (Exhibit 8.12). The rapid rise of energy prices increases hotel operating costs and discourages some leisure travel, mainly impacting the low end of hotel markets. Research data suggest that high-end hotels are able to pass on the additional costs to hotel guests through increased room rates and fees, while low-end hotels are experiencing notable declines in occupancy due to reduced travel demand.

According to a study conducted by PricewaterhouseCoopers, for every 10.0% increase in gasoline prices, hotel room demand declines by 0.5%. If energy prices stay elevated or continue to rise, they could pose a negative impact on hotel performance.

Expenses Generally under Control   Lodging total expense ratio is approximately 70 to 85% depending on the types of hotels and services provided.

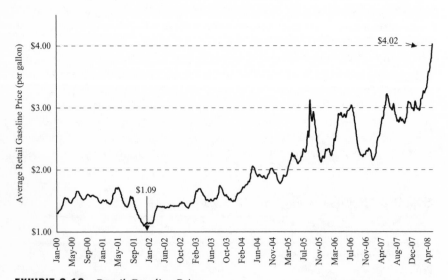

EXHIBIT 8.12   Retail Gasoline Prices
Source: ING Clarion Research & Investment Strategy and Moody's Economy.com, 2008.

Tighter cost control in response to diminished revenue growth, combined with fewer occupied rooms, has resulted in a slowdown in the pace of operating expense growth. In 2007, hotel operating costs grew by only 4.8% compared to the annual average of 6.3% from 2004 through 2006.[4] Labor costs are the largest component and account for approximately 47% of total hotel operating expenses.[5] With better staffing management control and an anticipated slowdown in demand, we expect that hotel expenses will increase by less than 4% in 2008 despite the rise in energy and food costs.

Airline Industry Impact on Hotel Sector Jet fuel costs for airlines have increased by about 80% over the previous year and now constitute 40% of airlines' operating costs, up from 25% in 2007. As a result, U.S. domestic airfares have risen 16% this year in an attempt to offset the surging costs.[6] Many airlines have not only increased the fuel surcharge per ticket, but have also instituted or raised additional fees for services such as checking bags and transporting pets.

While the rising fees are proving to be a nuisance for airline passengers, decreases in scheduled service by major U.S. carriers are also exacerbating the current situation. Domestic route networks are being targeted for downsizing: American Airlines recently announced an 11% to 12% reduction in domestic capacity in the latter half of 2008;[7] Delta Airlines also plans to reduce domestic capacity by 10%; and United Airlines will likely provide similar guidance as it plans to ground 15 to 20 Boeing 737s later this year.[8] Many of the cuts are expected to be on point-to-point routes, with feeder routes to international hubs remaining largely intact.

Despite the domestic downsizing, many U.S. airlines continue to increase international services as these routes tend to be more lucrative. Delta, for example, is expected to see 15% capacity growth on international routes in

---

[4]Robert Mandelbaum, "In Hindsight, 2007 Looks Great, Labor Costs Are a Concern," PKF Hospitality Research, http://www.pkfc.com/en/pkf-hr/ (accessed July 2008).

[5]Ibid.

[6]Ann Keeton, "US Airfares Up 16% in 2008, Expected to Climb Higher," *Dow Jones Newswires*, May 27, 2008.

[7]Mary Jane Credeur, "Fuel's Rise Hurts Pittsburgh, Cincinnati as Airlines Cut Flying," *Bloomberg L.P.*, May 28, 2008, http://www.bloomberg.com/apps/news?pid=20601207&sid=aPAhsNianPQU&refer=oil.

[8]Aaron Karp, "Delta, United to Ground Aircraft, Slash Domestic Capacity to Counter Slowdown," *Air Transport World Online*, March 19, 2008, http://www.atwonline.com/news/story.html?storyID=12103.

EXHIBIT 8.13 Year-to-Date Airline Passenger Traffic

	YOY % Change		
Airport	Domestic	International	Total
Chicago (O'Hare)[a]	−10.27%	−3.68%	−9.27%
Los Angeles[a]	−3.92%	2.34%	−2.19%
Miami[a]	−0.01%	9.39%	4.13%
Phoenix[b]	−1.10%	11.60%	−0.50%
San Diego[a]	5.50%	−4.90%	5.40%
San Francisco[b]	11.30%	7.12%	9.78%
Washington (Dulles)[b]	−7.51%	13.63%	−2.98%

[a]YTD as of April 2008
[b]YTD as of March 2008.
Source: ING Clarion Research & Investment Strategy and Bureau of Transportation Statistics.

2008.[9] This may bode well for global gateway cities, which should continue to attract both business and leisure travelers more so than domestically-oriented cities (Exhibit 8.13).

Should any one major airline cease operations as a result of the current economic environment, the tourism industries in some cities served by that airline may experience significant short-term downside. Of the airports listed above, American (hubs in Chicago and Miami), United (hubs in Chicago, Los Angeles, San Francisco, and Washington) and US Airways (hub in Phoenix) have the most significant operations in these markets. The health of these airlines will continue to play a major role in delivering business and leisure travelers to these regions.

Hawaii, as a case in point, is one example of a market that may suffer from the airline industry's woes. Two commercial airlines serving the state, Aloha Airlines and ATA Airlines, recently filed for bankruptcy and discontinued all passenger service as of March 31 and April 3, 2008, respectively. As a result, domestic passenger traffic to and from Hawaii experienced a year-over-year decrease of 10.3% for the month of April 2008 as well as a 15.7% reduction in total air seats available.[10] The long-term effects of

[9]Ibid.
[10]State of Hawaii Department of Business, Economic Development & Tourism, "Monthly Visitor Statistics," http://hawaii.gov/dbedt/info/visitor-stats/tourism/ (accessed April 2008).

EXHIBIT 8.14 Hotel Cap Rates Are on the Rise

	Average Cap Rate		
	2007 Q1	2008 Q1	Cap Rate Change
National average	7.98%	9.26%	128 bps
Full service hotels	7.48%	8.07%	59 bps
Limited service hotels	8.51%	10.60%	209 bps

Source: ING Clarion Research & Investment Strategy and Real Capital Analytics, 2008.

such an event are yet to be seen although the air seats capacity outlook for Hawaiian airports in the May–July 2008 period is for a decrease of 13.2%.[11]

Capital Market Trends

Hotel Cap Rates Are on the Rise As with other property sectors, hotel cap rates are rising because of risk re-pricing and weakened fundamentals. Nationally, as of March 2008, the average hotel transaction cap rate expanded by 128 bps compared to the same period a year ago. However, full service hotels held up relatively well compared to limited service hotels (Exhibit 8.14).

Public-to-Private Transactions In the past three years, hotel transaction volume has been driven mostly by public-to-private transactions and large portfolio deals highlighted by the $26 billion acquisition of Hilton Hotels by Blackstone in 2007 (Exhibit 8.15). There have not been any large hotel portfolio transactions announced since the beginning of the credit crisis in July 2007.

Transaction Dollar Volume Has Declined Sharply After reaching a peak in the fourth quarter of 2007 when the Hilton privatization deal was closed, U.S. hotel transactions fell to $5.2 billion during the first quarter of 2008 (Exhibit 8.16). With slowing RevPAR growth and a decline in occupancy rates, many hotel investors are uncertain about the near-term future of the hotel market.

---

[11]State of Hawaii Department of Business, Economic Development & Tourism, "Air Seats Capacity Outlook," http://hawaii.gov/dbedt/info/visitor-stats/air-seats/ (accessed May–July 2008).

EXHIBIT 8.15   Notable Public-to-Private Hotel Transactions in the United States

Year	Transactions
2007	Blackstone Group buys Hilton Hotels Corp. for $26 billion. Morgan Stanley buys CNL Hotels and Resorts for $6.6 billion. Goldman Sachs buys Equity Inns for $2.2 billion. Lightstone Group buys Extended Stay Hotels from Blackstone for $8 billion. JER Partners acquires Highland Hospitality Corp. for $2 billion. Apollo Investment Corp. buys Innkeepers for $1.5 billion. ING Clarion Partners buys Apple Hospitality Two for $890 million. APAIMCAP acquires Eagle Hospitality Properties for $238 million.
2006	Bill Gates and Alwaleed Bin Talal buy Four Seasons Hotels for $3.7 billion. Alwalled bin Talal and Colony Capital buy Fairmont Hotels & resorts for $3.3 billion. Seminoles buy Hard Rock Cafe chain for $965 million. Blackstone acquires MeriStar Hospitality for $2.6 billion.
2005	Blackstone buys Wyndham International for $3.2 billion. Blackstone acquires La Quinta for $3.4 billion.
2004	Blackstone buys Extended Stay for $3.1 billion.

Source: ING Clarion Research & Investment Strategy, 2008.

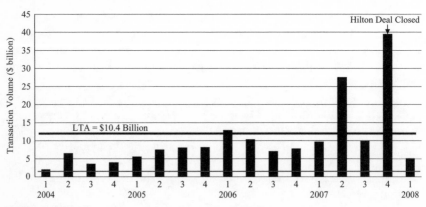

EXHIBIT 8.16   Hotel Quarterly Transaction Volume in Steep Decline
Source: ING Clarion Research & Investment Strategy and Real Capital Analytics, 2008.

EXHIBIT 8.17 U.S. Economic Forecast

	2008	2009	2010
Real GDP growth	1.6%	3.0%	3.6%
Office using employment growth	−0.5%	0.8%	2.6%
Inflation (CPI)	3.6%	2.1%	1.6%

Source: ING Clarion Research & Investment Strategy and Moody's Economy.com.

Hotel Sector Outlook

The U.S. Economy Is Expected to Recover by Late 2009 Our forecast calls for a recovery of the U.S. economy in late 2009 as the housing market downturn and credit crunch run their course. It is likely that hotel demand will be under pressure until then. Although currently higher than the long-term trend (2.5%), inflation is expected to retreat by the end of 2008 and move in line with or even below the long-term trend in 2009 and 2010 (Exhibit 8.17). In addition, office-using employment, a key driver for hotel demand, is forecast to recover fully by 2010. With the exception of financial, home building, and auto manufacturing companies, most U.S. companies have strong balance sheets, and their recent earning outlooks are generally positive.

U.S. National Hotel Forecast The current hotel sector slowdown, which began in fall 2007, is expected to last through 2008 and most of 2009 because of weakened demand and increasing supply coming online. As a result, the national average hotel occupancy rate is forecast to decline by 2.0% in 2008 and 1.7% in 2009 (Exhibit 8.18). Despite this decline in occupancy, the hotel sector is forecast to continue generating positive RevPAR, which is expected to grow by 2.3% and 0.9% in 2008 and 2009, respectively. Coinciding with a likely full U.S. economic recovery in 2010, RevPAR is expected to improve strongly to 4.7% as demand is forecast to outpace supply at that time.

Hotel Segment Forecast According to our forecast, the Luxury, Upper Upscale, and Midscale w/o F&B segments are expected to outperform the rest of the segments (Upscale, Independent, Midscale w/ F&B, and Economy) in 2008–2010 (Exhibit 8.19).

EXHIBIT 8.18 U.S. Hotel Sector Forecasts as of May 2008 (all segments)

Year	Occupancy Rate (%)	Change of Occupancy (%)	ADR ($)	Change of ADR (%)	RevPar ($)	Change of RevPar (%)	Supply Growth (%)	Demand Growth (%)
2001	59.8	−5.6	84.0	−1.44	50.2	−6.93	2.38	−3.35
2002	59.0	−1.3	82.8	−1.48	48.8	−2.71	1.57	0.33
2003	59.2	0.3	82.9	0.15	49.1	0.44	1.01	1.33
2004	61.3	3.6	86.3	4.16	52.9	7.90	0.41	4.01
2005	63.1	2.9	91.1	5.49	57.4	8.54	−0.10	2.78
2006	63.3	0.3	97.9	7.49	61.9	7.79	0.19	0.46
2007	63.1	−0.2	103.7	5.95	65.5	5.71	1.32	1.11
2008 F	61.8	−2.0	108.3	4.45	67.0	2.34	2.31	0.18
2009 F	60.8	−1.7	111.3	2.72	67.6	0.94	3.03	1.25
2010 F	61.1	0.5	116.0	4.23	70.8	4.71	2.08	2.55

Source: ING Clarion Research & Investment Strategy, Smith Travel Research, and Lodging Econometrics, Portsmouth, NH 03801.

The Luxury and Upper Upscale Segments The Luxury and Upper Upscale segments continue to maintain a favorable demand and supply balance. Unlike 2001–2002, the supply pipeline has been relatively constrained during this cycle. Despite a slight decline in occupancy rate, growth in ADR and RevPAR is forecast to remain relatively strong.

The outlook for these two high-end segments is good. The Luxury and Upper Upscale segments are the most difficult to source and build. They tend to have high barriers to entry because of the difficulty in finding suitable land (especially in infill markets), higher construction costs, and a much more complex development process. These constraints should mitigate new supply (especially in prime urban city centers) compared to other segments. Because of their high barriers to entry, luxury hotels have the highest operating income and the highest price appreciation potential.

The Luxury and Upper Upscale segments appear to be poised for continued strong performance, bolstered by an expanding price-insensitive customer base (Baby Boomers, affluent consumers, and mass affluent consumers) and a fair amount of insulation against economic cycles. Baby Boomers are the wealthiest generation and are beneficiaries of significant wealth transfer with more than $2 trillion in annual spending power.[12] They

---

[12]CNBC, "American Boomers Now a $2 Trillion Market," *MSNBC*, September 28, 2006, http://www.msnbc.msn.com/id/12288534/.

EXHIBIT 8.19 Forecast RevPAR Growth by Segment

| Segment | Historic | | | | | | | ING Forecast | | | | |
	2001	2002	2003	2004	2005	2006	2007	2008	2009	2010	3-Year Avg	Rank
U.S.	−6.9	−2.7	0.4	7.9	8.5	7.8	5.7	2.3	1.4	4.6	2.8	NA
Luxury	−14.2	−5.2	0.8	10.3	10.9	11.6	10.0	5.3	4.4	5.8	5.2	1
Upper Upscale	−11.6	−3.4	−1.8	8.2	9.7	7.1	7.2	2.8	3.8	5.0	3.8	2
Midscale w/o F&B	−1.6	−0.9	0.5	7.3	11.7	9.0	5.9	2.1	1.0	6.3	3.1	3
Upscale	−8.4	−4.8	−0.6	8.9	10.1	8.4	5.5	1.4	−2.4	4.3	1.1	4
Independent	−6.8	−2.5	1.4	7.8	5.1	6.8	7.0	1.2	1.9	−0.2	1.0	5
Midscale w/ F&B	−6.6	−4.0	−0.4	6.2	8.6	6.4	1.5	0.7	−0.9	3.0	0.9	6
Economy	−3.3	−3.6	−1.4	4.7	7.6	5.0	4.2	−1.4	1.1	2.8	0.8	7

Source: ING Clarion Research & Investment Strategy, Smith Travel Research, and Lodging Econometrics, Portsmouth, NH 03801, May 2008.

are approaching retirement age, and their demand for the Luxury and Upper Upscale chain scale segments should continue to expand. Additionally, affluent consumers have the tendency to continue spending even when the economy slows. Generation X, characterized by members who enjoy refined lifestyles and who also tend to spend heavily, will likely add additional demand. Furthermore, foreign visitors to the United States are increasing at a healthy pace (about 10% year-over-year).[13] They are typically affluent and willing to spend, further boosting the room demand for these two segments.

The Upscale and Midscale Segments   The Upscale and Midscale segments have the largest hotel supply pipeline with approximately 174,000 new rooms forecast to enter the market in 2008 and 2009. Occupancy rates are expected to decline, and RevPAR is forecast to be flat or even negative in 2009.

These segments are characterized by relatively lower construction costs, an expanding midscale franchise market, higher operating margins, and comparatively lower economic risk. The Midscale w/o F&B segment appeals to the needs of many travelers today who are seeking value accommodations. Demand for this segment should be relatively stable through the economic downturn. The Upscale segment could benefit as some business travelers might be pushed to move down the chain scale from Upper Upscale for cost savings. The Midscale w/ F&B segment has been in a secular decline since 2005 as this particular offering becomes less attractive.

Economy and Other Low-End Segments   The Economy and other low-end segments are feeling the squeeze from three fronts: higher operating costs, soaring gasoline prices, and weakened demand. Traditionally, these low-end segments have relatively weak pricing power. As of March 2008, occupancy levels declined nearly 5.0% over the same period in 2007. The sector is forecast to underperform because of flat room rates and a large decline in occupancy.

CONCLUSION

Given strong fundamentals, the Luxury and Upper Upscale segments seem to have strong momentum. Hotel operators in these two segments

[13]U.S. Department of Commerce, ITA, Office of Travel & Tourism Industries, "Summary of International Travel to the U.S.," http://tinet.ita.doc.gov/research/reports/I94/index.html (accessed May 2008).

demonstrated success in raising ADRs with only a minimum loss in occupancy rates. If priced properly, the addition of Luxury or Upper Upscale hotel properties could potentially boost portfolio investment returns during the ongoing commercial real estate slowdown.

U.S. hotels will likely remain under pressure in 2008 and 2009. Consequently, RevPAR growth projections are expected to be adjusted downward. Acquisition opportunities may arise as hotel assets' pricing declines. Luxury and Upper Upscale segments, especially business hotels and resorts located in international gateway cites, are expected to weather the slowdown better and will likely begin a recovery by 2010. They are forecast to outperform relative to the five other chain scale segments as well as the four core property sectors.

CHAPTER 9

Global Gateway Industrial Market Investment

Bohdy Hedgcock and David Lynn
Spring 2008[1]

Global gateway ports—the entry and exit point for goods moving through the distribution system—offer future growth opportunities as both U.S. consumption and international trade continue to expand. With the growing importance of international trade, the combination of reliability and speed to market has taken precedence over stacking and storing goods. While warehouse space remains a commodity, access to prime transportation hubs is a growing competitive advantage. The emergence of air, rail, and trucking as increasingly important modes for international trade is expanding these global gateway facilities from coastal ports to inland hubs as well. When combined with access to a strong population base, reasonable barriers to entry that keep supply in check, and an efficient transportation and infrastructure network, distribution facilities in global gateway ports may present a compelling investment opportunity. This chapter analyzes the changing dynamics in the industry, with a focus on trends that are influencing the expansion of existing and emerging gateway markets.

---

[1]This paper was originally produced in spring 2008. The data, opinions, and forecasts have not been updated for book publication.

BACKGROUND

Global gateway ports are a key element of the larger U.S. freight distribution system, including air, rail, trucking, and inland freight hubs. An increasingly sophisticated network of warehouse and distribution facilities support this system and make up nearly 60% of the 12.7 billion square feet of industrial space nationwide. Two long-term trends are impacting the supply and demand for warehouse space:

- The growing U.S. population coupled with increasing per capita consumption means that more and more products must be shipped, stored, and redistributed from manufacturers to the final consumer.
- The increasing reliance on foreign trade has steadily increased the volume of both imports and exports and is driving supply chain reconfiguration to encourage expanded activity in both existing and emerging port locations.

Traditionally, the distribution of goods has been linked to the place of production. As a result, warehouses and other types of industrial space have been established near manufacturing centers. Those manufacturing centers, in turn, selected locations based on proximity to natural resources, labor pools, and transportation corridors. With an increasing percentage of manufacturing moving overseas, access to suppliers and consumers primarily drives the location of distribution centers in the United States today.

Locations near hub and gateway cities that have access to efficient transportation networks are preferred, as they offer advantages in both reliability and efficiency (Exhibit 9.1). Retailers stocking their shelves with consumer products and manufacturers dependent on materials from disparate distributors are two examples of firms that increasingly rely on *just-in-time* (JIT) supply chains. Overall productivity and profit for these firms demand that supplies be delivered on schedule. In making their warehousing and distribution decisions, firms increasingly devote resources to those key markets that offer a combination of access to global and local markets with service from efficient and reliable transportation networks. As logistics and real estate gain importance, prime transportation hubs are expected to be a key driver of development and investment opportunities.

EXHIBIT 9.1   Major Global Gateway Markets
Source: ING Clarion Research & Investment Strategy, May 2008.

FACTORS INFLUENCING PORT EXPANSIONS

Global Trade Growth

Globally, export volumes of goods are expected to be strong in 2008, though the rate of growth may slow from the extraordinarily high rates of global trade experienced over the past four years. Of the 108 countries for which the Economist Intelligence Unit (EIU) forecasts export volume growth, only 10 countries are expected to have 2008 export volumes down from 2007 volumes.[2] The EIU forecasts a 4.8% increase over 2007 in the export volume for the developed world—that is, the OECD (Organisation for Economic Co-operation and Development) countries. This year-over-year growth rate would be lower than the historical averages for both the 10-year (5.4%) and 15-year (6.2%) periods. However, in the emerging economies, export volumes are considerably stronger with much of Asia and the countries of Eastern Europe appearing as solid sources of export markets in 2008 relative to last year. The weaker dollar has also made U.S. exports very competitive, and strong growth is forecast in 2008.

---

[2]ING Real Estate Research & Strategy, Economist Intelligence Unit, "Shipping Statistics Yearbook 2007," in *Containerisation International Yearbook 2008* (April 2008).

The United States is the only country expected to have a decline in imports in 2008, according to the EIU. The forecast drop of 0.4% would be only the third decline since 1981 (1982, 1991, and 2001 were the others). Several key emerging economies—China, Vietnam, India, Brazil, Russia, and Poland—are all forecast to experience double-digit growth in import volumes in 2008. The OECD average import growth rate for 2008 of 3.6% is expected to be the trough in the current cycle and is forecast to rebound to 4.9% next year and remain above 5.0% for the following three years. Even Japan, where import volumes were down in 2007 from the 2006 figure (by –2.7%) is forecast to have solid import volume growth this year of 3.9%. Canadian import growth will be strong this year (5.4%) as will growth in other large import markets which currently have strong currencies, including Germany (5.2%), the Netherlands (6.8%), and Australia (7.6%).[3]

Containerization—20-ft. Equivalent Units (TEUs)

Containerization is a system of intermodal cargo transport using standardized containers (known as *shipping containers* or *isotainers*) that can be loaded and sealed intact onto container ships, railroad cars, planes, and trucks. The standardization of these containers allows for improved efficiency in transporting materials across shipping modes—ship, rail, and trucking—and has greatly enhanced the flexibility and efficiency of global shipping systems.[4]

The volume of containers handled by U.S. ports has grown at an average annual rate of 6.6% since 1990. Total volume in 2007 was nearly 45 million TEUs, almost triple the 15.6 million TEUs recorded in 1990. Pacific Coast ports handled 55% of the total volume, compared to 40% for Atlantic ports and 5% for Gulf Coast ports. Total volume is highly concentrated, with the ports of Los Angeles, Long Beach, and New York/New Jersey accounting for 46.6% of the total volume in 2007, up from 41.2% in 2000. The top 20 U.S. ports handle more than 95% of the total TEU traffic. The top three U.S. ports—Los Angeles, Long Beach, and New York/New Jersey—are ranked

---

[3]Ibid.

[4]The use of these containers has become so ubiquitous that reporting agencies commonly provide shipping data in reference to standard container capacity. Container capacity is generally expressed in 20-ft. equivalent units (TEUs). An equivalent unit is a measure of containerized cargo capacity equal to one standard 20 ft. (length) × 8 ft. (width) container. The most common containers are 40 feet in length, permitting them to fit efficiently on a ship, truck, or railcar.

EXHIBIT 9.2 U.S. and Global Port Rankings by Volume, 2007

Top U.S. Ports by Volume (2007)			Top Global Ports by Volume (2007)		
Port	Total TEU (000s)	Percent of U.S. Total	Port	Country	Total TEU (000s)
Los Angeles	8,355	18.6%	Singapore	Singapore	24,792
Long Beach	7,316	16.3%	Hong Kong	China	23,539
NY/NJ	5,299	11.8%	Shanghai	China	21,710
Savannah	2,604	5.8%	Shenzhen	China	18,469
Oakland	2,388	5.3%	Busan	S. Korea	12,039
Hampton Roads	2,128	4.7%	Kaohsiung	Taiwan	9,775
Seattle	1,974	4.4%	Rotterdam	Netherlands	9,655
Tacoma	1,925	4.3%	Dubai	UAE	8,923
Houston	1,769	3.9%	Hamburg	Germany	8,862
Charleston	1,754	3.9%	Los Angeles	U.S.	8,355
San Juan	1,695	3.8%	Qingdao	China	7,702
Honolulu	1,125	2.5%	Long Beach	U.S.	7,316
Port Everglades	949	2.1%	Ningbo	China	7,068
Miami	885	2.0%	Antwerp	Belgium	7,019
Jacksonville	710	1.6%	Guangzhou	China	6,600
Baltimore	610	1.4%	Port Klang	Malaysia	6,326
Anchorage	505	1.1%	Tianjin	China	5,950
Wilmington (DE)	284	0.6%	NY/NJ	U.S.	5,299
Portland (OR)	260	0.6%	Tanjung Pelepas	Indonesia	4,770
Philadelphia	253	0.6%	Bremen/ Bremerhaven	Germany	4,450

Source: American Ports Authority Association

among the top 20 global ports in total TEU volume. Rankings of the largest ports by 2007 TEU volume for the United States and globally is provided in Exhibit 9.2.[5]

The Mega-Containership Trends and Implications for Global Ports

In order to capture additional economies of scale, shipping companies continue to employ increasingly larger freightliners. The emergence of

---

[5]All container volume data are for 2007 annual numbers as reported by the American Association of Port Authorities unless otherwise noted.

mega-ships allows for reduced logistics and transportation costs, as shippers and manufacturers are able to take advantage of economies of scale. Marine-based supply and distribution centers are increasingly focused around key load-center ports that have adequate waterside capacity to handle these vessels coupled with adequate landside access to serve key consumer markets.

The largest ships are referred to as *post-Panamax* due to their inability to travel through the Panama Canal. They are divided into three generations: Post I, with onboard capacity of up to 5,500 TEUs; Post II, with capacity of up to 10,000 TEUs; and Post III, with capacity greater than 10,000 TEUs. Post II ships with a capacity of 8,000 TEUs are the largest ships presently in operation. Post II ships are also becoming dominant in the Asia–North America transpacific trade. Post III ships are not in existence yet, although they are expected to emerge in the next 5 to 10 years. The channel depth requirement for unrestricted handling of Post II and III ships is 50 and 52 feet respectively.[6]

Three factors determine the ability of ports to accommodate larger ships: (1) water draft, or the depth of the water channel; (2) air draft, or the height of any surrounding bridges or overpasses; and, (3) turn-around, or the required space to maneuver the ships. Currently only two ports on the East Coast, Norfolk (Ports of Virginia) and Halifax (in Nova Scotia) are able to accommodate the Post II ships. These are also considered the only ports on the East Coast that will eventually be able to handle Post III ships. Most of the other major ports in the east, including Charleston, Savannah, Jacksonville, and Miami may be able to accommodate Post II ships eventually. However, substantial dredging and other upgrades that may not be economically feasible could be required. Both Savannah and Jacksonville are currently undertaking improvements to add additional capacity and service larger ships.

Most of the major West Coast ports, including Los Angeles, Long Beach, Seattle, Tacoma, and Oakland are currently able to handle Post II ships. All except Oakland should be capable of handling Post III ships at some point in the future, pending improvements. The high cost and significant environmental hurdles associated with dredging suggest that the actual number of ports capable of handling these largest ships will remain limited in the near term.

Port Congestion and Costs

While the amount of time to move goods from one place to another by ship has been decreasing over time, increasing congestion and fees in the area of

---

[6]A. Ashar, "Long Term Development Trends of U.S. Ports," Transportation Research Board, December 2004, www.trb.org/Conferences/MTS/4C%20AsharPaper .pdf.

some primary ports is adding new challenges. Any port is only as strong as the weakest link in its distribution system, so difficulties in moving goods from port to rail or port to truck can create significant costs. Congestion surrounding the Los Angeles/Long Beach ports is the most commonly cited example of increasing delays, but other large ports are also struggling to keep up with a growing volume of goods. Growing fees, particularly in the California ports, are also making shipping to those locations more expensive. Both trends are resulting in a shift in overall volumes, with some Gulf Coast and East Coast ports exploiting their cost advantage.

Many importers began rethinking their freight movements following the strikes and associated delays in the Los Angeles-area ports in 2004 and 2005. Shipping volume began to shift from the West Coast ports to Gulf and East Coast ports in order to gain more consistency in transit times. That trend has continued, with shippers increasingly looking away from the major ports of Los Angeles/Long Beach to decrease costs and increase efficiency. For example, the American Association of Port Authorities reports that the West Coast's share of Asian imports fell to 58% in 2005 from 86% in 1999, while the Panama Canal's share climbed to 40% from 11%.[7] From 2006 to 2007, the total volume of TEUs handled in Pacific ports declined by 0.57%, while the volume increased at Atlantic ports by 2.46% and at Gulf Coast ports by 13.18%.[8]

Capacity   The impact that a delay on the land side of a shipping system can create is described below:

> *At sea, container freight moves at 25 knots. The 6,300 miles from Hong Kong to Los Angeles can be covered in eleven or twelve days. That's when things grind to a halt. The ship may take three days to be worked in L.A. The container will reside for an average of five days more in the terminal. It will take another day to get out of the terminal and across the L.A. urban area, which is about 50 miles across. The average velocity of the freight drops to about 0.25 knots or 1% of its velocity at sea. All the wonderful technology built into maritime transport is stymied by the port system's ability to get the*

---

[7]Thomas Ward, "Port Congestion Relief: Attacking the Entire Chain," JWD Group, a division of DMJM Harris, p.1. Available at http://www.dmjmharris.com/media/4437.pdf.

[8]American Association of Port Authorities, "U.S. / Canada Container Traffic in TEUs (1990–2007)," online database at http://aapa.files.cms-plus.com/Statistics/CONTAINER%5FTRAFFIC%5FNORTH%5FAMERICA.xls (accessed April 2008).

*freight inland. All the while that the container is moving at such
a low speed, it is consuming valuable port and urban resources:
berths, terminal yards, urban roads, and regional highways. The
slower it moves, the more it consumes.*[9]

Traditionally, it has been cheaper to bring containers into West Coast
ports and move them via rail to distribution centers in the central and
eastern regions of the United States for distribution to the majority of the
U.S. population that lives east of the Mississippi. Delays in moving goods
from the West Coast ports are causing shippers to rethink this approach.
In California, the biggest problem is delays associated with moving freight
through the vast Los Angeles urban area and its congested road and rail
systems. In the Northwest ports, the problems are primarily associated with
an undersupply of rail capacity and the challenges posed by weather.

Shifting shipping routes to a larger number of ports is advantageous to
the overall system in the long run, as it provides more redundancy in the
system and the competition between ports can help to reduce overall costs.
However, these shifts can also cause disruption. Ward notes, "Shifting just
5% of the traffic out of Southern California to another port can increase
that port's traffic by as much as a third. How many ports can sustain such a
rapid onslaught?"[10] Careful planning is essential to insure that ports improve
each element of the transport chain, so that this added volume of shipments
can continue to be moved efficiently through the system. While the rise
of smaller ports creates wider opportunities for real estate, any investment
decision must consider whether the emerging port facility has appropriate
facilities in place to handle the increasing demand.

Increased Fees   In addition to the costs associated with transporting goods
from the marine port to inland distribution centers, a series of new container
fees in California to fund infrastructure improvements and environmental
impact mitigation are causing real concern for importers. Carriers that deliver to the ports of Long Beach and Los Angeles are facing a combination
of new fees that could amount to as much as $100 per fully loaded TEU.
The expectation is that these fees will eventually rise in Northern California
and Pacific Northwest ports, as well.

As an example of the mounting fees, as of June 1, 2008, a new $35 charge
will be placed on every loaded 20 ft. equivalent cargo container entering or

---

[9]Ward, p. 1.
[10]Ibid.

leaving the Long Beach or L.A. ports by truck. As a result of these new fees, which East Coast ports have not matched, West Coast ports have become increasingly less cost competitive for containers that will ultimately move eastward.[11]

Distribution Centers

Distribution centers have become the fundamental link between production and consumption. A distribution center is a warehouse or other specialized building that is stocked with products to be redistributed to retailers or wholesalers. An emerging pattern involves the location of megadistribution centers, particularly in retailing. This process is coinciding with the deindustrialization of the United States, making the retail sector more reliant on foreign production and imports. Thus, locations near international gateways are becoming relatively more important. Accessibility and land requirements induce major retailers to look for more suitable alternatives than the existing and heavily congested gateways.

The location of distribution centers is largely dictated by JIT. Just-in-time delivery is becoming the norm in various industries. It involves raising efficiency by eliminating large inventories. For example, instead of producing its own parts, Toyota relies on suppliers to deliver products in small batches, as required by Toyota's assembly lines, and within narrow time windows for immediate use. With few components in stock, there is little margin for error, forcing every firm in the supply chain to perform as required. As a result, freight customers demand carriers that can meet strict delivery deadlines. Because disruptions in the supply chain can create huge impacts in operations and sales, an increasing number of firms are incorporating some element of redundancy in their distribution system. While this seems counter to the efficiency goals of just-in-time, lessons learned from recent port closures has confirmed that the cost of some duplication in the system is preferable to strict reliance on a single entry/exit port.

The geography of distribution within mega-urban regions is changing as many freight distribution activities are being relocated to increasingly suburban areas. Traditionally, distribution centers were located close to central urban areas to enhance market proximity. As the size of warehouse and distribution centers expands, the ability to locate these facilities in central

---

[11]SCDigest Editorial Staff, "Global Logistics: With West Coast Port Congestion Gone for Now, Many Shippers Continue to Migrate to East Coast Ports," *Supply Chain Digest*, May 25, 2008, http://www.scdigest.com/assets/On_Target/08-03-25-3.php?cid=1570&ctype=content.

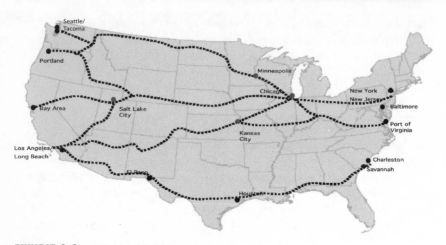

EXHIBIT 9.3 U.S. Land Bridges
Source: ING Clarion Research & Investment Strategy and Dr. Jean-Paul Rodrique, Department of Economics & Geography, Hofstra University.

cities has diminished, given high land costs. In addition, locating in suburban areas helps to avoid congested roadways and allows for increasing use of alternative modes such as rail and barges.

Rail Corridors

The role of railroads in the logistics system has gained renewed prominence in the last few decades, as highways began to clog and diesel prices escalated. For North America, rail transportation has seen the emergence of long-distance corridors, better known as *land bridges*. The North American land bridge is mainly composed of three latitudinal corridors that have been developed to deal with the increasing need to move containerized freight across the continent. These land bridges link the two major gateway systems of North America: Southern California and New York/New Jersey via Chicago (Exhibit 9.3). In addition to the U.S.-based corridors, a Canadian and a Mexican land bridge have also been developed.

The land bridge provides an alternative to freight shipments across the Panama Canal. For instance, a container coming from Singapore takes 36 days to reach New York using the Panama Canal sea route. The same journey takes about 19 days if shipped to the West Coast and then transferred by rail via a land bridge. Shipments from Europe can benefit from a similar time savings, reducing travel from Rotterdam, for example, to the West Coast from an average of five to six weeks to about three weeks, including an 80-hour railway journey across North America. The emergence of viable cross-continent shipping has allowed several maritime companies to abandon their reliance on the Panama Canal altogether. This has allowed them to shift to post-Panamax class containerships, improving overall efficiency.

Despite the increasing importance of land bridges, cross-continent rail freight transportation is complicated by the fragmented patterns of rail line ownerships. Rail companies have their facilities, customers, and markets along the segments they control. The liners particularly hinder sharing rail networks in order to gather market share and regional control over rail freight services. As a result, interconnectivity (the ability to connect from one rail system to another) is somewhat constrained and represents a major problem between segments controlled by different rail companies.

Mergers have improved coordination among different rail carriers; however, a limit has been reached in the network size of most rail operators. Because of the geography of rail ownership, there are six major locations suitable for the establishment of a hub system to support a rail freight distribution system in North America. These locations correspond to areas where changes in rail ownership have occurred, creating a link between different segments of the continental rail network. Chicago, Minneapolis/St. Paul, Kansas City, St. Louis, Memphis, and Dallas/Fort Worth are suitable locations since they are interface nodes in the rail system. Each hub is positioned to act as a gateway, collecting, sorting, and redistributing the containerized freight along major rail corridors. Chicago is obviously on the top of the list because it handles a very high share of the rail traffic, about 50% of the American rail freight. It acts as North America's primary consolidation and deconsolidation center and is implicitly the chokepoint of the continental rail system.

Another option being explored by some of the Chinese shipping lines and U.S. intermodal operators focuses on expanding Mexican ports and developing rail lines north of the U.S.-Mexico border. This offers an alternative to southern California ports which suffer significant bottlenecks. The port most often mentioned as a major entry point, Lazaro Cardenas, is a deepwater port about 1,000 miles south of the U.S. border. However, it is unlikely to impact the dominance of U.S. ports any time soon. In order to be part of a core intermodal network, a port city needs to be near a large metro; the Mexican markets have not developed to that point. Currently, Lazaro Cardenas handles less than 100,000 containers, though expansion plans will allow the port to handle 1.8 million containers by 2017. In comparison, the ports of Los Angeles and Long Beach handled more than 15 million containers in 2007.

The Panama Canal

The Panama Canal provides an alternative for freight movement from Asia to the East Coast through all water freight transport. The 50-mile canal shortens the trip distance for transoceanic shipments. For example, a ship sailing from Los Angeles to New York via the canal travels approximately 7,500 miles, half the distance it would take through the previous 15,000-mile trip route around Cape Horn.

The canal transports 4% of world trade and 16% of all U.S. originated trade. The total number of vessel transits (ships passing through the canal) rose by about 3% between 1999 and 2007; however, given the steady rise in average ship size and in the numbers of Panamax vessels passing, the total tonnage carried increased by more than 37% over that same period.[12]

Several factors have led to the importance of the Panama Canal in North American freight logistics, including the increasing congestion at the Ports of Los Angeles and Long Beach discussed previously. In addition, increasing costs and decreasing reliability on the U.S. intermodal system (particularly rail connections) has led to interest in other routes between the East and West Coasts of the United States. Furthermore, the increase of distribution and warehousing centers near ports along the Gulf and Southeast coasts of the United States have made the Panama Canal (also known as the "all-water" route) an increasingly attractive route for shippers serving these markets.

The Panama Canal Authority is undertaking a $5.25 billion expansion project that would involve the construction of two lock facilities, the excavation of new access channels and widening of existing channels, and the deepening of existing navigation channels. Panamanian voters approved the plan in October 2006 and construction began in 2007. The new locks are expected to begin operations in 2015. In addition to these significant infrastructure investments, the Panama Canal Authority has developed strategic partnerships with key U.S. ports, including the Port of Houston, to boost trade through the canal. This combination of wider navigation channels and locks (to allow large, post-Panamax ships to navigate through the canal), coupled with strategic marketing partnerships with key U.S. ports, should increase demand for the canal itself and for U.S. ports along the Gulf and East Coasts. The ability to accommodate larger ships will allow for economies of scale that will help the all-water route gain increased importance.

---

[12]Panama Canal Authority, "Panama Canal Traffic—Fiscal Years 1999–2007," http://www.pancanal.com/eng/maritime/statisti.html (accessed March 2008).

North American Free Trade
Agreement (NAFTA) Impacts

NAFTA was established in 1994, creating a trade bloc including Canada, Mexico, and the United States. According to data from the office of the U.S. Trade Representative (USTR), trade relations among Canada, Mexico, and the United States have broadened substantially since NAFTA's implementation. The USTR reports "from 1993 to 2007, trade among the NAFTA nations more than tripled, from $297 billion to $930 billion. Business investment in the United States has risen by 117% since 1993, compared to a 45% increase between 1979 and 1993."[13] Trade with NAFTA partners now accounts for more than 80% of Canadian and Mexican trade, and more than a third of U.S. trade.[14]

Mexican exports to the United States have quadrupled since NAFTA's implementation, from $60 billion to $280 billion per year. U.S. exports to Mexico have also increased sharply, more than tripling as Mexico's economy has grown. Canada, the leading exporter of goods to the United States, has arguably experienced the strongest economic growth since NAFTA's implementation of the three member countries.[15] Growth in this trade results in higher levels of international freight movement and the demand for expanded freight transportation services in the United States.

In Mexico, the historically inefficient and unreliable state-run rail service has made trucking the overwhelming choice for freight transportation. In 1999, trucking hauled 87% of Mexican land cargo by weight, versus only 13% for rail. Privatization of the Mexican National Railway in 1997 and 1998 permitted foreign companies to bid on 50-year leases for Mexico's three regional rail systems. The capital influx enjoyed by Mexico's newly privatized railroads has dramatically improved productivity and stimulated modernization in the Mexican rail industry. By capitalizing on privatization, Ferromex has also increased its freight volumes by over 45% since 1997. With greater consistency and the advent of refrigerated and double-stack container services, the railroads are better able to compete with trucking. In the next decade, Mexican rail is likely to continue to gain market share over trucking.

---

[13]Office of the United States Trade Representative, "NAFTA: Myth vs. Facts," March 2008, http://www.ustr.gov/assets/Document_Library/Fact_Sheets/2008/asset_upload_file855_14540.pdf.
[14]Lee Hudson Teslik, Council on Foreign Relations, "NAFTA's Economic Impact," *Backgrounder,* March 21, 2008, (http://www.cfr.org/publication/15790/.
[15]Ibid.

In addition, three highway corridors have emerged over the past decade as principal Canada–U.S.–Mexico trade routes. The NASCO Corridor is a 2,500-mile-long multimodal transportation network linking Mexico, the United States, and Canada. The corridor connects more than 71 million people, and supports $1 trillion in total business between the three countries. It stretches from Lazaro Cardenas, the deepwater port of Mexico, to the border crossing of Laredo, Texas, through eleven states, and to eastern and western Canada.[16]

Foreign Trade Zones

A Foreign Trade Zone (FTZ) is a port of entry, where "foreign and domestic merchandise is considered to be outside the country, or at least, outside of U.S. Customs territory. Certain types of merchandise can be imported into a Zone without going through formal Customs entry procedures or paying import duties. Customs duties and excise taxes are due only at the time of transfer from the FTZ for U.S. consumption. If the merchandise never enters the U.S. commerce, then no duties or taxes are paid on those items."[17] FTZs were developed as a means to attract new and foreign investments. The areas are typically locations for labor-intensive manufacturing centers that involve the import of raw materials or components and the export of factory products. Foreign and domestic merchandise may be moved into zones for operations, including storage, exhibition, assembly, manufacturing, and processing.

Exports (shipments to foreign countries) from facilities operating under FTZ procedures amounted to over $30 billion in 2006, up from about $5 billion in 1986. Industries accounted for most zone manufacturing activity included the oil refining, automotive, pharmaceutical, and electronic product sectors.[18]

Texas leads the United States in terms of the number of FTZs as well as trade volumes within FTZs. Texas also has the greatest number of companies active in FTZs, with 449 in total. California is second with 429 companies.

---

[16]North America's SuperCorridor Coalition (NASCO), *NASCO Conferénce 2008, Quebéc,*   http://www.nascocorridor.com/calendardetail.asp?id=2181&pageno=1 (accessed May 2008).

[17]National Association of Foreign Trade Zones, "The Coastal Foreign Trade Zone," http://www.naftz.org/ (accessed May 2008).

[18]Foreign-Trade Zones Board, *Annual Report—Fiscal Year 2006,* December 2007.

Similarly, Texas also leads in terms of employment within the zones with more than 70,000 jobs.

A MORPHOLOGY OF MODES

Water Freight Gateways

Maritime trade accounts for about 60% of U.S. trade by value. U.S. maritime trade rose from $434 billion in 1990 to $811 billion in 2006, an average annual growth rate of 5%. This robust growth highlights the rising importance of China, the rising level of trade with several Pacific Rim nations, and the increasing importance of the Port of Los Angeles as the nation's top freight gateway by value. Exhibit 9.4 shows the increasingly important role of China for U.S. trade.

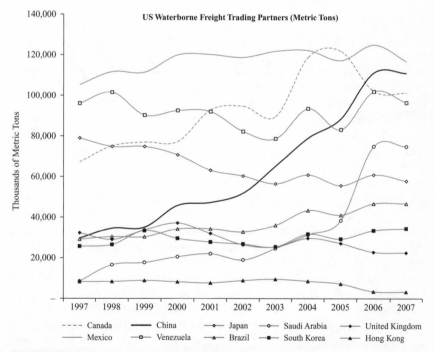

EXHIBIT 9.4 U.S. Container Trading Partners
Source: ING Clarion Research & Investment Strategy and U.S. Census Bureau, Foreign Trade Division, 2008, based on data from the World Shipping Council, 2006.

U.S. seaports are specialized in terms of handling commodities. The Pacific and Atlantic coast ports are characterized by a predominance of container trade, while the U.S. Gulf Coast ports are primarily involved in dry bulk and tanker trade. Gulf ports such as Houston, Texas, lead in terms of tonnage of international cargo shipments—agricultural, petroleum, coal, and other bulk commodities.

The growth of port traffic is directly related to the growth in container traffic and the demand for larger, faster, and more specialized vessels. Today, post-Panamax superfreighter vessels can carry up to 8,500 TEUs, and 10,000 TEU ships are in production. To handle these vessels, ports have had to invest in larger cranes, storage yards, improved information technology systems, and additional dredging. Given these requirements, a limited number of ports are able to handle these large ships.

Air Freight Gateways

Air freight accounted for 26% ($523 billion) of total U.S. trade in 2007. Between 1990 and 2006, the value of inbound and outbound air cargo handled at the U.S. gateway airports grew at an average annual rate of about 8%. Because the types of commodities transported by air are higher in value per ton (e.g., cut flowers, electronics, gemstones, and clothing) than those transported by other freight modes, the value of shipments is a better indicator of the importance of air gateways to the nation's international commerce, than weight.

The growth rate of air cargo is higher than for passenger traffic, with domestic and international revenue projected to increase at rates of 3.9% and 5.8%, respectively, between 2003 and 2014. The majority of demand for domestic cargo service is concentrated among all-cargo carriers, due to stricter security restrictions for transporting cargo on passenger aircraft and the faster growth of freight/express services relative to mail. The surging volume of air freight globally is just one indicator of a modern consumer trend which demands fast delivery of goods sourced from almost anywhere in the world. Cargo handled at the world's 20 largest cargo airports has increased in all but three of them over the past eight years (Exhibit 9.5).

The need to segregate unsecured cargo from passengers has increased the demand for all-cargo airliners. In addition, the growing congestion at the nation's leading hub airports has had a profound impact on air cargo operations. Many air express and cargo operations have moved to less congested venues. FedEx, UPS, DHL, and the U.S. Postal Service have relocated to medium-sized and underutilized airports. As a result, most large hub airports have experienced a decline in the share of enplaned cargo carried. Both medium and small hubs have benefited from capacity constraints at

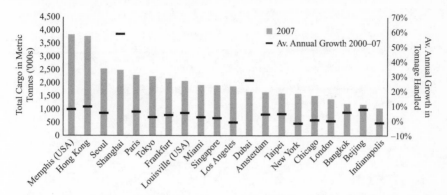

EXHIBIT 9.5 World's Leading Airports for Cargo Traffic by Volume
Refers to total cargo (loaded and unloaded freight and mail in metric tons) for
airports participating in the ACI monthly traffic statistics collection, excludes
Anchorage, Alaska, which also includes transit freight. Average annual growth for
all airports between 2000 and 2007 except Shanghai since 2002 and Dubai since
2001.
Source: ING Clarion Research & Investment Strategy and Airports Council International Annual Traffic Statistics Collection, March 2008.

the large hubs. Key U.S. air freight gateways include Memphis, Louisville,
Miami, Los Angeles, New York, and Anchorage.[19]

Land Freight Gateways[20]

The leading overall truck gateway ranked by value was Detroit, Michigan,
with $115 billion of freight, followed by Laredo, Texas ($79 billion), and
Buffalo–Niagara Falls, New York ($59 billion). The leading rail gateway was
Port Huron, Michigan, with $26 billion, followed by Laredo ($25 billion),
and Detroit ($21 billion).

While there are over 85 land cross-border ports with Canada, the leading
ports handle the majority of the transborder freight. The top 10 ports alone
handled $288 billion, or 92% of the truck freight crossing the northern
border. Two of the four largest U.S. land ports are in Michigan: Detroit,
and Port Huron. These two ports, combined, handled $200 billion of freight
transported by truck and rail.

---

[19]Anchorage was the nation's leading air gateway by weight, handling 26% of the
total international air-freight tonnage.
[20]Land freight gateways are entry ports using land transportation modes (truck, rail,
and pipeline).

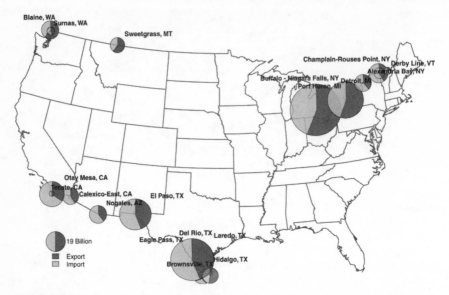

EXHIBIT 9.6 Major Land Border Gateways in the United States
Source: ING Clarion Research & Investment Strategy and U.S. Department of Transportation, National Transportation Statistics, 2007.

On the southern border, there are 25 land entry and exit ports with Mexico. The leading 10 ports handled $214 billion or 97% of the truck freight crossing the southern border. The land ports of Laredo, El Paso, and Hidalgo, all in Texas, handled over $170 billion (77% of truck freight value).

LEADING GLOBAL GATEWAY MARKETS

This section provides an overview of major U.S. industrial markets and clusters that are notable distribution centers (Exhibit 9.7). These markets are established, global gateway ports. In general, the highly populated markets command premium prices. Second- and third-tier distribution locations often attract small- and medium-sized businesses because of lower prices and (often) pro-business tax incentives. Areas with highly skilled logistics personnel, such as near U.S. military bases, are also growing in importance.

Markets are presented in the order of existing industrial square feet. Markets may consist of multiple MSAs. Investment in these markets may provide opportunities to capitalize on increasing global logistics operations.

EXHIBIT 9.7 Key Global Gateway Markets
Source: ING Clarion Research & Investment Strategy, May 2008.

New York/New Jersey[21]

The New York City metropolitan area is the most densely populated region in the United States and is home to a well-educated and ethnically diverse labor market. The metro area includes the New York, North/Central New Jersey (Edison), and Long Island markets.

The New York/New Jersey metropolitan region is one of the country's major platforms for freight movements due to both the significance of the Port of New York and New Jersey for international trade and the concentration of millions of customers in the metropolitan area. Warehouses and distribution centers were once concentrated in and around New York City, close to the port and customers. However, over the past few decades, the core region has suffered from traffic congestion and competition from competing land uses. As a result, distribution centers have been pushed out of the core region toward the region's periphery. The New Jersey Turnpike (I-95) functions as the backbone for this movement. Competitive distribution land markets also emerged in northern New Jersey. A more recent

---

[21]Information from U.S. Department of Transportation, *Bureau of Transportation Statistics, 2007*; and Port Authority of New York/New Jersey, http://www.panynj .gov/ (accessed May 2008).

market has emerged along I-80 in eastern Pennsylvania, near Harrisburg, where several distribution centers are taking advantage of affordable land and corridor-based accessibility.

The Port Authority of New York/New Jersey administers the largest port complex on the U.S. East Coast. The Port Authority is currently investing $1.7 billion to revamp existing port terminals, deepen the harbor's channels and berths, and improve inland rail and barge capabilities. The investments include the 50-foot harbor deepening project and the ExpressRail on-dock rail facilities. Additionally, the Port is spearheading development of the Port Inland Distribution Network, a hub-and-spoke system that will reduce inland distribution costs and increase throughput capacity.

The Port of New York and New Jersey handled 5.3 million loaded TEUs in 2007, representing an 11.8% increase over the previous year. The port's top five trading partners are China, Italy, India, Germany, and Brazil.

John F. Kennedy (JFK) International Airport in New York was the leading U.S. airport for international freight by value, handling 21% of U.S. air imports and exports in 2006, for a total value of $112 billion. The New York/New Jersey Air Cargo Center is unique among the world's air gateways because it is composed of three separate airports and interconnected by a vast road and rail network. With over 3,000 domestic and international movements daily from JFK International, Newark International, and LaGuardia, the right combination of international and domestic flights can speed cargo movement from its origin to its final destination in a matter of hours.

Los Angeles, California[22]

The Los Angeles cluster includes the Los Angeles, Riverside, and Orange County markets. The ports of Los Angeles and Long Beach together handle the highest volume of container traffic in the world. The ports have experienced a tremendous growth of shipments over the last decade and are facing capacity constraints. Logistics firms are facing problems of congestion, land availability, and labor shortages.

The Port of Los Angeles encompasses 7,500 acres, 43 miles of waterfront, and 26 cargo terminals. These terminals handle approximately 170 million metric tons of cargo annually and moved more than 7.3 million TEUs in 2007, when it achieved 34% of the West Coast container market share and 19% of the national share. Both figures represent a slight decline from 2006. The nearby Port of Long Beach moved more than 7.3 million TEUs in 2007, representing 30% of the West Coast market share and 16%

---

[22]Information from U.S. Department of Transportation, *Bureau of Transportation Statistics, 2007*; and Port of Los Angeles, http://www.portoflosangeles.org/ (accessed May 2008).

of the national share. Combined, the two ports handled more than one-third of total TEU volume in the United States.

A major effort to improve landside access to both ports is the Alameda Corridor freight rail expressway, which opened in April 2002. The Alameda Corridor, a $2.5 billion project, connects the ports of Los Angeles and Long Beach to the rail yards near downtown Los Angeles and the national railroad network. The project consolidates 90 miles of branch rail tracks into one 20-mile railroad expressway, thus allowing trains to travel more quickly and avoiding highway traffic congestion.

Further development has occurred in Vernon, Commerce, and City of Industry. More recently, Ontario is developing as a modern distribution hub in the inland empire, combining open land, freeway access, and proximity to air freight (Ontario International Airport). The intersection of I-15 and State Route 60 is emerging as a major node for warehousing and distribution centers. Developments are increasingly moving beyond the Greater Los Angeles area. The Swedish furnishing retailer IKEA at Tejon Ranch in Kern County operates one of the largest distribution centers in the West Coast. The site is located near Bakersfield, almost 70 miles north of Los Angeles, at the California State Route 99 and I-5 intersection. The distribution center is 1.85 million square feet in size and serves IKEA's western North America distribution.

Los Angeles International Airport (LAX) is the world's fifth busiest passenger airport and ranks eleventh in air cargo tonnage handled. In 2006 more than 61 million people traveled through LAX. LAX handled 70% of the passengers, 75% of the air cargo, and 95% of the international passengers and cargo traffic in the five-county Southern California region.

Chicago, Illinois[23]

The Chicago metropolitan area is the third largest city in the United States and the most important inland hub in North America, serving as the nation's primary consolidation and deconsolidation center for carload and intermodal freight. It functions as a network endpoint for both eastern and western railroad carriers and is the nation's largest rail-to-rail interchange point. About 50% of all American rail freight transits through Chicago, accounting for 500 freight trains per day. This staggering amount of freight volume involves large distribution facilities, including 200 truck terminals carrying more than 400,000 truckloads each day. Such a high concentration

---

[23]Information from U.S. Department of Transportation, *Bureau of Transportation Statistics, 2007*; and Port of Chicago, http://www.theportofchicago.com/index1a .html (accessed May 2008).

of freight activity is creating congestion problems, as the rail system is able to accommodate limited additional transcontinental traffic. In addition to its rail service, Chicago is home to two international airports and at the junction of seven interstate systems.

Bay Area, California[24]

The Bay Area cluster includes the Oakland, San Francisco, and San Jose markets.

In the case of the San Francisco Bay Area, the East Bay has been the traditional industrial and distributive "hub" of the region. The East Bay Area offers excellent access to all major locations in the region. This includes the old industrial corridor along I-880, the bridges connecting the East Bay with the San Francisco Peninsula, and the freeways to the Central Valley, connecting the region with the rest of California (via I-5). The Oakland area also offers intermodal access, via the Oakland International Airport and Port of Oakland, which serves as the fourth largest container port on the West Coast. Warehouses and distribution centers were traditionally concentrated along I-880 and close to the Port of Oakland. Because the port is situated in close proximity to the city center, road network connections are limited and land supply is constrained. In response to rising congestion and increasing land prices, distribution firms are moving to the Central Valley, located 50 to 70 miles east of the Bay Area. The site preferences for distribution and warehousing include: favorable access to freeways (I-205, I-580, and I-5); availability of rail lines; and proximity to ports and airports. The high cost of living in the Bay Area also increases the appeal of the Central Valley, as distribution activities are priced out of central areas.

Houston, Texas[25]

George Bush Intercontinental Airport is the eleventh-largest international air-cargo gateway to the United States, while the Port of Houston is the world's sixth-largest port and ranks first in the United States in total volume of foreign tonnage. In addition, the state is expected to have spent over $5 billion on area highway improvements by 2007. Houston also lies near a

---

[24]Information from U.S. Department of Transportation, *Bureau of Transportation Statistics, 2007*; Port of Oakland, http://www.portofoakland.com/; and San Francisco Port Commission, http://www.sfgov.org/site/port_index.asp (accessed May 2008).

[25]Information from U.S. Department of Transportation, *Bureau of Transportation Statistics, 2007*; and Port of Houston, http://www.portofhouston.com/ (accessed May 2008).

proposed I-69 NAFTA Superhighway that would offer direct over-the-road access between Canada, the United States, and Mexico.

The Port of Houston ranks first in foreign tonnage and imports. In 2007, it handled 1.8 million TEUs. The port is in the process of increasing its container capacity by investing more than $390 million. The container yards have been available since early 2007. Built out in phases over 15 to 20 years, parallel to market demand, the Houston port will have a maximum capacity of about 2.3 million TEUs—a 200% increase over current capacity.

Seattle-Tacoma, Washington[26]

Geographically closest to Asia, the Pacific Northwest has many opportunities to steal some economic development from other West Coast metros. But growing congestion issues, coupled with the Northwest's relative isolation from Midwest markets and the geographic bounds set by the Rocky Mountains, might make efficient redistribution of product moving eastward challenging. A high quality of life and well-educated population bode well for businesses that demand skilled labor.

Together, the ports of Seattle and Tacoma comprise the third largest marine container load center in North America, behind Los Angeles/Long Beach and New York/New Jersey. These West Coast ports provide critical network redundancy should one of the ports become impassable due to congestion or catastrophe.

The Ports of Tacoma, Seattle, and Everett are investing heavily to improve both the capacity and operations of their terminals. Burlington Northern Santa Fe (BNSF) Railway and Union Pacific (UP) are also investing in mainline rail infrastructure. These ports are also participating in the FAST Corridor program—a regional effort to increase the efficiency of moving freight in and around the Puget Sound. A total of $400 million is planned for 15 FAST Corridor projects in the Puget Sound area.

Time savings available by shipping through the Pacific Northwest are driving much of the expansion in these port facilities. The Pacific Northwest ports of Seattle and Tacoma (and to a lesser extent Portland) are about 600 to 700 nautical miles (NM) closer to Asia than the ports in the Los Angeles area, depending on the port pair. For example, the distance from Hong Kong to Seattle is 5,768 NM versus 6,380 NM to Los Angeles. The rail distances between the Pacific Northwest ports to the U.S. Midwest and Northeast are about the same as from the L.A. area. This translates to a time savings of about 1.5 days by going through a Pacific Northwest port.

---

[26]Information from U.S. Department of Transportation, *Bureau of Transportation Statistics, 2007*; Port of Seattle, http://www.portseattle.org/; and Port of Tacoma, http://www.portoftacoma.com/ (accessed May 2008).

Presently, the share of the nonlocal cargo in most PNW terminals already reaches 70–80%. Still, overall traffic as well as terminal size, is relatively small. Likewise, the two major U.S. ports, Seattle and Tacoma, both with on-dock yards, have limited land reserves.

Dallas, Texas[27]

Dallas/Fort Worth International Airport (DFW) encompasses more than 18,000 acres of land and has more than 2 million square feet of cargo warehouse space. DFW handled almost 65% of all international air cargo in Texas. DFW's international cargo has grown 75% since 2002. As the major midcontinent gateway to the world, DFW's strategic, central location facilitates cargo connections around the world. Its location offers superior trucking connections to four major interstate highways. Through the airport's integrated service network, shippers can quickly connect with airlines, major intermodal facilities, and regional and interstate highways.

Easy access to five interstate highways, ample rail service, intermodal facilities, and a capable cargo airport are some of the factors that motivated the development of the Dallas Logistics Hub, which upon completion will facilitate and expedite cargo flow to and from Mexico and Canada. The city has already signed agreements with the Port of Houston, four Mexican ports, and the Panama Canal to explore and utilize its inland port resources.

Columbus, Ohio[28]

Rickenbacker International Airport is one of the top U.S. ports of entry for textiles. Additionally, DHL-owned, all-cargo air carrier ABX Air operates out of Wilmington Airpark. With over-the-road deliveries to half the U.S. population in 24 hours, Columbus, Ohio, is an ideal option for shippers and consignees.

Due to congestion at gateway locations and long-distance accessibility provided by the interstate highway system, so called "inland hubs" are becoming more and more important, including the distribution center cluster across the Ohio River Valley. This cluster is affiliated with the interstate network and air cargo facilities, and not with a traditional port gateway.

---

[27]Information from U.S. Department of Transportation, *Bureau of Transportation Statistics, 2007*; and Dallas Fort Worth Airport, http://www.dfwairport.com/ (accessed May 2008).

[28]Information from U.S. Department of Transportation, *Bureau of Transportation Statistics, 2007*; and Rickenbacker Airport, http://www.rickenbacker.org/home.asp (accessed May 2008).

The distribution center clusters along the Ohio River Valley, including portions of Ohio, Indiana, and Tennessee. The area hosts warehousing, trucking, freight forwarding, and air cargo activities. The growth of the new economy has fostered such development. The "first generation" e-fulfillment providers are gravitating toward the preferred location for a single, centralized distribution facility. Industrial markets such as Columbus, Indianapolis, Indiana, and Louisville, Kentucky, have seen substantial demand from these users.

The Midwest is a preferred manufacturing location (with concomitant distribution networks in place). Midwest locations are also ideally suited to serve major markets both on the East Coast and along the center of the country. Columbus is within a 10-hour drive of 50% of the North American population. In general, 60% of the entire U.S. population can be reached by overnight trucks. In terms of logistics, major interstate and freeway intersections (I-70, I-72), rail connections, intermodal terminals, and two airports serve the location. Large investments by single firms can also have a strong impact on the industrial market, triggering "leader-follower"[29] impact chains. Major corporations continue to invest in distribution centers in the region, including Emery Worldwide (Dayton, Ohio), Lowe's Home Improvement (Allen, Ohio), UPS (Louisville), and FedEx (Memphis, Tennessee, and Indianapolis).

By adding the capacity to ship double-stacked containers (one on top of another), railways are seeking to further enhance their efficiency. The Heartland Corridor project, for example, is reengineering the shape and size of tunnels along rail lines from Norfolk through Columbus to Chicago to effectively double the freight capacity through double-stacking.

Indianapolis, Indiana[30]

Indiana's economy has diversified to include distribution and logistics. Indianapolis International Airport is the second-largest FedEx hub in the world. The airport also has spent $1 billion to expand a new terminal scheduled for completion in 2008. The expansion is intended to accommodate growing freight volume and raise the city's prominence in logistics and distribution centers. In terms of location, 75% of the U.S. and Canadian population can be reached within a one-day truck drive from the Indianapolis region.

---

[29] A business leader will soon attract competitors.

[30] Information from U.S. Department of Transportation, *Bureau of Transportation Statistics, 2007*; and Indianapolis International Airport, http://www.indianapolisair port.com/ (accessed May 2008).

Baltimore, Maryland[31]

Baltimore enjoys a strategic location with convenient access to both the Northeast and mid-Atlantic regions. It is 200 miles closer to the Midwest than any other East Coast seaboard city. The city is also geographically close to three major airports—Dulles International Airport, Ronald Reagan Washington National Airport, and Baltimore Washington International Thurgood Marshall Airport. In addition, I-95, the Northeast's main north-south thoroughfare, runs directly through the city, offering companies overnight delivery options to two-thirds of the nation's population.

Memphis, Tennessee[32]

Memphis is a promising distribution hub due to its strategic location and well-developed transportation infrastructure. Situated at a major east-west, north-south crossroads, shippers can deliver product within a 48-hour window to nearly all 50 contiguous states as well as Canada and Mexico.

Memphis International Airport is central to the city's logistics and distribution. Federal Express Corporation (FedEx), the world's largest express transportation company, is headquartered in Memphis and operates its primary overnight package sorting facility at the airport. FedEx dominates the cargo business at the Memphis International Airport, transporting approximately 95% of all cargo handled at the airport last year. FedEx's share of cargo at the airport has been at least 95% since 1992.

In addition, the Port of Memphis ranks as the country's fourth-largest inland port and the city is the third-largest rail center in the nation.

Louisville, Kentucky[33]

Louisville is a major global distribution hub due to the UPS world-port air cargo facility. UPS has spent $1.1 billion since 2002 in developing its main hub. Two-thirds of the U.S. population lives within a day truck

---

[31]Information from U.S. Department of Transportation, *Bureau of Transportation Statistics, 2007*; and Port of Baltimore, http://pob.mpa.state.md.us/ (accessed May 2008).

[32]Information from U.S. Department of Transportation, *Bureau of Transportation Statistics, 2007*; and Memphis International Airport, http://www.mscaa.com/ (accessed May 2008).

[33]Information from U.S. Department of Transportation, *Bureau of Transportation Statistics, 2007*; and Louisville International Airport, http://www.flylouisville .com/Default.aspx (accessed May 2008).

drive from Louisville. In addition, Louisville is in the heart of the Midwest, and Louisville International Airport is the ninth-largest cargo airport in the world in terms of tonnage. Furthermore, convenient access to three inter-state highways makes Louisville one of the best areas in the United States for distribution and logistics activities.

Port of Virginia[34]

The Port of Virginia, which includes port facilities in the nearby cities of Nor-folk, Hampton Roads, and Portsmouth, is among the East Coast's fastest-growing container ports. The port facilities are undergoing an expansion valued at $500 million. Six major interstates crisscross the state. Virginia lays claim to more than 3,000 miles of railroad track and is host to the headquarters of rail carrier Norfolk Southern. A well-educated workforce and strong military presence at Norfolk are convincing many businesses to invest in Norfolk. The ports enjoy a strategic mid-Atlantic location, which offers shippers access to two-thirds of the U.S. population. Norfolk has the best natural deepwater harbor on the U.S. East Coast. Fifty-foot-deep unob-structed channels provide easy access and maneuvering room for the largest of container ships currently in operation. Virginia ports are located just 18 miles from the open sea on a year-round, ice-free harbor. The port also has good intermodal connections, with six direct-service trains to 28 major cities each day (more than any other port).

Jacksonville, Florida[35]

Jacksonville is well-located to serve one of the fastest-growing consumer regions in the United States. Jacksonville leverages strong marine logistics infrastructure with solid rail and road transportation capabilities. The Jack-sonville Port has long been one of the U.S.'s top intermodal facilities. In addition, a diverse number of carmakers and automotive parts companies support port operations.

The addition of Mitsui O.S.K. Lines and potentially Hanjin Shipping Co. to the Jacksonville Port Authority has significantly increased the potential for warehouse and distribution activity in Jacksonville. Local officials estimate

---

[34]Information from U.S. Department of Transportation, *Bureau of Transportation Statistics, 2007*; and Virginia Port Authority, http://www.vaports.com/ (accessed May 2008).

[35]Information from U.S. Department of Transportation, *Bureau of Transportation Statistics, 2007*; and Jacksonville Port Authority, http://www.jaxport.com/ (accessed May 2008).

that the increased capacity will place Jacksonville among the top ten ports in the United States in terms of cargo traffic. Major industrial players are positioning themselves to take advantage of this growth, with the amount of new development at a record-setting pace. While the long-term picture for the metro is strong, the lack of supply constraints in the metro could lead to oversupply in the near term.

Savannah, Georgia[36]

As with other Southeastern cities, Savannah's economic development potential is largely tied to increasing container volume at its port and interest from retailers looking to tap into the growing Florida and Southeast markets.

The Port of Savannah is ranked among the five largest container ports in the country and is the largest single terminal container facility on the East and Gulf Coasts. From Savannah, companies can move product by rail overnight to Atlanta and to key inland hubs, such as Charlotte, North Carolina, Chicago, Dallas, and Memphis, in three days or less.

Charleston, South Carolina[37]

The Port of Charleston handled 1.75 million TEUs in 2007, placing it in the top 10 for U.S. ports. Top commodities across Charleston docks include agricultural products, consumer goods, machinery, metals, vehicles, chemicals, and clay products.

The Port Authority completed a $148-million harbor deepening project in 2004 which took the inner harbor channels to 45 feet, allowing service of larger ships. Planned projects include construction of a new three-berth, 280-acre marine terminal at the former Charleston Naval Base. Work is already underway and the first phase of the terminal is expected to open in six years. The Port Authority has also announced its intention to acquire property for an additional port facility in Jasper County on the Savannah River.

Hanjin Shipping, K Line, and Yang Ming are joining CSAV Norasia to introduce a new service that will provide additional capacity from the east coast of South America to the U.S. East Coast. The SNA (South and

---

[36]Information from U.S. Department of Transportation, *Bureau of Transportation Statistics, 2007*; and Georgia Ports Authority, http://www.gaports.com/ (accessed May 2008).

[37]Information from U.S. Department of Transportation, *Bureau of Transportation Statistics, 2007*; and Port of Charleston web site, http://www.port-of-charleston.com/ (accessed May 2008).

North America) service will deploy five ships with average capacity of 2,500 TEUs. The SNA service replaces the existing NSA service, which was operated by Hanjin, K Line, Yang Ming, and Hyundai Merchant Marine with four 1,800-TEU vessels. The service offers calls in Sao Francisco do Sul, Santos and Salvador, Brazil; Puerto Cabello, Venezuela; and Rio de Janeiro. Charleston is the last U.S. port outbound, offering exporters quick transit times to overseas markets.

OPPORTUNITIES IN EMERGING FACILITIES

This section describes inland ports that have emerged close to transportation infrastructure and that are expected to become attractive locations for warehouse/distribution activities. The projects include satellite marine terminals, logistic and intermodal parks, airports, and network corridors. Investment in these areas present more risk than in established markets, but may also present stronger returns over time.

Markets are ordered by geographic area.

Global III, Rochelle, Illinois[38]

The Union Pacific Global III Intermodal Facility, located in Rochelle, Illinois, was built to meet the growing need for intermodal terminal capacity in the Chicago market. Unlike other intermodal terminal developments, this facility was built to address the area's limited railroad capacity and to create a distribution corridor featuring warehouse, distribution, and logistics centers.

UP began construction in November 2001 and officially commenced operations in fall 2003. Spanning 843 acres, Global III includes a large switching yard to expedite resegmentation of trains and cars, and the intermodal terminal with 720,000-pound lift capability.

Global III is strategically located at the edge of Chicago's westward commercial frontier. A short distance outside the city, this in-demand area is experiencing enormous growth as industries locate warehouse and distribution facilities outside of Chicago's congested downtown area. This new facility offers direct access to interstate highways to major east-west and north-south markets.

Many midsize and several major markets (cities over 250,000 population) are located within a 350-mile radius of the site. Via interstate highway I-39, Rochelle is connected to Chicago; Milwaukee,

---

[38]Information from Union Pacific Railroad, http://www.up.com/ (accessed May 2008).

Wisconsin; Minneapolis-St. Paul, Minnesota; Omaha, Nebraska; Kansas City, Missouri, and Kansas City, Kansas; St. Louis, Missouri; Louisville, Kentucky; Lexington–Fayette County, Kentucky; Indianapolis, Indiana; Cincinnati, Ohio; Columbus, Ohio; Toledo, Ohio; and Detroit, Michigan. An analysis of population data reveals that, within the 350-mile radius of Rochelle resides 20% of the U.S. total population.

Joliet Arsenal (JADA), Illinois[39]

The Joliet Arsenal was developed by the U.S. Army in the early 1940s as a munitions plant. Located on a 26,500-acre site near Joliet, Illinois, the site is about 40 miles southwest of Chicago. In 1976, the Arsenal was decommissioned and the site was subdivided for both public and private use. The Joliet Arsenal Development Authority (JADA) was established to facilitate the redevelopment of 3,000 acres of Arsenal property. The cornerstone of this redevelopment was a complex of over 2,000 acres being developed by CenterPoint Properties. The CenterPoint Intermodal Center (CIC) is a multimodal rail transportation system on the site. CIC's industrial park is currently located on 1,100 acres and encompasses up to 12 million square feet of rail-served industrial buildings suitable for warehousing, distribution, and light manufacturing.

The plan for CIC includes a BNSF transportation complex named Logistics Park Chicago (LPC). It includes a major intermodal container terminal, an automobile loading/unloading facility, and a car loading facility. Currently, the terminal handles over one million lifts.

California Integrated Logistics Center (CILC), Bakersfield, California[40]

CILC is an effort to develop an inland port near the City of Shafter, north of Bakersfield, connected to both the Port of Oakland and Los Angeles by rail shuttle. Shafter is roughly equidistant by rail from Oakland and Long Beach (approximately 280 miles). Two major rail liners, UP and BNSF, border Shafter. In addition, two main highways (State Route 99 and I-5) border Shafter and provide easy backdoor access to Los Angeles and to the east through State Route 58. Shafter is also situated 300 miles from approximately 40 million potential customers. The city of Shafter is within close proximity to major distribution centers with major imports, such as Sears, IKEA, and Target.

---

[39]Information from Joliet Arsenal Development Authority, http://jada.org/ (accessed May 2008).

[40]Information from City of Shafter, http://www.shafter.com/ (accessed May 2008).

March Global Port, Moreno Valley, California[41]

March is a 350-acre "joint-use airport" governed by the Air Force and the March Joint Powers Authority. The plan was to convert approximately 350 acres of land for civilian aviation facilities. March does not have any distinct inland port functions, although it does have a rail connection. In October 2005, DHL opened its West Coast distribution hub at March Global Port.

March is well-suited for transporting shipments because it is served by four major freeways: I-215 (serving the High Desert and San Diego), I-10 (serving Los Angeles), State Route 91 (serving Orange County), and State Route 60 (serving Los Angeles to the west, and the Coachella Valley and Arizona to the east). In addition, March is conveniently located and within a one-hour drive to most of Southern California.

San Bernardino International Airport (former Norton AFB), California[42]

The San Bernardino International Airport (SBD) is located 60 miles east of the Los Angeles International Airport (LAX). San Bernardino International Airport is surrounded by three major interstate freeways (I-10, I-215, and I-210) and is within two miles of the BNSF intermodal facility.

Alliance California is a project by the Hillwood Group, also the developers at Alliance, Texax, in partnership with ING Clarion. Rail intermodal service is available through the nearby BNSF San Bernardino terminal but is not located on site. The project has attracted aircraft-related business centers and commercial distribution centers.

Global Access at Victorville, California[43]

Global Access is an 8,500-acre multimodal freight transportation hub supported by air, ground, and rail connections. Global Access is comprised of three development divisions which include:

- Southern California Logistics Airport (SCLA), a 2,500-acre world-class aviation and air cargo facility serving domestic and international needs.

---

[41]Information from March Global Port, http://www.marchglobalport.com/ (accessed May 2008).

[42]Information from San Bernardino Airport, http://www.sbdairport.com/ (accessed May 2008).

[43]Information from Global Access, http://www.logisticsairport.com/page.aspx (accessed May 2008).

- Southern California Logistics Centre, a 2,500-acre commercial and industrial complex totaling 60 million square feet of diverse development.
- Southern California Rail Complex, a planned 3,500-acre intermodal rail and multimodal complex including rail-served facilities.

The City of Victorville and Stirling, a Foothill Ranch, California-based development company, have a public and private partnership arrangement to redevelop the former George Air Force Base into Global Access. George Air Force Base is located in Victorville, California, in the Mojave Desert approximately 90 miles northeast of Los Angeles.

By combining aviation, trucking and rail service, the former George Air Force Base is considered a major international cargo distribution center. Carriers currently utilizing the airport include FedEx Express, ASB Air, and MK International.

Alliance Logistics Park, Texas[44]

AllianceTexas, is located 15 miles north of downtown Fort Worth and 15 miles west of Dallas/Fort Worth International Airport. Covering some 15,000 acres, Alliance is one of the largest and most successful master-planned industrial developments in the country. Existing air, rail, and highway systems have been greatly expanded and upgraded in order to connect Alliance with domestic and international markets. Business activity is further enhanced at Alliance by a foreign trade zone, an enterprise zone, and high-tech telecommunications facilities.

The business park houses more than 140 companies, including 62 from Fortune 500, Global 500, and Forbes' Top Private Companies. These firms have invested more than $5 billion to build 24.4 million square feet of office space and create 24,000 full-time jobs. A key factor in the success of the project is the Free Port Tax Incentive program, which allowed for a waiver of inventory taxes for up to 175 days from local jurisdictions. In addition, Alliance offers access to a large workforce, proximity to intermodal facilities, and relatively affordable land and development prices.

Alliance also offers the network services to build and market data centers across the country. Alliance has been labeled an "e-commerce fulfillment center" because of companies that are engaged in filling business-to-business and business-to-consumer orders via the Internet.

---

[44]Information from Hillwood Development Company, *AllianceTexas*, http://www.alliancetexas.com/ (accessed May 2008).

Kelly USA/Port of San Antonio, Texas[45]

Port of San Antonio (PASA) is a master-planned, 1,900-acre aerospace, industrial complex, and international logistics platform, centrally located in San Antonio, Texas. Created from the former Kelly Air Force Base, Port San Antonio is approximately equidistant from the East and West Coasts of the United States and at the center of the NAFTA Corridor between Mexico and Canada.

Transportation offerings include an airport; accessibility by two class I railroads, UP and BNSF; and three interstate highways: I-35, I-10, and I-37. Markets surpassing 90 million people are within a two-day drive from Port San Antonio. Five major seaports are accessible within a three-day drive: the Ports of Houston, Corpus Christi, Manzanillo, Lazaro Cardenas, and Veracruz.

PASA is currently developing a master plan for development of 700 acres of industrial and commercial property at Port of San Antonio. The plan calls for three types of development, aerospace and aeronautical at Kelly Airport, commercial and mixed-use at Kelly Town Center, and rail-served industrial at East Kelly Railport.

Rickenbacker/Columbus Inland Ports[46]

Columbus is a city of 1.6 million people located in central Ohio, 300 miles east of Chicago and 500 miles west of New York City. The Limited, Honda of America, and Kroger are very large local, logistics-intensive employers. The city is well located along major interstate highways I-70 (east-west) and I-71 (northeast southeast). It is also serviced by three major rail liners: Conrail, BNSF, and CSX with three intermodal terminals. Together, these terminals handled 180,000 containers, more than most other Midwest cities except Detroit, Chicago, and St. Louis.

Columbus has the opportunity to become a significant inland port in the United States, providing multimodal distribution across the Midwest and parts of Canada. About half of the U.S. population is within a one-day truck drive from Columbus.

Rickenbacker is a 5,000-acre all-cargo airport. It is a former Air Force base with 12,000-foot runways. The airport contains over 22 million square

---

[45]Information from Port of San Antonio, http://www.portsanantonio.us/Homepage .asp?WPID=1 (accessed May 2008).

[46]Tioga Group, et al., *Inland Port Feasibility Study: Project No. 06-023, Inland Port Case Studies*, June 30, 2006, http://www.scag.ca.gov/goodsmove/pdf/SCAG-InlandPortCaseStudies063006.pdf.

feet of class "A" distribution space. Ample room still exists for additional growth; only 40% of the land suitable for industrial projects has been developed so far. FedEx, UPS, and a number of logistics companies have established operations in Rickenbacker.

Virginia Inland Port[47]

Operated as an intermodal container transfer facility, the Virginia Inland Port (VIP) provides an interface between truck and rail for the transport of ocean-bound containers to and from the Port of Virginia. Virginia Inland Port's annual throughput volume was 14,000 in 2003, 28,000 in 2004, and 35,000 in 2005. In conjunction with Washington–Dulles International Airport, ongoing efforts have been made to develop the corridor between the two facilities as a principal freight distribution center/hub. This involves attracting warehouse and distribution facilities to the area, and expanding the foreign trade zone and facilities surrounding the port. These developments have used multimodal infrastructure (air-rail-truck or sea-rail-truck) as the core of business/industrial parks.

CONCLUSION

Expanding shipping activity in both established and emerging gateway markets presents increased demand for warehouse facilities. These markets are benefiting from expanding global trade, reliable and efficient transportation networks (often multimodal), and proximity to a strong population base for consumer goods. Investment in both established facilities and new development present compelling investment opportunities, particularly in markets with reasonable barriers to entry that help to keep supply in check. Markets with expanding port facilities or that offer efficiencies that help reduce overall cost and time of delivery, including inland markets benefiting from expanding ground transportation from Mexico, are among the most attractive markets today.

[47]Ibid.

CHAPTER 10

The Opportunity in Senior Housing

Tim Wang and David Lynn
Summer 2008[1,2]

With favorable demographic fundamentals and the achievement of higher yields relative to conventional apartments, we believe that the senior housing sector is emerging as an increasingly attractive investment opportunity. The senior population, defined as persons age 65 and older, is growing at twice the national average, with many baby boomers entering retirement. Consequently, the senior housing market is expected to transition from a niche market to a major specialized market, with the long-term outlook for this property sector becoming increasingly positive. Facilitated by a restrained supply pipeline over the past six years, occupancy levels for senior housing assets rebounded from lows recorded in 2001–2002 to near 90% today in many metro areas. Operating business models are better defined, contributing to strong revenue growth and higher profit margins. Annual rent growth in the sector remains a healthy 4 to 5%. In response to improved operations and increased investor interest, asset prices are increasing to record levels while cap rates are falling to single digits, ranging from 7 to 9%. The cap rate spread between senior housing and

---

[1] This paper was originally produced in summer 2008. The data, opinions, and forecasts have not been updated for book publication.

[2] This paper was originally published by The Counselors of Real Estate in *Real Estate Issues* 33, no. 2 (2008) 33–51. Reprinted with the permission of *The Counselors of Real Estate*.

conventional apartments has declined from 300 bps to 150 to 175 bps. Since the senior housing market is driven by surging senior population and not directly related to external economic factors such as economic growth and the unemployment rate, the addition of senior housing assets to a portfolio could increase diversification and lower market risk. Different investment strategies are outlined and discussed.

BACKGROUND

A relatively young industry, senior housing development took flight in the early 1980s when developers and investors recognized the potential to benefit from the anticipated surge of the elderly population in the United States. Numerous small mom-and-pop and not-for-profit operators dominated the industry during its nascency.

The industry expanded significantly in the late 1980s when a U.S. Department of Housing and Urban Development (HUD) program was implemented, with the senior housing sector in mind, to insure lenders against losses on mortgage defaults. As a result, private capital began to flow into the sector.[3]

The mid-1990s witnessed the rapid growth of real estate investment trusts (REITs) and the emergence of the private commercial mortgage-backed securities (CMBS) market. The securitization of loans collateralized by senior apartments and skilled nursing homes increased steadily during the late 1990s.

Because of excess capital available from the public markets, the senior housing sector, especially the assisted living segment, was overbuilt during the late 1990s. The market outpaced itself as developers built properties at a rate that well exceeded demand, resulting in oversupply.[4] Compounding the problem was the fact that product designs did not meet the needs of target markets. Consequently, average occupancy rates declined, and many projects failed to meet investment expectations.

Depressed stock prices from 1999 to 2000 limited the supply of new equity financing, but offered attractive valuations for acquisition targets, prompting a surge of mergers and acquisitions (M&A) among senior housing

---

[3]National Investment Center for the Seniors Housing & Care Industries (NIC), *The Case for Investing in Seniors Housing and Long Term Care Properties* (2001). See also the NIC web site, http://www.nic.org/overview/faqs.asp.
[4]Ibid.

REITs. At the same time, several health care REITs shifted from growth strategies to liquidation strategies in order to address debt problems. Finally, accounting scandals, operational issues, higher interest rates, and excessive debt caused the industry to restructure and consolidate.[5]

Today, industry business models have become more defined. Occupancy and operating margins are improving to near six-year highs and the industry is reporting healthy year-over-year revenue and net operating income (NOI) growth. As a result, institutional investors are increasing their acquisitions in the sector, the result of which is helping to drive cap rates to new lows. Although a variety of reimbursement and operational issues remain, both the near- and long-term outlooks for the senior housing sector are increasingly positive.

Defining Senior Housing

The senior housing sector is generally composed of five segment types, defined by the level of care and amenities provided in conjunction with the living setting. The industry has developed well-defined business models for each segment.

- *Active adult communities and senior apartments (for-sale and for-rent).* Active adult communities are typically condos, co-ops or single-family homes with minimal or no services offered. These communities have an age requirement of 55-plus and offer a number of amenities, such as clubhouses, which appeal to active adult homeowners. Senior apartments tend to be larger, multi-unit facilities with a rental payment structure. In addition to age restrictions, many communities have income restrictions because they are developed under low-income housing tax credit programs.
- *Independent living facilities (ILFs).* Also known as *congregate care facilities*, ILFs offer a multifamily design to those seniors who are less active and who may have difficulty with routine housekeeping. These facilities are similar to senior apartments, but offer several additional services, such as meals, housekeeping, transportation and organized group activities. Residents typically rent apartments at ILFs at a premium to local market rents in order to cover the cost of common area charges and the additional services provided.
- *Assisted living facilities (ALFs).* ALFs are multifamily properties with personalized support services for seniors. Typically, ALFs cater

---

[5]Ibid.

to individuals who need assistance with daily activities, but do not require nursing home care. The units and common areas are designed to accommodate a higher level of support, while still retaining the characteristics of residential apartments. ALFs are a cost-efficient alternative to in-home care because they primarily provide nonmedically intensive support activities. A property that specializes in the care of residents with Alzheimer's or other forms of dementia is also considered an assisted living property. These memory care facilities can be freestanding properties or wings or floors within a traditional assisted living property.

■ *Skilled nursing facilities (SNFs)*. SNFs provide the highest level of care, are hospital-like in nature and are, consequently, the most expensive of all senior housing options. In addition, SNFs are also the most highly regulated of the senior housing facilities, typically requiring state licenses. Many SNFs offer acute and intensive medical care, and post-hospitalization and rehabilitation therapies. Medicare and Medicaid programs cover a large portion of these expenses, with such government reimbursements accounting for a significant portion of revenue at these facilities.

■ *Continuing care retirement communities (CCRCs)*. CCRCs combine attractive residential living with high levels of service designed to address the comfort, health, wellness, security, and developing needs of aging seniors. Essentially a "one-stop shop," CCRCs offer comprehensive, continuing-care services at one location, by providing skilled nursing facilities mixed with large numbers of independent living and assisted living units. Residents may also receive medical care onsite, the costs of which are all reimbursable by Medicare and Medicaid programs. In addition to a monthly fee, there is typically a large, one-time entry fee to enter a CCRC. CCRCs, many of which are not-for-profit and are religiously affiliated, are the smallest segment within the senior housing market because they are costly to build, and due to the complex local regulatory approval process, time intensive to develop.

■ *Real estate vs. service*. Whether senior housing constitutes a real estate investment or a service industry investment is determined by the specific type of facility. The services provided by most senior housing facilities include hospitality, health care, education, and recreation. Clearly, active adult communities provide residences, which represent real estate investments. Conversely, skilled nursing facilities provide support services, and logically should be considered primarily a service business investment. The remaining types of facilities provide a mix of both services and housing. Independent living facilities provide meal and linen services but, for the most part, are primarily considered a real estate investment.

EXHIBIT 10.1 Medical Acuity Level among Senior Housing Segments (as of 2007)

Medical Acuity Level	Continuum of Elderly Care	Independence Level
75%	Skilled nursing facility (SN)	25%
40%	Assisted living units (AL)	60%
25%	Congregate living units (CL)	75%
10%	Independent living units (IL)	90%
0%	Community living options/ Active adult (AA)	100%

Source: ING Clarion Research & Investment Strategy and National Investment Center.

The more support-intensive segments, such as assisted living, should logically be considered a form of health care real estate—a combination of an operating business and a real estate investment. Finally, CCRCs blend substantial care services with residential services.

The previous five senior housing segments target different subgroups within the elderly population by providing different levels of housing needs and services. Monthly fees for senior housing increase as the required level of service increases. Historically, the service business has generated higher yields than residential real estate and, not surprisingly, the more service-intensive categories, such as assisted living and skilled nursing, generate higher yields than the less service-intensive active adult communities and independent living categories. We believe the perceived investment risk for the individual categories appears to rise as the service business component increases (Exhibit 10.1).

TARGETED SENIOR GROUPS

There are mainly three large, distinct groups that comprise the senior population:

1. *Baby boomers (age 44–62).* The baby boomers are the largest generation in U.S. history, constituting a sizable demographic wave. With 82.8 million people born between 1946 and 1964, the baby boomers represented about 30% of the U.S. population in 2007,[6] with estimated annual spending of $2 trillion.

---

[6]U.S. Census Bureau.

EXHIBIT 10.2 Product Offering among Segments

	Active Adult	Independent Living	Assisted Living	Skilled Nursing
Target age group	55–65	65–75	75+	As needed
Service level	No	Medium	High	High
Care level	No	No	Medium	High
Structure	Condo Rental (limited)	Rental Condo (limited)	Rental	Rental
Real estate product	Single-family, Multifamily	Multifamily	Multifamily	Multifamily
Recreational amenities	Clubhouse	Typically on 1st floor	Typically on 1st floor	Typically on 1st floor

Source: ING Clarion Research & Investment Strategy and American Seniors Housing Association.

Baby boomers tend to seek maintenance-free living, easy lifestyles, more leisure time, new experiences, and prefer multiple options, customization, and control. As they enter their peak earning years, baby boomers' lifestyle preferences and spending patterns should be closely monitored. By 2011 the first wave of baby boomers will turn 65 years old.

2. *Silent generation (age 63–83).* Nearly 50 million Americans were born into the Silent Generation between 1925 and 1945. Members of this cohort experienced the Great Depression in the 1930s and were raised prior to the fast-paced growth of the 1950s. Most of this generation is now retired.

3. *GI generation (age 80-plus).* The members of the GI Generation are the World War II-era seniors. In general, this group is fiscally conscious and conservative. Because of their age, members of the GI Generation tend to need considerable medical support and personalized care. Different products target different age groups with different needs (Exhibit 10.2).

DEMAND FACTORS

There are several factors contributing to increased demand for senior housing including: demographic trends, geographic distribution, lifestyle preferences and needs, market penetration, and affordability.

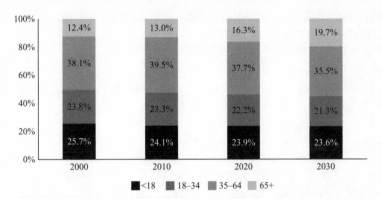

EXHIBIT 10.3 Market Share by Age
Source: U.S. Census Bureau and ING Clarion Research & Investment Strategy, 2006.

Demographic Trends

The share of the population age 65 and older has been steadily increasing since 2000, with more than a half million people joining that cohort each year. The U.S. Census Bureau projects that the senior population will account for approximately 20% of the U.S. population by 2030, up from less than 13% today (Exhibit 10.3). It is projected that within five years, the population of persons age 65 and older will increase from 16 million today to about 40 million.[7] Thereafter, the senior population will be the only major age cohort to gain share in the overall U.S. population. By 2010, the senior housing market is expected to transition from a niche market into a major specialized market.

Demographic trends underscore the growing demand for senior housing. In the short term (2005–2010), demographic trends are expected to support strong demand growth in two groups: the population age 55–64 and the population age 85 and older. The population growth rate for the United States is expected to be slightly less than 1% per year over the next 10 years. Notably, the population age 85 and older is projected to grow at approximately three times the national rate through 2010 (Exhibit 10.4).[8]

In the midterm (2010–2015) and long term (2015–2020), the population age 65–74 is expected to realize the strongest growth, averaging more than

---

[7]Ibid.
[8]Ibid.

EXHIBIT 10.4 Compound Annual Growth Rate (as of 2007)

	Short Term 2005–2010	Intermediate Term 2010–2015	Long Term 2015–2020
Population 55–64	3.60%	2.40%	1.70%
Population 65–74	2.80%	4.50%	4.00%
Population 75–84	−0.30%	0.70%	2.00%
Population 85+	3.10%	2.00%	1.60%

Source: U.S. Census Bureau and ING Clarion Research & Investment Strategy.

4% growth annually (Exhibit 10.4).[9] This rapid acceleration is expected to commence in 2010, as the baby boomers begin to reach their mid-70s, prompting yet another surge in senior housing demand. The population age 85 and older is expected to grow at a steady level over the projection period, a result largely attributable to advances in medical care and increasing longevity.

Geographic Distribution

The largest concentration of senior population growth is in the nation's southern and western states. Indeed, Florida, Texas, Virginia, Maryland, North Carolina, South Carolina, and Tennessee are projected to account for about 40% of population increase in persons age 65 and older in this decade, with California, Arizona, Washington, Nevada, and Colorado expected to account for another 26% of the same (Exhibits 10.5 and 10.6).[10]

Lifestyle Preferences and Needs

Demographics play just one role in this complex market as demand from seniors also depends on the nature of their housing preferences. As people age, their need for assistance in daily living activities such as eating, dressing, standing, sitting, walking, and taking medications properly will inevitably increase. However, today's seniors are comparatively healthier and tend to live longer than previous generations (Exhibit 10.7).[11] Not surprisingly, many seniors prefer to remain in their own homes for as long as possible, with the majority preferring to own rather than rent. Therefore,

---

[9]Ibid.
[10]State Population Forecasts, U.S. Census Bureau and Moody's Economy.com.
[11]National Center for Health Statistics.

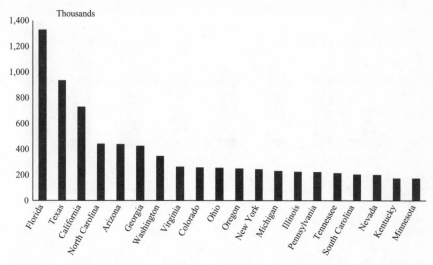

EXHIBIT 10.5 States with the Greatest Numerical Change in Population 65-plus (projected), 2005–2010
Source: ING Clarion Research & Investment Strategy and Moody's Economy.com, 2008.

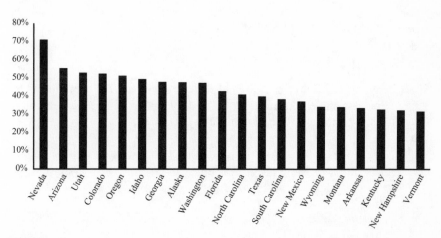

EXHIBIT 10.6 States with the Greatest Percentage Change in Population 65-plus (Projected), 2005–2010
Source: ING Clarion Research & Investment Strategy and Moody's Economy.com, 2008.

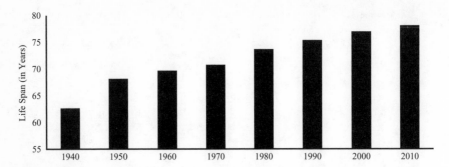

EXHIBIT 10.7   Average U.S. Life Expectancy
Includes all races and both sexes.
Source: National Center for Health Statistics and ING Clarion Research & Investment Strategy, 2006.

the homeownership payment structure and residential qualities of senior housing facilities are becoming increasingly popular.

Growing numbers of seniors are occupying senior-specific residential real estate, suggesting increased acceptance of the senior housing lifestyle. The penetration rate, or percentage of senior households choosing to move to senior housing, has recently been increasing at a rate of approximately 4% per year. The overall compound growth rate of this trend over the past 10 years has been approximately 6% per year.

Age Restriction

Specific age restriction is a gray area in such an age-restricted community. In 1995, Congress passed the Housing for Older Persons Act (HOPA) defining the criteria for an age-restricted community:[12]

- It is intended and operated for occupancy by persons 55 years or older.
- At least 80% of the units are occupied by at least one person who is 55 years or older; or 100% of units are occupied by persons 62 years or older.
- It complies with and enforces the age restriction through written policy and age verification.
- It is noted that the Housing for Older Persons Act is concerned with who is residing in the unit, not who owns the unit. Furthermore,

---

[12]U.S. Department of Housing and Urban Development.

state and local regulations could be stricter than the federal standards. In this case, the community must comply with the stricter legal requirements.

Market Penetration

Market penetration is a major factor of demand. The total pool of seniors is actually much larger than the number of seniors currently residing in senior housing. Many of the published estimates for demand, which include individuals already residing at these facilities, understate potential demand. Notably, even without an increase in the penetration ratio of the industry to the larger pool, favorable demographic trends are expected to produce annual demand growth of approximately 2% or greater.

However, not all the senior population will constitute effective demand for senior living facilities. First, a substantial number of elderly continue to reside in self-owned single-family homes. Second, many seniors reside with spouses, roommates, or family. After adjusting for these factors, the current estimate for the number of seniors who are renting or will rent senior housing in the target demographic cohort of persons age 75 and older is approximately three million (out of 18.2 million). At present, this senior renter group is increasing by approximately 100,000 households per year.

Affordability

Cost effectiveness may play a significant role in the demand for senior housing. A study by the Assisted Living Federation of America (ALFA) determined that the average daily rate at an assisted living facility is approximately 85% of home health care cost, and 65% of the cost of residence at a skilled nursing facility.[13]

SUPPLY FACTORS

Historic Perspectives

Since the late 1990s, the development pipeline for senior housing has declined significantly. New senior construction in 2002 was approximately 80% less than that in 1999.[14] This decrease was largely attributable to the

---

[13] Assisted Living Federation of America (ALFA).

[14] National Investment Center for the Seniors Housing and Care Industry (NIC).

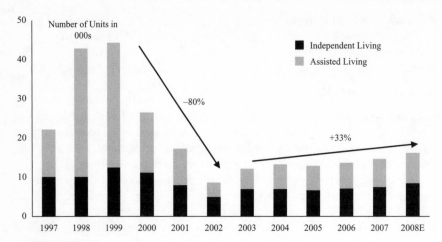

EXHIBIT 10.8   Senior Housing Construction.
The construction data are from NIC/ASHA surveys and may not represent the
national total.
Source: ING Clarion Research & Investment Strategy and National Investment
Center/American Seniors Housing Association, 2007.

decline in investment interest and invested capital after the late 1990s. Over
the past few years, senior housing construction activities have increased;
however, the net new construction for independent living and assisted living
is still relatively constrained (Exhibit 10.8).

New Development

The 2007 American Seniors Housing Association (ASHA) and National
Investment Center (NIC) Senior Housing Construction Survey identified
35,880 senior housing units that began construction between April 1, 2006
and March 31, 2007, while 14,772 units remained under construction in
properties that started construction before this period.[15] These pipeline units
represent an approximate 1.6% increase to the total national stock of senior
housing.

Geographic Distribution

While it may be expected that current development follows regional demographic trends, the geographic distribution of new construction reveals a

---

[15] American Seniors Housing Association (ASHA), *The State of Seniors Housing*
(2007).

different picture. The F. W. Dodge construction pipeline indicates that the Northeast and Midwest each account for a comparatively larger share of the 100,000-plus senior housing units currently under construction.[16] While the West and the South are, together, expected to account for more than 75% of growth in the senior population, the regions only account for a combined 45% of senior housing in development. Notably, there are twice as many senior housing units under construction today in Illinois as in Florida.[17]

There are two reasons for the remarkable difference between the regional distribution of new senior housing and the regional growth of the senior population. First, there is simply more existing senior housing in the South and West; regions which, historically, have higher shares of the senior population. In fact, these two regions already account for more than half of the nation's senior population, and well over half of the existing senior housing inventory. Second, increasing numbers of seniors are choosing to remain in their present states after retirement rather than moving to the Sunbelt regions. One recent survey named Chicago as one of the possible retirement destinations for aging baby boomers. Notably, Chicago is typically more affordable than many sunny destinations in parts of Florida and California. Those individuals currently living in Chicago may choose to remain there as they reach retirement, and in so doing, are likely to demand more service-oriented housing to meet their needs as they age.

Product Characteristics of Active Adult Communities

Active adult communities can be for-sale or for-rent and are typically single-family homes, cluster homes, and multifamily housing targeted to adults age 55 and older, offering amenities such as clubhouses, walking trails, exercise rooms, and onsite security. Unlike the various forms of assisted living facilities, active adult communities do not provide any form of medical care; rather, services are focused on activities. Not only must developers of active adult communities accurately define the buyer profile and design to appropriate price points, they must also deliver housing that is superior, in terms of community planning, lifestyle, and amenities, to the currently available product.[18] Because of their locations and pricing structures, active

---

[16] F. W. Dodge, McGraw Hill Construction, 2007.

[17] Ibid.

[18] Building Owners and Managers Association (BOMA) International, *Developing, Leasing and Managing Healthcare Real Estate* (2003).

adult communities are indicative of the various nontraditional ways in which baby boomers are planning for their golden years.

Active senior demand is similar for both for-sale and for-rent housing, though there remain some general differences. For-sale active senior developments have traditionally been built in Sunbelt locations. These properties tend to be more amenitized, offering larger units, golf courses, higher-end furniture, and fixtures, and generally are more suburban. For-rent active senior developments are geared to more mobile tenants, who may still be working and living part-time at the property; using the rental as a second home to be near family or familiar surroundings. These properties are often built as urban infill, in or around the central business district (CBD), and in close proximity to shopping and public transportation. For-rent active senior developments are especially attractive to residents who prefer to live without the burden of a mortgage, and the maintenance and capital expenses associated with homeownership. Unit sizes in for-rent senior properties are typically smaller than that of for-sale properties, and amenities are typically lower-end. The market for rental-active senior housing is generally wider and more diverse than for-sale senior market.

Building and Community Design

The most successful active adult properties offer spacious units, state-of-the-art amenities, quality locations, and high levels of services. The size, in terms of total units, of the typical active adult for-sale community is decreasing.[19] Sun City, Arizona, one of the first retirement communities to be built in the 1960s, had 25,000 homes. In 1996, the average community had more than 1,800 homes, and by 2004, that number had declined to 393. Active senior rental communities typically range from as small as 20–30 units to as large as 300–400 units, but are seldom greater than 500 units. This trend is partially attributable to the dearth of large tracts of buildable land in more established urban areas.

Homeownership

There is a renewed focus on ownership models such as condos and co-ops in senior housing because 80% of seniors age 65 and older are accustomed to being homeowners rather than tenants. The rise in home values over the past five years has likely fueled this trend, as homeowners can enjoy the benefits of building equity and private ownership.

---

[19] Ibid.

Industry Players

The emergence of larger, well-capitalized owners and managers will likely provide investors with reduced uncertainties concerning operations. At the same time, the larger owners and managers will likely gain greater access to investment capital. This trend is expected to fuel future M&A activities because the industry is highly fragmented with many midlevel and small players.

The top 10 managers and top 10 owners account for 58% and 55% of the total units, respectively. The top brands include Sunrise Senior Living, American Retirement Corp., Horizon Bay, Erickson Retirement Communities, and Encore Senior Living.[20] No single brand or company is dominating the senior housing industry at this point, presenting an opportunity to build a brand name and increase market share.

SEGMENT PERFORMANCE

Improved Occupancy and Margins

The senior housing industry has successfully emerged from a period during which developers and investors, with several different business models, flooded the market. Skilled housing management operators are beginning to dominate the landscape, resulting in improved operations. Average margins for quality properties have increased across all sectors, with the independent living sector reporting margins in excess of 40%, while assisted living margins have risen to more than 30% for larger communities.

Since 2005, absorption in the senior housing industry increased significantly, thereby increasing the average occupancy rates in the top 30 metropolitan statistical areas (MSAs).[21] If this positive trend in absorption continues, occupancy rates will likely remain healthy in 2008. In addition, the number of units under construction increased only moderately in 2007, further improving occupancy levels (Exhibit 10.9).

Cap Rates

Average cap rates range from 7.4% to 9.0% for independent living and assisted living facilities as of the third quarter of 2007.[22] It is likely that

---

[20] ASHA, Largest 50 U.S. Managers/Largest 50 U.S. Owners, survey (2007).
[21] NIC.
[22] Ibid.

EXHIBIT 10.9   Occupancy Rates, 2007Q3

Property Type	Occupancy Rates (Mean)	Number of Properties Sampled
Independent living	91%	581
Assisted living	88%	1,412
Skilled nursing homes	86%	1,002
CCRCs	92%	167
Independent units in CCRCs	93%	165
Assisted living units in CCRCs	88%	133
Skilled nursing beds in CCRCs	88%	142

Source: ING Clarion Research & Investment Strategy and National Investment Center.

EXHIBIT 10.10   Capitalization Rates, 2007Q3

Property Type	Low	Average/Chg from 2006Q3	High
Independent living	4.9%	7.4% (−40 bps)	10.0%
Assisted living	6.0%	9.0% (+10 bps)	12.5%
Skilled nursing homes	9.0%	12.8% (−10 bps)	14.5%
CCRCs	6.5%	9.1% (+20 bps)	14.0%

Source: National Investment Center.

single-digit cap rates will remain in 2008 as institutional investors continue to show interest in the sector. The average cap rate stabilized in the second half of 2007, while the cap rate for independent living continues to decline by approximately 40 bps (Exhibit 10.10).

Investment Activity

Senior housing has continued to post strong performance in terms of loan volume, loan performance, and equity investment as investors are increasingly interested in the sector. According to National Investment Center, total senior housing loan volume outstanding grew to $20.5 billion during the third quarter of 2007, 8.5% higher than the previous quarter. Loan performance continued to be strong with a delinquency rate of only 0.6% as of the third quarter of 2007.[23]

---

[23] Ibid.

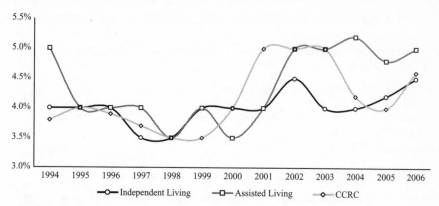

EXHIBIT 10.11 Annual Rent Growth in Senior Housing Facilities
Source: ING Clarion Research & Investment Strategy and American Seniors Housing Association, 2007.

Rent Growth

Rents have increased at an average rate of 4.5% annually over the past 20 years, with rental growth trending upward in 2006–2007.[24] It is likely that rent growth for senior housing will range from 4 to 5% over the next few years, depending on quality, types, and geographic location of the properties (Exhibit 10.11).

RISK FACTORS

Although the investment outlook has improved considerably for the senior housing market, significant risks still remain.

Regulatory Risk

A large component of the senior housing industry is affected by complex regulatory requirements at the federal, state, and local levels. Development of skilled nursing facilities and CCRCs requires the receipt of special permits from local governments, and the process can be quite time intensive. Indeed, it may take three to six years from planning to final development of such facilities.

---

[24] ASHA, *The State of Seniors Housing.*

Health Care Policy   The reimbursement requirements of the industry are also complex and unpredictable. Skilled nursing and CCRC facilities receive significant reimbursement for health-care-related services from Medicare and Medicaid, programs which face increasing budgetary constraints.

Age-restricted and independent living facilities are typically nonregulated. As such, Medicaid payments account for just a small amount of revenue to these types of facilities and have no impact on the revenue of independent living facilities.

Operating Risk

The senior housing industry is both an operating service business and a real estate investment and, depending on the level of service provided, may require up to five times the amount of operating personnel than does a multifamily property.[25] It is difficult for management to realize operating efficiencies through the various activities of staffing, catering, administrative expenses, and insurance. Operating licenses, too, are difficult to transfer. Finally, health care costs are rising much faster than the pace of inflation and show no signs of abating, the result of which we believe could deleteriously affect the medical service aspect of the business.

Operating risk can be mitigated by careful selection of experienced, professional operators who have demonstrated successful business performance. We believe that the selection of operators should be based on both financial strength and industry expertise. Desirable operators are those leading companies with at least five years of experience in the senior housing industry.

Business Risk

As a relatively young industry, senior housing has a short track record from which to gauge investment risk. We believe that investment should be diversified not only in different geographic areas, but also by engaging with different operating partners. Institutional investors can establish joint ventures or partnerships with a few large, well-established operating partners. For example, California Public Employees' Retirement System (CalPERS) does not allow more than one-third of its senior housing investment to be associated with a single operator.

---

[25] Arthur E. Gimmy, Susan B. Brecht, and Clifford J. Dowd, *Senior Housing, Looking Toward the Third Millennium* (Chicago: Appraisal Institute, 2003).

Volatility and Turnover   In general, the annual turnover rates for independent living and assisted living are approximately 30% and 50%, respectively, which is much less than the annual turnover rate for conventional apartments.[26] Although skilled nursing facilities have a higher turnover rate, seniors in general tend to be a very stable population with little reason to move. On a risk-adjusted basis, senior housing returns are significantly higher than conventional apartment investments. Cap rates are still approximately 150 bps higher for senior housing product, despite the fact that occupancy rates tend to be more stable than those of conventional apartments.

We believe that most of the mistakes in the senior industry have been made on the development side, with the lease-up period often being long and unpredictable. However, once the property is stabilized, the turnover tends to be less volatile. As such, vacancy loss, marketing, and redecorating costs of stabilized properties are comparatively lower.[27]

Market Penetration Risk

There are risks associated with the perception that many seniors view these facilities as less desirable than remaining in their own homes. The preference for homeownership and certain lifestyle preferences may significantly undermine market penetration. In addition, some fiscally conscious seniors may find the "entry fee" pay structure unappealing, making them reluctant to give what is essentially an interest-free loan to the facility (assisted living and CCRCs). Finally, there is a lack of clear industry-specific definitions and performance benchmark measures.

Generation Gap Risk

There is a big gap between the two largest generations: baby boomers and echo boomers (born between 1980 and 2001). Many baby boomers are counting on cashing in their homes to fund their future retirement. However, their houses may not fetch their current prices several years from now as sellers will likely outnumber potential buyers at that time. The situation certainly poses a significant risk for seniors to make a smooth transition from traditional home ownership to senior living.

---

[26]NIC.
[27]Ibid.

SECTOR OUTLOOK

The senior housing industry today is very different from its profile in the 1990s, and in fact has improved significantly in several aspects:

- A rapidly growing and more affluent senior population has been driving demand for updated facilities with a residential look and feel, and recreational activities.
- Many seniors prefer to retire and live near their social network, instead of migrating to the Sunbelt states.
- Improved research and reporting by industry organizations is leading to improved transparency of supply and demand trends and better estimates of the industry scope.
- The decline in new development is resulting in higher occupancy rates and profit margins.
- Several large, well-established operators with national presence are emerging through industry consolidation. These operators leverage experience and scale leading to improved operating margins.
- The rapid maturation of new channels for real estate finance and investment are providing adequate capital to fuel industry expansion.
- Institutional investors are buying high-quality assets because of improved fundamentals and relatively high yields.
- Cap rates are declining to new lows, and stabilized properties are being sold at record prices.

Near-Term and Long-Term Outlook

Strong underlying demographics, which are projected to persist for several decades, especially after 2010, support industry demand growth at current levels of penetration. Total potential demand greatly exceeds current industry capacity. Growing industry concentration and improved fundamentals will likely provide investors with an industry structure conducive to institutional investment. Therefore, the long-term outlook for the senior housing industry is positive, suggesting that this secular trend will most likely provide one of the best investment opportunities in the apartment sector over the next 10 to 20 years.

Because of relatively constrained construction activities over the past few years, demand is outweighing available supply. Occupancy rates and operating margins are at five-year highs; therefore, in the near-term, the cyclical trend is also positive. However, because the senior population is growing at just 2% each year, and peak baby boomer demand is not likely to occur for a few more years, a sudden increase in supply could easily tip the balance to oversupply.

EXHIBIT 10.12 SWOT Analysis

Strengths	Weaknesses
• Long-term favorable demographics with rapid growth of senior population. • Cost-effective living options based on well-defined business models. • Near-term low supply and high demand. • High occupancy levels, low turnover rates, and excellent cash flows. • Good portfolio diversification due to low correlation with external economic factors.	• Peak of the senior population still a few years away. • Some segments have high non-real estate component. • Long lease-up period, service intensive; requires an experienced operator. • CCRCs have low transaction liquidity.
Opportunities	**Threats**
• Focus on major market with large, growing senior populations, and high occupancy. • Rehab and reposition old senior housing properties. • Target the booming 2nd homes for the baby boomers and possible retirement communities near university campuses. • Explore redevelopment projects in high growth markets.	• Uncertainty in market penetration—more seniors prefer homeownership to renting. • Record prices and low cap rates. • Low barriers to entry and new supply can disrupt the market and reduce occupancy. • Rising health care costs; dependent on government health care policy.

Source: ING Clarion Research & Investment Strategy.

As more capital flows into the senior housing sector and properties continue to sell at near record prices, new construction activity will likely increase. The extent to which construction will increase, however, is unknown. It is likely that the slowdown in the conventional residential housing market will encourage some builders to enter the senior housing sector (see Exhibit 10.12).

STRATEGIC OPTIONS

Target Active Adult Community and Independent Living

We believe that the current supply and demand balance strongly favors active adult communities/senior apartments and independent living properties. Expected population growth in these two segments will likely exceed supply in the foreseeable future due to limited supply growth over the past few years, a consequence of the scarcity of construction financing available to this sector. Active adult community and independent living properties are not constrained by health care service requirements, and as such, may be considered as part of an apartment allocation (Exhibit 10.13). Based on the underlying demographic fundamentals, the returns of active adult community and independent living properties are not closely correlated with the returns of conventional multifamily properties and can potentially increase portfolio returns and mitigate risk.

Selectively Buying Assisted Living

The assisted living segment, which targets the fast-growing 85-plus population, was drastically overbuilt in the late 1990s, well in excess of demand for the product. Today, occupancy rates and operating margins are increasing, but remain below their previous peaks achieved in the mid- to late 1990s. However, because more seniors prefer homeownership to renting, the effective increased demand in the segment is growing at approximately 2% per year, with a more significant increase in demand likely in the future. Moreover, the real estate component accounts for just 50% to 60% of the assisted living segment. It is projected that between 2005 and 2010, the population of persons age 85-plus will grow to approximately 6.1 million, a compound annual growth rate of 3.1%. Notably, the existing bed stock is only 1.9 million. Overall, it appears that the assisted living segment has the strongest potential within the senior housing sector going forward, with the ideal investment period occurring two to four years from today. As such, we believe that current investments in assisted living must be selectively based on the quality of assets and their locations (Exhibit 10.13).

Avoid Skilled Nursing and Continuing Care Retirement Communities (CCRCs)   Despite improved operating margins, the skilled nursing segment is not expected to perform favorably. A highly regulated sector, its profits are likely to be squeezed due to the rapidly rising costs of direct medical care and changes in Medicare coverage. We believe that proposed cuts in Medicaid and pending health care reforms are likely to negatively impact medical-related services going forward. More important, real estate represents approximately 30% of the skilled nursing segment and, as such, investments may not meet required returns.

CCRC is a segment that warrants close monitoring, as the product is gaining popularity among seniors, and current occupancy rates and

Segment		Comments	Attractiveness
Active adult community/Senior apartments	Pros	Continued home ownership, appealing to baby boomers, suitable for their 2nd homes, 100% real estate.	Attractive
	Cons	Competing with conventional single-family residential or condo market, more supply in pipeline	
Independent living	Pros	Simple, cost-effective operation, in demand, preferred by seniors, first mover advantage—waiting for baby boomer wave.	Attractive
	Cons	Not the peak of population yet, renting instead of owning.	
Assisted living	Pros	Improved margins, 85+ population growing fast, supply slowing, room for further improvement in occupancy.	Neutral
	Cons	Big wave still a few years away, renting instead of owning, large non-real estate component.	
Skilled nursing	Pros	Revenue dependent on government reimbursement, recent Medicare bill positive, cap rates still high.	Less Attractive
	Cons	Regulated, some nonprofit, health care reform uncertainty, increasing health care costs, proposed Medicaid cut negative, larger non-real estate component.	
CCRC	Pros	High occupancy, improved margins, gaining popularity.	Less Attractive
	Cons	Complex to operate, difficult to develop, low liquidity.	

EXHIBIT 10.13 Senior Housing Segment Attractiveness
Source: ING Clarion Research & Investment Strategy.

operating margins are impressive. However, CCRC facilities are challenging to build and must comply with stringent regulatory requirements. Consequently, such facilities are arguably best suited for local operation and ownership. Few CCRC facilities are traded each year, suggesting the sector's low liquidity, and therefore likely making the sector less attractive for institutional investors (Exhibit 10.13).

Focus on a Few Top Markets—Both Sunbelt and Non-Sunbelt Locations

It is essential to identify those markets that are most conducive to the growth of the senior housing sector, and to clearly understand the supply and demand dynamics of such markets. Of particular interest are those affluent markets (large MSAs) with high percentages of older baby boomers. Because the entitlement process tends to be less rigorous, there is generally more flexibility in selecting locations for new active senior developments than for other multifamily projects. As such, we believe that senior housing development need not be confined to the Sunbelt suburbs. Potential locations include those in relatively close proximity (up to two hours drive time)

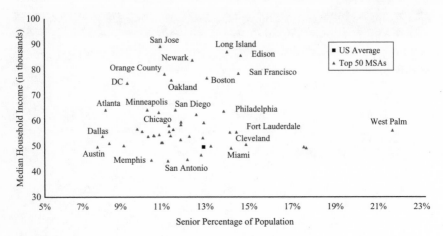

EXHIBIT 10.14   Top 50 Metropolitan Statistical Area Markets for Senior
Housing
Source: ING Clarion Research & Investment Strategy.

to MSAs with populations greater than 5 million. We believe that new active
senior development is likely to occur on the periphery of major metropolitan
areas and in exurbs in which residents will have broader recreational options. The greatest new opportunities may well be in non-Sunbelt locations
that are close to urban areas, but with plentiful, inexpensive, and devel-
opable land with more relaxed entitlement and development regulations.
Ideal locations, as with other multifamily developments, are those that are
supply constrained and have a high barrier to entry.

Based on senior population and median household income, the top
50 MSAs are mapped in comparison to the U.S. average (Exhibit 10.14).
Clearly, markets with both higher share of senior population than the national average and higher median household income than the nation are
desirable for senior housing investment. Accordingly, we believe that it is
imperative to design a strategy that accurately matches the appropriate products to their target markets.

Investment Criteria

For most facilities, the breakeven occupancy is typically 80%, and occupancy
levels in excess of this figure will immediately enhance net operating income
(NOI). We believe that a sound investment portfolio will include active
adult communities, senior apartments, and independent living assets with
stabilized occupancy. To further diversify the portfolio, investment in several

geographic regions and partnerships with two to three operators and/or managers is desirable. A properly selected portfolio for investment purposes has the potential to generate 5% to 7% cash returns and a total leveraged internal rate of return (IRR) ranging from 9% to 12%.

An ideal senior housing property in this scenario has the following characteristics:

- Located in a major MSA with a large and growing senior population.
- In areas with household income above $75,000.
- Demonstrated high occupancy and limited new supply in the pipeline.
- Private pay structure with a minimum nonprofit component.
- A minimum of 110 units in the property.
- In close proximity to medical providers and public transportation.
- Limited competition within a 10-mile radius of the property.
- Relatively high barriers to entry.

Value-Added/Development Opportunities

Many senior housing properties are ideally located but require extensive renovation and upgrades. As cap rates continue to compress, the opportunity to engage in value-added redevelopment is increasingly appealing. With the land already selected, such projects have the potential to be quite profitable. Investors, however, must be willing to assume the additional risks associated with the initial lease-up period.

Target the Luxury Upper End of the For-Sale and Rental Segments

Baby boomers are the wealthiest generation in history, and many are entering their retirement years having accumulated significant wealth. With discerning taste and a willingness to pay for quality, baby boomers will likely seek luxury developments that offer a wide range of services. Of particular appeal are locations near resort, recreation, and social destinations. Investment in the luxury segment offers the potential to realize the highest sale and rent premiums. Moreover, investment in this niche affords both the opportunity to stand apart from commodity developers and to build a brand and reputation.

Target the Cost-Sensitive Middle Market

Many baby boomers subsist on moderate, fixed incomes, and do not want to live above their means. For this group, active senior housing could provide an economically prudent lifestyle. In a form of *housing cost arbitrage,* many empty-nesters (people whose children have moved out) realize that they have more house than they need, which may prove expensive to maintain. Notably, many empty-nesters' homes are located in high property tax jurisdictions in the Northeast. By selling their homes and buying new residences that are smaller and more energy efficient, we believe that baby boomers can accumulate significant equity while living more cost-efficient.

Retirement Communities near College Campuses

A unique investment strategy is the development of senior residences aimed at university alumni wishing to live near their alma maters. With a wealth of educational and recreational offerings, universities have clear potential to attract alumni to the vicinity. Because such alumni tend to be well-educated, affluent, and willing to donate, universities should benefit greatly from their presence.

Strategic alliances and joint ventures with universities are especially attractive because colleges have the credibility, capability, and potential for comparatively lower land costs. In 2005, Hyatt, in conjunction with Stanford University, built a $170 million four-story upscale retirement residence in Palo Alto, California. Current residents include two Nobel laureates, a former Cabinet member, and the inventor of the cherry-picker truck. Similar new developments have sprung up near Cornell University in Ithaca, New York, and Dartmouth College in Hanover, New Hampshire. It is likely that this trend will continue and attractive investment opportunities will arise near other renowned college campuses.

Opportunity to Build Brand Equity

The senior housing industry is highly fragmented with no single player dominating the market. We believe that the continued consolidation of owners and operators is likely. Opportunities exist to gain market share and build a national brand through strategic portfolio and property acquisitions.

Partnering with a Seasoned Operator

The senior housing sector, with the exception of the active adult community segment, is service-oriented and, as such, operating efficiency is critical to achieving target profit margins. Further, due to frequent turnover of units and a slow initial lease-up period, strategic marketing is essential to reaching and maintaining target occupancy rates. A large, well-established operator can leverage its experience and economies of scale to achieve high occupancy levels and operating margins.

The senior housing industry is still relatively young and investors are still in the process of learning to understand the industry. Thus, in choosing an operating partner, it is essential to review the potential partner's management experience and financial position. Because most senior housing operators have less than 20 years of operating experience, a thorough credit evaluation and review of auditor opinions can prove informative. Just as diversification by property type is important to ensuring a healthy investment portfolio, diversification by partnering with several operators can similarly mitigate operating risk.

CHAPTER 11

Active Portfolio Management Using Modern Portfolio Theory

David Lynn and Yusheng Hao
Summer 2008[1]

In this chapter, we apply Modern Portfolio Theory, or the mean-variance framework, to a hypothetical multibillion-dollar diversified core real estate private equity fund (the "Hypothetical Fund"). This analysis can help identify the potential risk and return features of the Hypothetical Fund, potentially favorable and unfavorable markets for future acquisitions, and properties for potential future disposition. Hypothetical risks and returns are measured against the National Council of Real Estate Investment Fiduciaries (NCREIF) property index benchmarks.[2]

THE INVESTMENT UNIVERSE BY SECTOR, REGION, AND METRO

The first step of the analysis is to define an investment universe. An investment universe contains all investment options for a series of allocation strategies. In this study, three different but interrelated investment groups are examined for different purposes.

---

[1] This paper was originally produced in summer 2008. The data, opinions, and forecasts have not been updated for book publication.

[2] For an overview of the NCREIF Index, see the important disclosures at the end of this chapter.

Sector

The sector analysis considers the appropriate balance between the apartment, industrial, office, retail, and hotel sectors within the hypothetical portfolio. The sector analysis provides recommendations intended to maximize hypothetical absolute returns and risk-adjusted returns. The NCREIF annual total return series from 1978 to 2007 for each sector and metro level forecasts, aggregated to the sector level, are used to generate the forecast hypothetical expected returns.

Region

The regional analysis addresses the appropriate balance within the Hypothetical Fund between the East, Midwest, South, and West regions, as defined by NCREIF (Exhibit 11.1) in order to maximize hypothetical returns or risk-adjusted returns. The historical return data consists of the NCREIF

EXHIBIT 11.1   Region Investment Universe
Source: NCREIF.

annual total return series from 1978 to 2007 for each region, and the hypothetical expected returns over a three-year period (2008 to 2010) are based
on recent metro forecasts, aggregated to the regional level.

Metro

The metro analysis addresses the appropriate balance between metro areas
within the Hypothetical Fund to maximize hypothetical returns or risk-
adjusted returns. The analysis considers a universe of 50 metro areas for the
apartment, industrial, office, and retail sectors; the hotel sector is considered
only at the national level (Exhibit 11.2). The analysis is based upon the
NCREIF annual total return series from 1978 to 2007 for each metro (where
available), and hypothetical expected returns over the next three years (2008
to 2010) based on recent metro forecasts, aggregated to the regional level.

For this analysis, the Hypothetical Fund includes assets in 28 of the
50 markets (selected randomly) for which we regularly forecast supply
and demand fundamentals (Exhibit 11.2), plus two additional, nontarget
markets.

The efficient frontiers and hypothetical risk and return expectations of
the hypothetical portfolio vary, due to the different investment options and
data available within the sector, region, and metro investment universes.

EXHIBIT 11.2 Investment Universe by Metro

East	Midwest	South	West
Baltimore	**Chicago**	**Atlanta**	**Denver**
Boston	Cincinnati	Austin	Portland
Charlotte	Cleveland	**Dallas**	Salt Lake City
Edison	Columbus	**Fort Lauderdale**	Las Vegas
Long Island	**Detroit**	Fort Worth	**Los Angeles**
New York	Indianapolis	**Houston**	**Oakland**
Newark	Kansas City	**Jacksonville**	**Orange County**
Philadelphia	Minneapolis	**Orlando**	**Phoenix**
Richmond	Nashville	Miami	**Riverside**
Stamford	St. Louis	Raleigh	**Sacramento**
Washington		**Tampa**	**San Francisco**
		San Antonio	**San Jose**
		West Palm Beach	**San Diego**
			Seattle
			Tucson

Bold markets are where the Hypothetical Fund would have investments.
Source: ING Clarion Research & Investment Strategy.

HYPOTHETICAL FUND PERFORMANCE EXPECTATIONS

The expected total return of the Hypothetical Fund is forecast and compared to the NCREIF Index benchmark. Results are consistent with our expectation that hypothetical core real estate investment returns would likely be in the high single digits (between bonds and equities). Based on our market forecasts, the Hypothetical Fund would be expected to outperform the NCRIEF Index on all metrics over the next three years (2008–2010). Hypothetical returns could be 30 bps higher, while hypothetical risk could be 109 bps lower (Exhibits 11.3 and 11.4).

HYPOTHETICAL FUND SECTOR EXPOSURES

In this example, the Hypothetical Fund would have exposure to properties across all five major property sectors: apartment, industrial, office, retail, and hotel. More specifically, the investments would include:

- 20 apartment properties with a market value of $1.5 billion, accounting for 22% of the Hypothetical Fund assets.
- 50 industrial properties with a market value of $1.25 billion, accounting for 18% of the Hypothetical Fund assets.
- 30 office properties with a market value of $2.0 billion, accounting for 29% of the Hypothetical Fund assets.
- 35 retail properties with a market value of $1.5 billion, accounting for 22% of the Hypothetical Fund assets.
- 5 hotel properties with a market value of $650 million, accounting for 9% of the Hypothetical Fund assets.

EXHIBIT 11.3 Hypothetical Fund vs. NCREIF: Expected Performance, 2008–2010[a]

	Expected Return	Standard Deviation	Return per Unit of Risk	Sharpe Ratio[b]
Hypothetical Fund	4.92%	5.25%	0.937	0.174
NCREIF Index	4.62%	6.34%	0.729	0.098

[a]This uses the Sharpe Ratio, which is a measure of the excess return (or risk premium) per unit of risk in an investment asset or a trading strategy.
[b]Risk free rate is 4.0%.
Source: ING Clarion Research & Investment Strategy, as of March 2008.

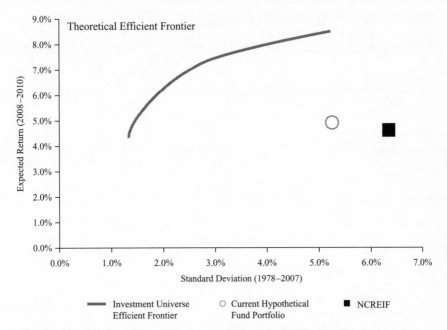

EXHIBIT 11.4   Hypothetical Fund vs. NCREIF on the Efficient Frontier
Source: ING Clarion Research & Investment Strategy and NCREIF.

HYPOTHETICAL FUND INVESTED MARKETS VS. NATIONAL AVERAGE

Fundamental drivers of the Hypothetical Fund's potential performance can be better understood by comparing the economic and demographic compositions of the markets the Hypothetical Fund would be invested in with the national average.

Overall Portfolio

For the overall portfolio, the Hypothetical Fund markets exhibit higher concentrations in Information Services, Back Office, Financial Services, and Government employment sectors (Exhibit 11.5), all of which tend to be heavy office users. In addition, the Hypothetical Fund markets have higher expected employment growth and population growth in coming years, along with above-average market capital growth and market total returns. Overall,

EXHIBIT 11.5 Hypothetical Fund Portfolio vs. National Average

Employment Sectors	Portfolio	National	Portfolio
	Share	Share	LQ
Basic materials	2.7%	4.0%	0.68
Back office	7.8%	6.8%	1.16
Consumer service	27.2%	27.4%	0.99
Financial service	6.0%	5.4%	1.11
Government	22.5%	21.3%	1.06
Health service	10.4%	11.4%	0.91
High-tech manufacturing	1.8%	1.8%	1.01
Information services	8.7%	5.7%	1.53
Traditional manufacturing	3.3%	5.3%	0.62
Transportation	6.6%	6.7%	0.98
Industry Statistics	Portfolio	National	Ratio
Current employment growth	1.6%	1.4%	1.20
Forecast employment growth	1.1%	1.0%	1.04
Current population growth	0.9%	0.8%	1.14
Forecast population growth	1.0%	0.9%	1.17
Current market yield	5.8%	5.9%	0.98
Current market capital growth	12.7%	10.9%	1.17
Current market total return	19.0%	17.3%	1.10

All current growth is based on trailing 12 months. All forecasts are annual growth based on next 3 years.
Source: ING Clarion Research & Investment Strategy, Moody's Economy.com, and NCREIF, as of March 2008.

those markets in which the Hypothetical Fund would invest outperform the national average.

Apartment

Those markets in which the Hypothetical Fund would have apartment investments have higher concentrations in Information Services, Back Office, Financial Services, Government, and Consumer Services employment sectors (Exhibit 11.6), implying a younger and wealthier population with positive employment and population growth expectations. The current real estate market performance is slightly below average, however, since those markets are already expensive—that is, there was less capital appreciation (cap rate compression) to add to total returns.

EXHIBIT 11.6 Hypothetical Fund Apartment Portfolio vs. National Average

Employment Sectors	Portfolio	National	Portfolio
	Share	Share	LQ
Basic materials	2.6%	4.0%	0.64
Back office	8.3%	6.8%	1.23
Consumer service	28.3%	27.4%	1.03
Financial service	6.0%	5.4%	1.10
Government	22.5%	21.3%	1.05
Health service	10.4%	11.4%	0.91
High-tech manufacturing	1.6%	1.8%	0.86
Information services	8.3%	5.7%	1.45
Traditional manufacturing	2.9%	5.3%	0.56
Transportation	6.3%	6.7%	0.93
Industry Statistics			
Current employment growth	1.8%	1.4%	1.34
Forecast employment growth	1.2%	1.0%	1.15
Current population growth	1.1%	0.8%	1.43
Forecast population growth	1.2%	0.9%	1.38
Current market yield	2.57%	5.80%	0.44
Current market capital growth	2.9%	4.6%	0.62
Current market total return	4.8%	5.0%	0.97

All current growth is based on trailing 12 months. All forecasts are annual growth based on next 3 years.
Source: ING Clarion Research & Investment Strategy, Moody's Economy.com, and NCREIF, as of March 2008.

Industrial

The Hypothetical Fund's industrial investments would be located in markets that not only have high concentrations in Information Services, Financial Services, and Back Office employment sectors, but are also highly concentrated in High-Tech Manufacturing and Transportation sectors (Exhibit 11.7). These markets have above-average employment and population growth expectations as well as strong growth in current capital and total returns.

Office

Office assets in the Hypothetical Fund's portfolio would be situated in markets with above-average concentrations in Information Services, Financial

EXHIBIT 11.7 Hypothetical Fund Industrial Portfolio vs. National Average

Employment Sectors	Portfolio	National	Portfolio
	Share	Share	LQ
Basic materials	3.0%	4.0%	0.74
Back office	8.2%	6.8%	1.21
Consumer service	28.2%	27.4%	1.03
Financial service	6.2%	5.4%	1.14
Government	19.7%	21.3%	0.92
Health service	9.8%	11.4%	0.86
High-tech manufacturing	2.7%	1.8%	1.48
Information services	7.5%	5.7%	1.31
Traditional manufacturing	4.1%	5.3%	0.78
Transportation	7.4%	6.7%	1.10
Industry Statistics	Portfolio	National	Ratio
Current employment growth	1.8%	1.4%	1.33
Forecast employment growth	1.3%	1.0%	1.30
Current population growth	1.1%	0.8%	1.35
Forecast population growth	1.2%	0.9%	1.41
Current market yield	8.3%	9.3%	0.90
Current market capital growth	5.6%	5.8%	0.96
Current market total return	6.4%	6.4%	1.00

All current growth is based on trailing 12 months. All forecasts are annual growth based on next 3 years.
Source: ING Clarion Research & Investment Strategy, Moody's Economy.com, and NCREIF, as of March 2008.

Services, Back Office, Government, and High-Tech Manufacturing employment sectors (Exhibit 11.8), all of which are heavy office-using sectors. These markets have above-average employment and population growth expectations as well as growth in current capital and total returns.

Retail

The Hypothetical Fund's retail investments would be in markets with above-average concentrations in Information Services, Back Office, Financial Services, Government, and Transportation employment sectors (Exhibit 11.9). These markets also have above-average current capital growth.

EXHIBIT 11.8 Hypothetical Fund Office Portfolio vs. National Average

Employment Sectors	Portfolio	National	Portfolio
	Share	Share	LQ
Basic materials	2.6%	4.0%	0.65
Back office	7.5%	6.8%	1.10
Consumer service	27.0%	27.4%	0.99
Financial service	6.0%	5.4%	1.11
Government	23.1%	21.3%	1.08
Health service	10.5%	11.4%	0.92
High-tech manufacturing	1.8%	1.8%	1.00
Information services	9.4%	5.7%	1.64
Traditional manufacturing	2.7%	5.3%	0.52
Transportation	6.2%	6.7%	0.92
Industry Statistics	**Portfolio**	**National**	**Ratio**
Current employment growth	1.6%	1.4%	1.19
Forecast employment growth	0.9%	1.0%	0.94
Current population growth	0.8%	0.8%	1.05
Forecast population growth	0.9%	0.9%	1.07
Current market yield	10.3%	12.4%	0.83
Current market capital growth	9.4%	5.6%	1.70
Current market total return	5.8%	6.0%	0.97

All current growth is based on trailing 12 months. All forecasts are annual growth based on next 3 years.
Source: ING Clarion Research & Investment Strategy, Moody's Economy.com, and NCREIF, as of March 2008.

SECTOR REBALANCING STRATEGIES

Compared to NCREIF, the Hypothetical Fund would be overweighted in industrial and hotel sectors, while underweighted in the office sector (Exhibit 11.10). The low volatility of the industrial sector, combined with low correlation between the hotel sector and other major property types, would lower the Hypothetical Fund's volatility below the NCREIF Index.

Sector target ranges are typically established by a fund's business plan. For the Hypothetical Fund, these ranges were developed by considering expected sector returns, historical volatility, and sector correlations, as well as the goal to resemble a core fund comparable to the NCREIF composition (Exhibit 11.11).

EXHIBIT 11.9 Hypothetical Fund Retail Portfolio vs. National Average

Employment Sectors	Portfolio	National	Portfolio
	Share	Share	LQ
Basic materials	2.7%	4.0%	0.67
Back office	7.7%	6.8%	1.14
Consumer service	25.9%	27.4%	0.95
Financial service	6.0%	5.4%	1.11
Government	23.6%	21.3%	1.11
Health service	11.2%	11.4%	0.98
High-tech manufacturing	1.4%	1.8%	0.79
Information services	8.8%	5.7%	1.53
Traditional manufacturing	3.7%	5.3%	0.70
Transportation	6.9%	6.7%	1.02
Industry Statistics	**Portfolio**	**National**	**Ratio**
Current employment growth	1.1%	1.4%	0.83
Forecast employment growth	0.9%	1.0%	0.85
Current population growth	0.6%	0.8%	0.69
Forecast population growth	0.7%	0.9%	0.83
Current market yield	5.8%	7.1%	0.82
Current market capital growth	4.2%	4.2%	1.00
Current market total return	6.0%	6.0%	1.00

All current growth is based on trailing 12 months. All forecasts are annual growth based on next 3 years.
Source: ING Clarion Research & Investment Strategy, Moody's Economy.com, and NCREIF, as of March 2008.

EXHIBIT 11.10 Hypothetical Fund vs. NCRIEF Sector Allocation

	Hypothetical Modeled Assets	Hypothetical Value of Assets ('000)	Percent of Hypothetical Fund	NCREIF
Apartment	20	1,500,000	22%	24%
Industrial	50	1,250,000	18%	15%
Office	30	2,000,000	29%	38%
Retail	35	1,500,000	22%	21%
Hotel	5	650,000	9%	2%
Total	140	6,900,000		

Source: ING Clarion Research & Investment Strategy and NCREIF, as of March 2008.

EXHIBIT 11.11 Hypothetical Fund Sector Allocation and Target Ranges

	Current Allocation	Target Ranges
Apartment	22%	15%–20%
Industrial	18%	15%–20%
Office	29%	30%–40%
Retail	22%	20%–25%
Hotel	9%	5%–10%

According to sector target ranges established by the Hypothetical Fund's potential investment plan, the Hypothetical Fund would be currently overweight in apartment assets (Exhibit 11.11). With the changing market situation, the Hypothetical Fund would want to consider rebalancing its hypothetical portfolio by buying and selling properties, in order to achieve higher hypothetical returns or better hypothetical risk-adjusted returns.

Historically, the hotel sector is the most volatile sector in terms of NCREIF total returns, followed by office, industrial, and apartment. The retail sector is the least volatile, largely due to the prevalence of long-term leases.

Our 2008 forecasts project a sharp drop from double-digit total returns in the past few years to zero or even negative returns in every sector in 2008, followed by a bounce back in 2009, and a recovery in 2010 (Exhibit 11.12).

The hotel sector is the least correlated to other property types, so it can generally be used as a good diversifier for a traditional four-sector-heavy portfolio. The retail sector is in second place in terms of its low correlation with other types, while the office and industrial sectors are the most correlated pair because both are heavily influenced by the macroeconomic climate (Exhibit 11.13).

Looking forward, the Industrial sector is expected to outperform other sectors, generating an average 6.4% annual total return in the next three years. During the same period, the retail and office sectors are expected to generate average annual total returns of 5.0% and 4.0%, respectively, while the hotel sector (3.6%) and apartment sector (3.4%) will likely generate the lowest returns (Exhibit 11.14).

Strategies

In order to measure the impact of rebalancing the hypothetical portfolio, a series of scenarios are analyzed to assess the impact on risk, return, and

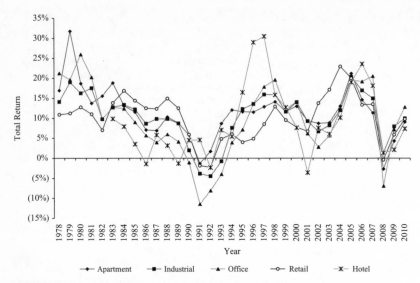

EXHIBIT 11.12   NCREIF Total Return History and Forecasts by Sector
Source: ING Clarion Research & Investment Strategy and NCREIF.

EXHIBIT 11.13   NCREIF Sector Total Return Correlations, 1978–2007

	Apartment	Industrial	Office	Retail	Hotel
Apartment	1.00				
Industrial	0.80	1.00			
Office	0.78	0.94	1.00		
Retail	0.45	0.61	0.54	1.00	
Hotel	0.52	0.61	0.67	0.12	1.00

Source: ING Clarion Research & Investment Strategy and NCREIF.

EXHIBIT 11.14   NCREIF Sector Total Return History and Forecasts

	Expected Return (2008–2010)	Historical Volatility (1978–2007)	Return per Unit Risk	Sharpe Ratio
Apartment	3.4%	6.0%	0.57	(0.09)
Industrial	6.4%	6.1%	1.04	0.39
Office	4.0%	9.1%	0.44	0.00
Retail	5.0%	5.7%	0.88	0.18
Hotel	3.6%	9.2%	0.39	(0.05)

Source: ING Clarion Research & Investment Strategy and NCREIF, as of March 2008.

EXHIBIT 11.15 Sample Hypothetical Efficient Portfolios after Sector Rebalancing

Risk	Return	Sharpe Ratio	Apartment	Industrial	Office	Retail	Hotel
5.87%	4.47%	0.080	22%	18%	29%	22%	9%
5.78%	4.49%	0.085	18%	17%	30%	25%	10%
5.80%	4.54%	0.092	17%	18%	30%	25%	10%
5.82%	4.59%	0.101	15%	20%	30%	25%	10%
5.92%	4.60%	0.101	15%	20%	32%	25%	8%
6.07%	4.61%	0.101	15%	20%	35%	25%	5%

Source: ING Clarion Research and Strategy and NCREIF.

risk-adjusted returns of shifting the sector allocations. A comparison of the current allocation (shaded row) and some select alternatives are shown in Exhibit 11.15.

The scenario analysis suggests potential adjustments to the hypothetical portfolio. Depending upon the Hypothetical Fund's goals, those adjustments could favor increasing total returns, reducing risk, or increasing risk-adjusted returns. For example, given the expectations of underperformance in terms of total returns in the apartment sector, it may be appropriate to decrease the allocation to that sector. In addition, the Hypothetical Fund is already overallocated to that sector, given the hypothetical target allocations. Increasing the allocation in the retail sector to the maximum level suggested by the target allocations, on the other hand, would help improve the overall hypothetical portfolio risk-return profile. Increasing the allocation to the industrial sector would be expected to help to increase the hypothetical portfolio returns. While the hotel allocation is near the top of the target range, an increase may be merited in order to further diversify the hypothetical portfolio, given historically low correlations with other sectors. This would improve the hypothetical risk-adjusted return. Numerous iterations of the scenario analysis may be tested to determine the sector balance that best matches the Hypothetical Fund's priorities.

Based upon this analysis, the Hypothetical Fund could potentially achieve higher hypothetical total returns by shifting allocations among sectors. Exhibit 11.16 compares the current Hypothetical Fund sector allocations (left column) with potential rebalancing options. Total hypothetical expected returns increase with each option to the right of the current allocation. From the risk-adjusted return perspective, the new allocations could move the Hypothetical Fund closer to the theoretical efficient frontier (Exhibit 11.17).

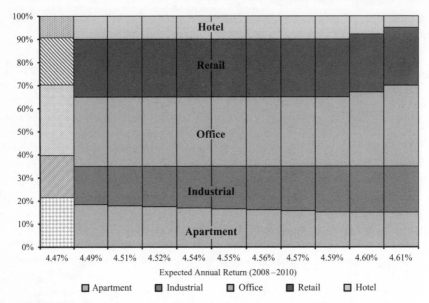

EXHIBIT 11.16 Sample Hypothetical Efficient Portfolio Sector Compositions
The left-hand column represents the sector composition of the current Hypothetical
Fund.
Source: ING Clarion Research & Investment Strategy.

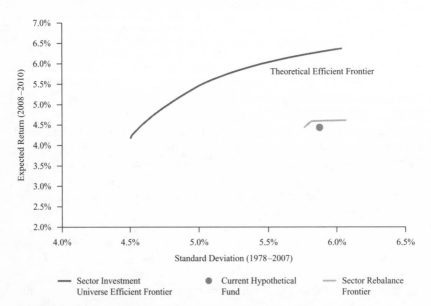

EXHIBIT 11.17 Hypothetical Fund Sector Rebalance Frontier
Source: ING Clarion Research & Investment Strategy.

REGIONAL REBALANCE STRATEGIES

Regional allocations in the Hypothetical Fund were selected at random, for illustrative purposes. Compared to NCREIF, the Hypothetical Fund would be overweighted in the West, while underweighted in the South (Exhibit 11.18). Based upon metro and regional forecasts for the next three years, we expect that the West will likely outperform the nation while the South will underperform. Therefore, the current regional allocation could likely help the Hypothetical Fund achieve higher hypothetical returns than NCREIF. Furthermore, the current allocation would be within the hypothetical target range for each region (Exhibit 11.19).

Regional target ranges are typically established by a fund's business plan. For the Hypothetical Fund, these ranges were developed by considering expected sector returns, historical volatility, and sector correlations, as well as the goal to resemble a core fund comparable to the NCREIF composition (Exhibit 11.18).

Historically, the East is the most volatile region in terms of NCREIF total returns, followed by the West, the South, and the Midwest. In our latest forecasts, a sharp drop from the double-digit total return in the past few years to zero or even negative returns is expected in every region in 2008, followed by a bounce back in 2009, and a recovery in 2010 (Exhibit 11.20).

EXHIBIT 11.18 Hypothetical Fund vs. NCRIEF Regional Allocation

	Modeled Asset	Value of Assets ('000)	Fund	NCREIF
East	29	2,484,000	36%	34%
Midwest	25	828,000	12%	10%
South	36	897,000	13%	21%
West	50	2,691,000	39%	35%
Total	140	6,900,000		

Source: ING Clarion Research & Investment Strategy, NCREIF, as of March 2008.

EXHIBIT 11.19 Hypothetical Fund Regional Allocation and Target Ranges

	Current Allocation	Target Ranges
East	36%	30%–40%
Midwest	12%	10%–20%
South	13%	10%–20%
West	39%	30%–40%

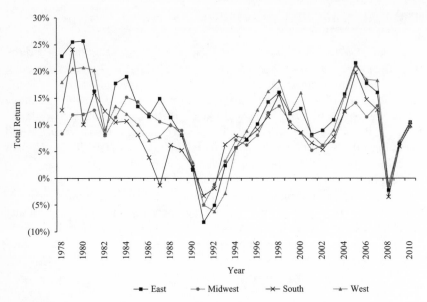

EXHIBIT 11.20 Total Return History and Forecasts by Region
Source: ING Clarion Research & Investment Strategy and NCREIF.

Among regions, the East and West exhibit the highest correlation because both regions are economically active and strongly linked. The South exhibits slightly different behavior vis-à-vis other regions due to its somewhat distinctive demographics, such as retirees, and industries, such as oil (Exhibit 11.21).

Looking forward, we expect the West to outperform all other regions, generating an average 5.3% annual total return in the next three years, followed by the East (4.8%) and the Midwest (4.7%). The South, especially in Florida, will likely be the hardest hit and is expected to return 4.0%, equivalent to the assumed risk-free rate (Exhibit 11.22).

EXHIBIT 11.21 Regional NCREIF Total Return Correlations, 1978–2007

	East	Midwest	South	West
East	1.00			
Midwest	0.86	1.00		
South	0.77	0.68	1.00	
West	0.91	0.82	0.84	1.00

Source: ING Clarion Research & Investment Strategy and NCREIF.

EXHIBIT 11.22 NCREIF Regional Total Return History and Forecasts

	Expected Return (2008–2010)	Historical Volatility (1978–2007)	Return per Unit Risk	Sharpe Ratio
East	4.8%	7.9%	0.60	0.10
Midwest	4.7%	4.7%	1.02	0.16
South	4.0%	6.0%	0.66	(0.01)
West	5.3%	7.4%	0.72	0.17

Source: ING Clarion Research & Investment Strategy and NCREIF, as of March 2008.

Strategies

In order to measure the impact of rebalancing the hypothetical portfolio, a series of scenarios are analyzed to assess the impact on risk, return, and risk-adjusted returns of shifting the regional allocations. A comparison of the current allocation (shaded row) and some select alternatives is shown in Exhibit 11.23.

The scenario analysis suggests potential adjustments to the hypothetical portfolio. Depending upon the Hypothetical Fund's goals, those adjustments could favor increasing total returns, reducing risk, or increasing risk-adjusted returns. For example, the high volatility in the East region suggests a potential reduction in holdings in order to reduce potential risk. The expected underperformance by assets in the South, relative to other regions, suggests reducing investment in that region to help improve expected hypothetical total return performance. Increasing the allocation in the Midwest could help diversify the hypothetical portfolio (lowering risks) given its low historical volatility. For the West, since the hypothetical portfolio would already be approaching its upper target range limit, there would be two options.

EXHIBIT 11.23 Sample Hypothetical Efficient Portfolios after Regional Rebalancing

Risk	Return	Sharpe Ratio	East	Midwest	South	West
6.63%	4.84%	0.127	36%	12%	13%	39%
6.36%	4.85%	0.134	30%	20%	12%	38%
6.37%	4.86%	0.135	30%	20%	12%	38%
6.39%	4.87%	0.136	30%	20%	11%	39%
6.40%	4.88%	0.137	30%	20%	10%	40%
6.76%	4.88%	0.131	40%	10%	10%	40%

Source: ING Clarion Research and Strategy and NCREIF.

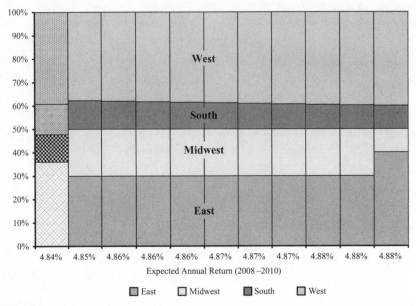

EXHIBIT 11.24   Sample Hypothetical Efficient Portfolio Region Compositions
The first column represents the regional composition of the current
Hypothetical Fund.
Source: ING Clarion Research & Investment Strategy.

Decreasing exposure to the West could likely help lower the potential risk, while increasing could likely help improve the hypothetical total returns.

From the return perspective, the Hypothetical Fund could likely achieve higher returns by allocating differently among the regions. Exhibit 11.24 compares the current Hypothetical Fund sector allocations (left column) with potential rebalancing options. Hypothetical total expected returns increase with each option to the right of the current allocation. From the risk-adjusted return perspective, the new allocations could likely move the Hypothetical Fund closer to the theoretical efficient frontier (Exhibit 11.25).

IDENTIFICATION OF HYPOTHETICAL SALES CANDIDATES

Selling Strategies

Based upon conclusions from the sector and regional analysis, the Portfolio Manager of the Hypothetical Fund could then develop a strategy to accomplish the desired portfolio rebalancing. That strategy should include

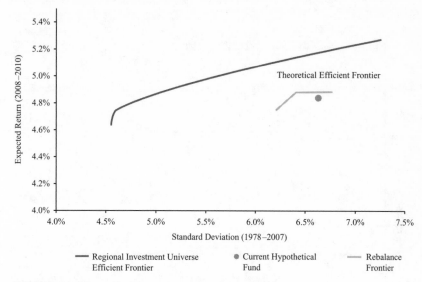

EXHIBIT 11.25 Hypothetical Fund Regional Rebalance Frontier
Source: ING Clarion Research & Investment Strategy.

both identifying targets for future acquisitions and identifying candidates for sale from the hypothetical portfolio. Depending on current market conditions, selling out of existing assets may be a more direct method of moving toward the preferred portfolio allocations.

The selection of hypothetical sales candidates can be based on any of four basic strategies (Exhibit 11.26). In these four strategies, the first three are based on ranks of individual assets, while the fourth is based on the impact of each asset's effect on the portfolio.

When identifying assets for sale, individual assets are assumed to perform the same as the metro average or the return from the beta. In realty, it is not uncommon that the performance of an asset is largely driven by the

EXHIBIT 11.26 Selling Strategies and Considerations

Strategies	Primary Impact
1. Sell assets with the lowest expected returns.	Return
2. Sell assets with the lowest Sharpe ratios.	Return, risk
3. Sell assets with the lowest Sharpe ratios in "Dogs."	Return, risk
4. Sell "Quadrant I" assets that hurt the portfolio.	Return, risk, correlations

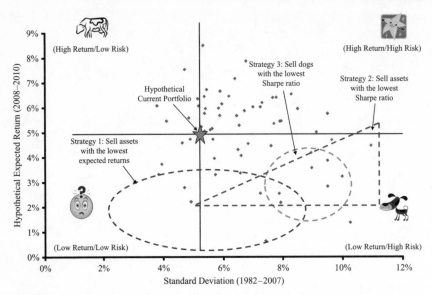

EXHIBIT 11.27 Assets in Dogs-Cows Quadrants
Source: ING Clarion Research & Investment Strategy (adapted from Boston Consulting Group framework).

alpha if, say, a property is located in a prime location of a market, or it was acquired at a handsome discount. Therefore, the assumption used should be considered when implementing the various strategies.[3]

Strategy Formulation Using the Dogs-Cows Matrix

Utilizing the Boston Consulting Group's Growth-Share Matrix[4] "Dogs," "Cows," "Stars," and "Question Marks" are defined in the context of a real estate portfolio (Exhibit 11.27). In this matrix, each dot represents a market where the Hypothetical Fund would currently have investments. The X-axis is the standard deviation of historical annual market total returns from 1982 to 2007, the proxy of market risks, and the Y-axis is the three-year projected annual market total returns from 2008 to 2010. The star at

---

[3]For purposes of this hypothetical analysis, the details of specific market selections for sales candidates within each sector is not provided. However, any complete analysis would include recommendations for dispositions by market. That analysis would be based upon forecast expected returns, risk, and market correlations.

[4]The Growth-Share Matrix analyzes business units or product lines by considering their relative market shares and market growth rates.

the center reflects the current relationship between risk and return of the hypothetical portfolio.[5]

- *Dogs.* Those markets with high historical volatilities but low expected returns. These markets are risky. The expected returns may not compensate that risk. Therefore, rational investors should avoid these markets unless there are great deals that can generate abnormal alpha returns.
- *Cows.* Those markets with low historical volatilities but high expected returns. Institutional investors normally favor this type of market. For new entrants, however, the cost of entry, especially in a low-cap rate environment, may be too high.
- *Stars.* Those markets that have both high historical volatilities and high expected returns. These markets are generally cyclical and are sensitive to overall economic cycles.
- *Question marks.* Markets with low historical volatilities as well as low expected returns. Markets of this type may be lackluster but could be good diversifiers by lowering risk to the overall portfolio.

The Four-Quadrant Analysis

As a contrast to the quadrants used in the Dogs-Cows matrix that map individual assets, the quadrants used in the Four-Quadrant Analysis measure the expected returns and the risks of portfolios by removing one asset at a time (Exhibit 11.28).

Quadrant I. Removing a "Quadrant I" asset decreases the volatility of the hypothetical portfolio and increases the hypothetical expected return. These assets hurt the overall performance of the portfolio and should be sold to improve the portfolio performance.

Quadrant II. Removing a "Quadrant II" asset will increase the hypothetical portfolio risk; retaining the asset lowers the hypothetical risk.

Quadrant III. Removing a "Quadrant III" asset will decrease the hypothetical portfolio's expected return; retaining the asset raises the hypothetical portfolio return.

---

[5]One important shift is necessary when applying the original BCG Matrix to a real estate application. In the original approach, a dot can shift into one of two neighboring quadrants when the market situation changes. In the context of real estate markets, each dot can only shift between the high expected return quadrant and the low expected return quadrant (between "Cows" and "Question Marks," or between "Dogs" and "Stars"). This is because the historical volatility has already been determined by its 30-year history.

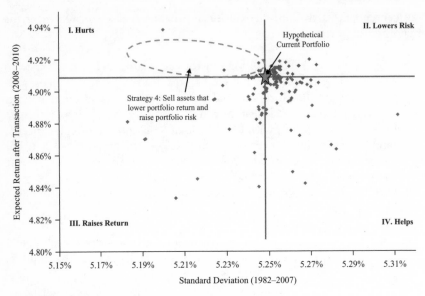

EXHIBIT 11.28 Hypothetical Portfolio Positions
Source: ING Clarion Research & Investment Strategy.

> *Quadrant IV.* Removing a "Quadrant IV" increases the hypothetical
> portfolio risk and lowers the hypothetical expected return. Selling
> these assets will diminish the portfolio's hypothetical performance.

Sales Strategy Conclusions

Selling those assets in underperforming markets under various strategies
could improve hypothetical portfolio returns and risk-adjusted returns for
the Hypothetical Fund (Exhibit 11.29). Beyond the performance objective,
there would be other benefits of selling hypothetical assets—raising cash for
distributions or for more attractive investment opportunities, lowering the
leverage ratio and divesting unwanted assets. Therefore, selling hypothetical
assets in selected markets could add value to the overall hypothetical portfolio management strategy.

  Among the four strategies presented above, only the fourth strategy—
selling Quadrant I assets—is structured from the portfolio perspective; that
is, selling assets that lower the portfolio return while increasing the potential risks. Therefore, in the efficient frontier, only strategy IV could help
improve the hypothetical portfolio in terms of both return and risk to move
the hypothetical portfolio closer to the theoretical frontier (Exhibit 11.30).

EXHIBIT 11.29 Hypothetical Portfolio Performance Summary after Sales

	Number of Assets Sold	Amount Sold (millions)	Expected Return[a]	Standard Deviation	Return per Unit Risk	Sharpe Ratio
Hypothetical Fund			4.92%	5.25%	0.937	0.175
NCREIF Index			4.62%	6.34%	0.729	0.098
1. Sell low return	19	$1,087	4.96%	5.35%	0.927	0.179
2. Sell low Sharpe ratio	26	$1,093	4.96%	5.40%	0.919	0.178
3. Sell low dogs	13	$899	4.94%	5.27%	0.937	0.178
4. Sell Quadrant I	3	$187	4.94%	5.19%	0.952	0.181

[a]Assume 2% transaction costs.
Source: ING Clarion Research & Investment Strategy.

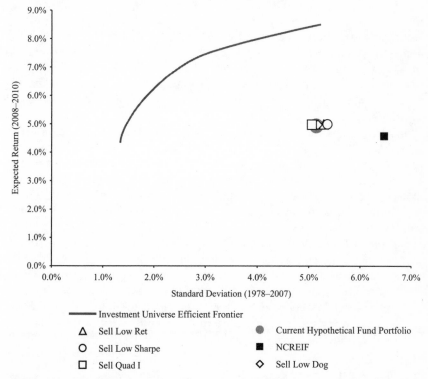

EXHIBIT 11.30 Hypothetical Portfolio Positions after Sales of Candidates
Source: ING Clarion Research & Investment Strategy, as of March 2008.

In contrast, the first three strategies consider only selling candidacy at the asset level. Selling a low performer would not necessarily help the entire hypothetical portfolio because the sold asset could have been a good diversifier, even though, as a single asset, it would not be as competitive as others. Therefore, the suggested portfolios created by the first three selling strategies would not move the hypothetical portfolio toward the theoretical efficient frontier. From the portfolio timing perspective, it would be suggested that Quadrant I assets be sold first.

ACQUIRING $1 BILLION OF NEW INVESTMENTS

In addition to potential sales, the Hypothetical Fund should also consider targeted acquisitions to improve performance, in terms of hypothetical total and risk-adjusted returns. In this scenario, the Hypothetical Fund would have $1 billion of new capital to invest over a period of 12 months.

Adding constraints to the amount of investment in a single market results in a more realistic analysis because no single market is liquid enough or sufficiently large enough to quickly absorb all the capital. The hypothetical analysis assumes that each market cannot absorb more than $100 million of additional investments during the one-year investment period. We also assume that there will be no increase in the apartment sector because the current weight is already above the upper limit of the target allocation range for that sector.

Our analysis identified three scenarios, all of which would improve hypothetical total returns while reducing risk. In all three scenarios, the selection of individual markets for each sector's investment is critical. The market analysis should consider total expected returns, market volatility, and correlations between individual markets and the sector as a whole. Based upon this analysis, target metro areas may be selected.[6]

> *Scenario I.* In order to achieve an increase in portfolio returns by 10 bps, it is suggested that $100 million would be invested in selected office markets, $296 million would be invested in selected retail markets, and the remaining $604 million would be invested in selected industrial markets. Hypothetical risk could be reduced by 44 bps, thereby increasing the hypothetical return per unit of risk by 11% and the hypothetical Sharpe Ratio by 20%.

---

[6]For purposes of this hypothetical analysis, the details of specific market selections within each sector are not provided. However, as part of any complete analysis the acquisition recommendations would include allocations to specific markets based on expected returns, risk, and market correlations.

Scenario II. To increase the hypothetical portfolio returns by 20 bps, it is suggested that an investment of $222 million would be made in selected retail markets, with the remaining $778 million invested in selected industrial markets. Hypothetical risk would be reduced by 37 bps, increasing the hypothetical return per unit of risk by 12% and the hypothetical Sharpe Ratio by 31%.

Scenario III. To maximize the expected returns, $200 million should be allocated to selected retail markets, and the remaining $800 million should be invested in selected industrial markets. Hypothetical returns could be boosted by 33 bps, hypothetical risk could be decreased by approximately 7 bps, and hypothetical return per unit of risk and the hypothetical Sharpe Ratio could be increase by 8% and 38%, respectively.

In addition to increasing the hypothetical portfolio return by 10, 20, and 33 bps under the three scenarios, the new acquisitions could also help lower the hypothetical portfolio risks by selecting markets with low correlations to those in which the Hypothetical Fund could already have investments. Hence, the hypothetical risk-adjusted returns, measured by return per unit risk and the Sharpe Ratio, could also make noticeable improvements (Exhibit 11.31).

By investing additional money into selected markets, the new hypothetical portfolio could find a position on the constrained incremental frontier,

EXHIBIT 11.31 Hypothetical Portfolio Performance Summary after New Acquisitions

	Number of Assets Sold	Amount Sold (millions)	Expected Return[a]	Standard Deviation	Return per Unit Risk	Sharpe Ratio
Hypothetical Fund			4.92%	5.25%	0.94	0.18
NCREIF Index			4.62%	6.34%	0.73	0.10
1. Increase Return by 10 bps	10	$1,000	5.02%	4.81%	1.04	0.21
2. Increase Return by 20 bps	11	$1,000	5.12%	4.88%	1.05	0.23
3. Maximize Return (33 bps)	10	$1,000	5.25%	5.18%	1.01	0.24

[a] Assume 2% transaction costs.

Source: ING Clarion Research & Investment Strategy and PPR.

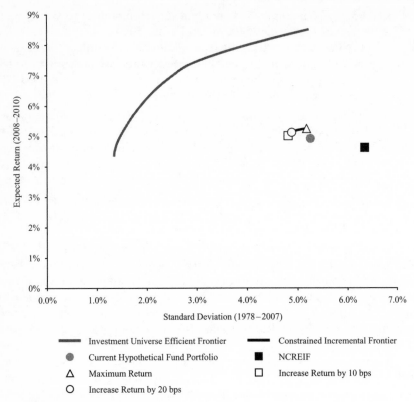

EXHIBIT 11.32   Hypothetical Portfolio Positions after New Investments
[a]Assume 2% transaction costs.
Source: ING Clarion Research & Investment Strategy.

which would shift left and up to be closer to the theoretical efficient frontier
than the current hypothetical portfolio (Exhibit 11.32).

CONCLUSIONS

- The Hypothetical Fund would be expected to outperform the NCREIF
  Index on all metrics in the next three years.
- Rebalancing at sector or regional levels could improve the Hypothetical Fund portfolio by increasing hypothetical expected returns while
  lowering the hypothetical potential risk.
- By selling selected hypothetical assets, the Hypothetical Fund portfolio could slightly improve its hypothetical expected return while

maintaining a hypothetical risk-adjusted return similar to the current Hypothetical Fund portfolio.

- By selectively adding $1 billion in additional investments with constraints, the Hypothetical Fund could likely target a range of risk and return opportunities.

Important Information: Hypothetical Disclosure

The discussion in this chapter is based in part on hypothetical information using the following data sources and assumptions:

- NCREIF market yield, capital growth, and total return historic data as of March 2008 at the national, regional, metro, and sector levels.
- Historic market data including construction, absorption, vacancy, rent levels, and rent growth from Torto Wheaton Research (TWR), Property & Portfolio Research (PPR), and REIS, as of 2007 Q4.
- Proprietary market fundamental forecasts, including construction, absorption, vacancy, and rent growth, prepared by ING Clarion Research & Investment Strategy as of March 2008. Forecasts were based on 2007Q4 data from TWR, PPR, REIS, and Economy.com.
- Demographic, employment, and economic historical data and forecasts from Economy.com as of March 2008.
- Transaction costs of 2% for all disposition and acquisition analysis.
- For acquisitions analysis, a maximum of $100 million allocation to any individual metro area during the 12-month acquisition period.

No representation is being made that any actual investment activity will or is likely to achieve results comparable to those shown, to make any profit at all, or to be able to avoid incurring substantial losses. In fact, there can be significant differences between hypothetical performance results and the actual results subsequently achieved by any particular investment strategy. The actual performance may differ significantly from the hypothetical results shown based, among other things, on: (1) the ability to obtain terms similar to the assumptions used to generate the hypothetical performance; (2) the size and composition of any given real estate portfolio, including asset allocation across property types, regions and markets; and (3) differing market, regulatory, economic, and political conditions. Given the unique economic environment at present, results are not likely to be the same under current market conditions. No representation or warranty is made as to the reasonableness of the assumptions made or that all assumptions used in achieving the returns have been stated or fully considered.

The results shown are provided for illustration purposes only. They have inherent limitations because they are not based on actual transactions or an actual real estate portfolio, but are based on the historical returns of the benchmark indexes and hypothetical selected investments, as well as various assumptions of past and future events. The results do not represent, and are not necessarily indicative of, the results that may be achieved in the future; actual returns may vary significantly. In addition, the historical returns used as a basis for this analysis are based on information gathered by ING Clarion Partners or from third-party sources, and have not been independently verified.

There can be no assurance that an investor's performance would have been the same as the results shown had the hypothetical fund existed in earlier or later periods. No independent party has audited the hypothetical performance, nor has any independent party undertaken to confirm that they reflect the trading method under the assumptions or conditions specified hereafter.

Hypothetical or simulated performance results have certain inherent limitations. Unlike an actual performance record, simulated results do not represent actual transactions or performance. Simulated portfolio analyses in general are also subject to the fact that they are designed with the benefit of hindsight. Also, since the hypothetical transactions have not actually been conducted, the results may have under- or overcompensated for the impact of various market factors, including but not limited to the availability of appropriate properties for acquisition, the availability of buyers for "for sale" properties, and the availability of financing necessary to complete any such transactions. In addition, hypothetical transactions do not involve financial risk. There are numerous other factors related to the economy or markets in general or to the implementation of any specific strategy that cannot be fully accounted for in the preparation of hypothetical performance results, all of which can adversely affect results.

Benchmark Disclosure

The NCREIF Property Index (NPI or NCREIF Index) is used as a benchmark for measuring the performance of private equity real estate portfolios. NCREIF describes the NPI as:

> ... *a quarterly time series composite total rate of return measure of investment performance of a very large pool of individual commercial real estate properties acquired in the private market for investment purposes only. All properties in the NPI have been acquired,*

at least in part, on behalf of tax-exempt institutional investors—the great majority being pension funds. As such, all properties are held in a fiduciary environment.[7]

The benchmark is a broad-based index used for comparative purposes only and has been selected as the most widely used and well-known measure of private equity real estate performance. Comparisons to benchmarks have limitations because benchmarks have volatility and other material characteristics that may differ from the Hypothetical Fund. For example, investments made for a fund may differ significantly in terms of asset allocation across sectors and markets from the benchmark. Accordingly, investment results and volatility of the Hypothetical Fund may differ from those of the benchmark. Also, the index noted in this chapter is unmanaged, is not available for direct investment, and is not subject to management fees or other types of expenses that the Hypothetical Fund may incur. Readers should carefully consider these limitations and differences when evaluating the comparative benchmark data performance.

---

[7]NCREIF, "Frequently Asked Questions About NCREIF and the NCREIF National Property Index (NPI)," p. 7; http://www.ncreif.org/pdf/Users_Guide_to_NPI.pdf (accessed June 2008).

CHAPTER 12

Derivatives in Private Equity Real Estate

Jeff Organisciak, Tim Wang, and David Lynn
Summer 2008[1]

A liquid property derivatives market would allow real estate investors to use new financial tools to manage real estate portfolios. Strategies for using property derivatives could add additional value to client portfolios and protect or enhance the returns of real estate funds. Though the market in the United States is nascent, rapid growth in the United Kingdom suggests that the concept has significant potential. While the widespread use of derivatives may be premature, especially given turmoil in the economy and capital markets, it is important to understand the strategic opportunities and risks that property derivatives present.

- Derivatives are not a completely novel concept in real estate investment. In fact, they are already widely used in the form of forward contracts, options on land, and interest rate swaps.
- The total return swap is the most prevalent structure for property derivatives. It involves one party paying the total return of an asset or index to another in exchange for a fixed- or floating-rate payment. Property derivatives are based off of indexes that measure changes in real estate prices (residential or commercial).
- The U.S. property derivatives market has potential for significant growth. Currently, the global volume of the property derivatives market is about $20 billion of outstanding notional, a very small amount of

---

[1]This paper was originally produced in summer 2008. The data, opinions, and forecasts have not been updated for book publication.

volume relative to established derivatives markets of other asset classes. The UK is by far the largest market for property derivatives, with 85% of total global volume.

- The risks of property derivatives are counterparty risk, basis risk, liquidity risk, and interest rate risk. Understanding and quantifying these risks is crucial for executing a derivative transaction successfully.

Three useful strategies for applying property derivatives to real estate investment are hedging ("portfolio insurance"), asset allocation and rebalancing, and speculation:

1. Hedging a commercial real estate portfolio using property derivatives involves either taking a short position on a real estate index using a total return swap, or buying a put option on an index. This strategy is similar to portfolio insurance and protects the portfolio from risks to the downside.
2. Asset allocation and rebalancing is a strategy that allows portfolio managers to execute strategic or tactical asset allocation decisions in a faster and more cost-efficient way than has ever been possible.
3. Speculation is a strategy that leverages the forward looking views and forecasts of a firm to take long or short positions on property derivatives.

BACKGROUND

A *derivative* is "a financial instrument whose value depends on the values of other, more basic, underlying variables."[2] The underlying variable is often a traded asset, such as a stock or commodity, *but it can also be an index*. Derivatives are generally used as tools for isolating and pricing financial risks involved with holding the underlying variable.

Current Use of Derivatives in Real Estate Investment

The most common types of derivatives are *forwards, futures, options*, and *swaps*. These tools are commonly used by real estate investors.

- A *forward contract* is an agreement to buy or sell an asset at a certain future time for a certain price. This type of derivative contract is applied in direct real estate investment as a forward purchase agreement.

---

[2]John C. Hull, *Options, Futures and Other Derivatives*, (Upper Saddle River, NJ: Prentice Hall, 2006), 1.

- A *futures contract* is similar to a forward, but deal terms are highly standardized and contracts are traded on exchanges. These are not commonly used in private real estate investment.
- An *option contract* gives the holder the right, but not the obligation, to buy or sell a specific quantity of an underlying asset at a specified price at some point in the future. This form is widely used in land investment by home builders and land investors.
- A *swap* is a contract whereby two parties agree to exchange cash flows according to a specified procedure, with no cash exchanged up front. Swap contracts are often used in real estate financing to hedge interest rate risk.

Benefits of Property Derivatives

Property derivatives differ from the types just listed in that they are based on composite real estate market performance as measured by indexes. Because of this, they offer a synthetic means to invest in the private real estate market. The synthetic nature of the investment has several attractive characteristics that may benefit real estate investors.

- *Quick execution.* Sourcing and executing private real estate investments is a time-consuming process. Property derivatives offer quick execution, which could benefit investors by allowing them to act on new information, strategies, or allocation preferences immediately.
- *Low transaction costs.* Round-trip transaction costs on direct investment are approximately 6–8% in the UK, and 3–5% in the United States. Derivatives costs would be lower and could therefore help to improve returns.
- *Short positions.* Taking a short position on the private real estate market has generally not been possible. Property derivatives enable the use of strategic hedging, which can protect the value of portfolios.
- *Flexible.* The size, length, and structure of property derivatives contracts can be tailored to meet individual needs. This gives investors flexibility to meet specific investment objectives and more easily achieve asset allocation targets.
- *Diversified.* Because property indexes measure aggregate market performance, investment in property derivatives does not include property or site-specific risks.

Property Derivatives and Mechanics

The most prevalent property derivative structure is the total return swap. A total return swap involves one party paying the total return of an asset or

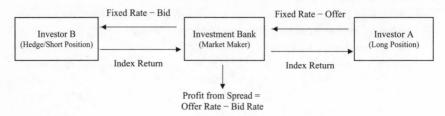

EXHIBIT 12.1 Over-the-Counter Swap Transaction
Source: ING Clarion Research & Investment Strategy.

index to another in exchange for a fixed- or floating-rate payment. The total return swap is the standard trading instrument in the European markets, where it is based on the International Property Databank (IPD) Index. In the United States, most swaps are based on the NCREIF Property Index (NPI), but they can also be based on other indexes.

Swap contracts are often customized to fit the needs of particular investors, and therefore they are traded over-the-counter (directly negotiated with a market maker or counterparty) (Exhibit 12.1). This is in contrast to options and futures, which are generally traded on exchanges, because the contracts are highly standardized.

Mechanics of the Total Return Swap

Motivation Investor A believes that the real estate index will outperform the market's expectations and, therefore, wants to take a long position. Investor B believes that the index will under perform expectations and, therefore, wants to take a short position (either as a hedge on underlying real estate holdings or as a speculative play).

Pricing An investment bank (or other market maker) brings the two sides together by setting a price:

- Investor A (long position) agrees to pay a fixed percentage rate (offer) of a referenced notional principal amount (or receive a rate if the quoted rates are negative) in exchange for a cash flow that is the index total return percentage of the notional amount.
- Investor B (short position/hedge) agrees to pay the index total return percentage in exchange for the fixed rate (bid).

Result Investor B has locked in a fixed rate of return and is protected from the market performing below expectations in exchange for any potential upside. Investor A gains exposure to future market movements; if the market performs below expectations, he will lose money, but if the market performs above expectations, he will make money. The market maker profits from a spread between the bid and offer rates. Essentially, Investor A is selling return insurance by participating in the upside, while Investor B is buying return insurance by giving up the upside.

CURRENT STATE OF THE DERIVATIVES MARKET

Property Derivatives in the Global Market

The global commercial property derivatives market is still nascent, with about $20 billion of outstanding notional (a small fraction of total global derivative volume for all asset classes). The vast majority of activity has been in the UK, as this market constitutes about 85% of global volume. France has the next largest market, with approximately $1.7 billion outstanding notional. Germany accounts for over $750 million in outstanding notional.[3] The United States is estimated to have only between $500 and $600 million notional outstanding, mainly based on the NPI (Exhibit 12.2). However, this volume has been building over the past two to three years.

Outlook for the Commercial Property Derivatives Market

There is potential for considerable growth in the property derivatives market. Exhibit 12.3 shows the rapid growth that the UK market has experienced over the past few years. Professors David Geltner (MIT) and Jeffrey Fisher (Indiana University) estimate that the U.S. market could develop to $120 to $150 billion per year in trading volume if it follows a similar trend.[4]

The UK property derivatives market has grown much faster than the U.S. market for two major reasons:

1. *Superior index.* The IPD index in the UK has greater coverage of real estate assets and is calculated with a more transparent methodology. This boosts investor confidence in the index as an accurate measure of real estate values.

---

[3] Activity in Europe is based on IPD (Investment Property Databank) indexes.

[4] David Geltner and Jeffery Fisher, "Pricing and Index Considerations in Commercial Real Estate Derivatives," *Journal of Portfolio Management*, Special Real Estate Issue (2007), 99–118.

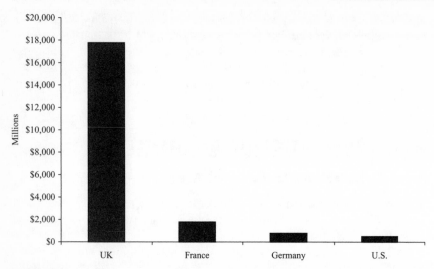

EXHIBIT 12.2   Total Outstanding Notional for Commercial Property Derivatives
As of Q1 2008; 1.96 USD = 1 GBP.
Source: ING Clarion Research & Investment Strategy and Investment Property
Databank.

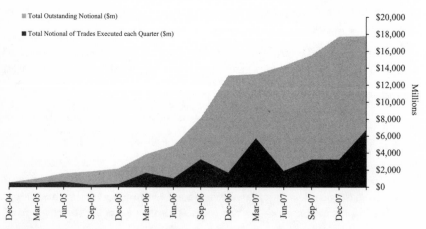

EXHIBIT 12.3   Growth of UK Property Derivatives Market
As of Q1 2008; 1.96 USD = 1 GBP.
Source: ING Clarion Research & Investment Strategy, Investment Property Data-
bank.

2. *Higher transaction costs.* Transaction costs for private real estate investment are higher in the UK due to the stamp tax, which makes property derivatives relatively more attractive.

Our survey of internal portfolio managers suggests that investors believe the U.S. property derivatives market will take four years or more to develop. All participants responded positively about the benefits of property derivatives just listed, though issues such as liquidity, pricing, and potential negative perception by investors were revealed to be impediments to market growth.

Current Pricing in the U.S. Swaps Market

Exhibit 12.4 shows the current price levels for NPI total return swaps by sector. The price levels are predominantly negative, indicating that the market has a bearish view on the future performance of the NPI.

Exhibit 12.5 shows the implied NPI market expectations for each year over the next five years. The market makers assume that the income component of the index will be 6.0% each year; as a result, the implied capital appreciation returns are negative through 2010.

Indexes and Market Players

A number of indexes have been developed to measure real estate values. While no index is perfect, each handles the challenges of measuring commercial real estate values differently. These indexes are in various stages

EXHIBIT 12.4 NPI Market Total Return Swap Pricing Sheet

Sector	Expiration	Bid	Offer
All Property	Dec 08	− 3.75%	− 2.00%
All Property	Dec 09	− 3.50%	− 2.00%
All Property	Dec 10	− 2.25%	− 0.75%
All Property	Dec 11	0.00%	1.50%
Apartment	Dec 10	− 3.50%	− 1.50%
Industrial	Dec 10	− 3.00%	− 1.00%
Office	Dec 10	− 3.50%	− 1.50%
Retail	Dec 10	− 4.00%	− 2.50%

Effective date for all markets is 12/31/07.
Source: Merrill Lynch, July 2008.

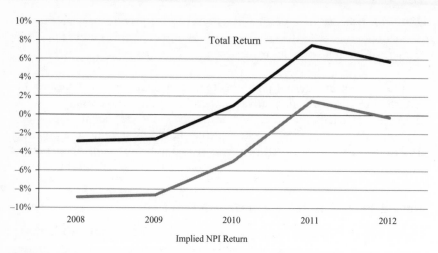

EXHIBIT 12.5 Implied NPI Return per Year (forward curve)
Source: ING Clarion Research & Investment Strategy and Merrill Lynch, July 2008.

of coming to the market for use in derivatives trading. They are the NPI, the Moody's/REAL Commercial Property Price Index (CPPI), the S&P/GRA Commercial Real Estate Index, the REXX Index, and the HQuant Hotels Index. For a comparison of the different indexes available, see Appendix D.

The most active players in the U.S. property derivatives market have generally been investment banks and interdealer brokers. The product is usually seen as an extension of the commercial mortgage-backed securities (CMBS) or commodities trading desk of the bank, and most personnel work on property derivatives part-time, along with their other duties. Bank management seems to view investment in the property derivatives market as a strategic option for the firm. After witnessing the success in European markets, they are leveraging their current employees at a relatively low expense to lay the groundwork for growth in the market, so that they can capitalize on it if it occurs. Banks most active in the U.S. market are Merrill Lynch and Morgan Stanley, though Goldman Sachs, UBS, Barclays, Bank of America, and Credit Suisse are involved to varying degrees. Interdealer brokers involved in the market include CBRE Melody/GFI Group, ICAP, and Vyapar Partners.

RISKS

The risks of trading in property derivatives are common to many derivative products and are magnified because the product is new and illiquid.

Liquidity Risk

Lack of market liquidity could seriously constrain a market participant's ability to sell a position at a fair value. This is especially true because there may only be one bank active in making a market for these products, if any.

Due to the low liquidity of the property derivatives market, the price discovery mechanism may not function reliably. This could push market pricing to levels inconsistent with property market fundamentals or hypothetical swap market equilibrium pricing.

Basis Risk

Type 1 basis risk is the risk that the value of a financial instrument does not move in line with the underlying exposure.

For a hedging strategy to be effective there should be a high correlation between the underlying exposure (e.g., a real estate portfolio) and the hedging instrument (contract based on a real estate index). The hedge is only effective if these move together closely.

Type 2 takes place when each property index attempts to derive theoretical value and price changes in real estate markets. Because there are methodological problems with every available index, there is the risk that the value changes measured by the index are different from the actual price changes in the real estate market. It is important to understand the idiosyncrasies of each index to know how they relate to your underlying exposure.

Counterparty Risk

Counterparty risk is the risk that the counterparty to a trade will not make the expected payments. Exchange-traded markets eliminate virtually all counterparty risk by requiring daily cash settlements.

Interest Rate Risk

Market prices of property derivatives are ultimately based upon interest rates—specifically LIBOR (London Interbank Offered Rate). Movements in interest rates will affect swap prices. Unless interest rate risk is hedged away, a swap contract contains an embedded bet on the future direction of interest rates.

STRATEGIC APPLICATIONS TO REAL ESTATE INVESTMENT

There are a variety of strategies for implementing property derivatives into real estate investment. While using property derivatives in investment does not inherently increase risk, the novelty of the concept may not make it appropriate for all investment styles. Exhibit 12.6 summarizes the strategies that may be appropriate for each real estate investment style.

Hedging as a Form of Portfolio Insurance

Hedging the capital values of portfolios using property derivatives could mitigate risks to the downside. There are two potential methods for hedging a real estate portfolio:

1. *Short real estate capital appreciation index (NPI, Moody's/REAL, SPCREX) through a swap on the index.* It would be possible to execute this strategy today given the products available in the market, but using the NPI would be the most likely choice. An example of a hedging strategy is shown in Exhibit 12.7. This strategy protects the downside risks, but gives up any upside. It is therefore not an ideal solution.
2. *Buy put options on a real estate capital index.* This strategy would protect the portfolio's downside while maintaining the upside. This would be an ideal strategy, but given current market liquidity is not practical.

One of the main problems with a hedging strategy in the current stage of the market's development is that the cost of the hedge may be prohibitive.

EXHIBIT 12.6 Derivatives Strategies by Investment Style

Investment Style	Strategy
Core	Hedging
	Asset allocation and rebalancing
	Index-linked structured note
Value-add	Hedging
	Asset allocation and rebalancing
Opportunistic	Speculation (long or short positions)
	Hedging
	Asset allocation and rebalancing

Source: ING Clarion Research & Investment Strategy.

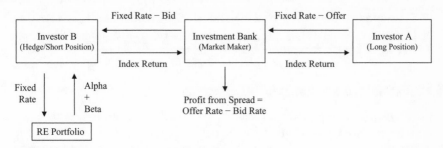

EXHIBIT 12.7   Portfolio Hedging Transaction with Swaps
Source: ING Clarion Research & Investment Strategy.

Exhibit 12.8 shows the downside protection that the hedge offers if the index falls below negative 5% total return. A portfolio initially worth $100 million is protected from falling below $95 million, but if the index return is greater than zero the hedge will have cost the portfolio approximately $7 million of upside. This cost is prohibitive to this strategy being implemented given future expectations about NPI performance.

Another problem with hedging at the portfolio level is the basis risk of the index. According to FAS 133, correlation tests must be met to qualify as an effective hedge; the adjusted R^2 (a measure of correlation) of the index should generally be above 0.80 compared with the asset hedged. For example, to hedge a portfolio of Boston central business district (CBD) office, the closest index available for hedging would be the NPI U.S. Office subindex. The adjusted R^2 for Boston CBD is 0.57 compared to the NPI U.S.

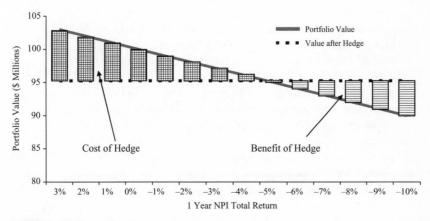

EXHIBIT 12.8   Hedge Cost
Source: ING Clarion Research & Investment Strategy.

Office subindex, the closest tradable index.[5] This would not be an effective hedge. Due to limitations on granularity of real estate indexes, hedging would work best at the national, sector, or regional level.

Allocation and Rebalancing

Inefficiencies in the private real estate market make strategic asset allocation difficult to execute in a timely manner. Property derivatives offer efficient access to real estate market exposure, which can facilitate more efficient portfolio management strategies, such as:

- *Diversification.* Diversify holdings regionally, internationally, or by asset class. Assembling a diversified real estate portfolio is a very difficult, expensive, and time-consuming process. An index offers diversification that is much faster and easier than direct investment, because the index tracks a large number of properties. Also, index exposure can be purchased in small sizes, where a diversified real property portfolio is inherently large.
  - A diversification strategy would be most appropriate for smaller portfolios that are heavily weighted in a few regions or sectors due to their small size.
  - Accomplished by going long on commercial property index with a total return swap, buying futures, or buying options.
- *Asset allocation.* Gain short-term access to specific asset classes, regions, or markets based on macrolevel outlook. Portfolio managers who wish to make tactical investment decisions could use property derivatives to execute these strategies quickly and with minimal costs. Also, it would be useful for gaining access to specific regions, property types, or markets when acquisition of quality assets in the real property market is difficult. Derivatives could be implemented and unwound as investments in the real property market are acquired. The strategy would also be appropriate for disposition, as exposure to markets or asset classes can be reduced without having to sell a trophy building.
  - This strategy would be appropriate for all funds regardless of size or scope.
  - Accomplished by going long or short on commercial property index with a total return swap.

---

[5]S. Naylor and A. Mansour, *U.S. Private Equity Real Estate Derivatives: Is Now the Time?* (San Francisco: RREEF Research, December 2007).

- *Portfolio rebalancing.* Adjust portfolio weights by sector or asset class to maximize risk-adjusted returns. Based on portfolio analytics, recommendations can be made on adjustments between sectors or regions to move the portfolio closer to its efficient frontier.
  - This strategy would be most appropriate for large diversified portfolios.
  - Accomplished by going long or short on a commercial property index, or swapping between two regional or sector specific indexes, using total return swaps.

Hedging for Development Projects

Investment in development projects is a high-risk strategy, with standard investment horizons of three to five years. Adverse changes in market pricing over the investment horizon can be extremely detrimental to the project's return. Because some development projects have high return expectations, it may be worth the cost of hedging to lock in a certain rate of return. Commercial and residential property derivatives may be helpful in hedging these risks. Each development strategy has a different potential hedging tool:

- *Land, condominiums.* A major variable in these investments is the price of residential housing; therefore, it may be possible to hedge these investments with residential property derivatives (see Case Study 3 in this chapter).
- *Apartment, industrial, office.* It may be possible to lock in an exit cap rate by using price indexes that follow these sector subtypes.
- *Hotel.* The HQuant hotel index tracks average daily rate (ADR), and could potentially be used to hedge hotel development projects.

Speculation

Property derivatives markets enable investors to take speculative long or short positions on real estate indexes. A speculative strategy for investing in property derivatives should include both a thorough underwriting process of the proposed investment as well as a clearly defined exit strategy.

When considering property derivatives for potential investment purposes, there are a number of factors to consider, including: market liquidity, notional size, contract length, expected returns, custom structures, and market sentiment. Each of these factors is a variable that alters the risk profile of the swap contract.

The expected return of a derivative transaction is a function of the market pricing and the expected return of the index. The expected index returns should be based on forecasts considering both property market fundamentals as well as index specific characteristics, such as a lag. An example of an econometric forecast model for the NPI is included in Appendix E. A model calculating the future cash flows and returns based on future expectations of the index is included later in this chapter in Exhibit 12.10.

An exit strategy should be defined before entering into a derivatives investment.

- Due to the general lack of liquidity for these products, any investment should be underwritten as a hold until contract expiration. Selling before this could entail a significant discount depending on market liquidity.
- After the contract is purchased, the value of the remaining cash flows will fluctuate as future expectations and swap market pricing change. At some point, it may be profitable to unwind the contract and lock in the profits before the expiration of the contract. An exit strategy should be determined in advance that outlines the returns expectations of the investment; and the strategy should be to sell (unwind) should market pricing reach a level that would generate the initially underwritten returns.

Index-Linked Structured Note

Index-linked notes pay interest based on the performance of an index, such as the S&P 500 Index. This structure offers investors a way to participate in equity market returns, while ensuring that the principal is returned at maturity. The structured note is similar to a bond. It requires the entire notional amount to be paid up front and pays a coupon rate determined by pricing in derivative markets. The principal is returned at the expiration of the note.

This structure can also be applied to a real estate index. Currently, notes linked to the NPI are available in amounts up to $100 million and pay a yearly coupon rate of NPI plus 300–500 basis points for two years.

Case Study 1: Hypothetical Portfolio Hedge

An investor with a hypothetical portfolio highly correlated to the NPI decided to hedge the portfolio by taking the short side of an NPI capital return swap in June 2007. At that time, the midpoint pricing to short the NPI capital return was 2.5% per year.

During third and fourth quarters of 2007, the hypothetical swap resulted in negative net cash flow, but the cash flow turned positive in the first quarter of 2008 (Exhibit 12.9). Midpoint pricing for the NPI capital return

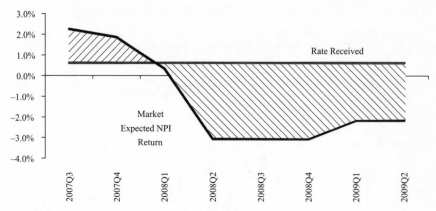

EXHIBIT 12.9 NPI Capital Swap Short Position
Source: ING Clarion Research & Investment Strategy.

declined from 2.5% in June 2007 to −8.5% in July 2008. Because of this, the hypothetical future cash flows became much more valuable, with a net present value of about $1.6 million (Exhibit 12.10). The investor can sell his position for a profit, unwind the position to lock in a fixed rate of return for the remainder of the contract, or hold the contract until expiration.

The proceeds of the hypothetical hedge transaction could go toward paying investor redemptions, protecting a promote threshold, or supporting fund returns.

Case Study 2: Fund Rebalancing

Property derivatives can potentially enable portfolio managers to execute rebalancing strategies more quickly. This case study discusses a hypothetical allocation rebalancing strategy using a total return swap of the apartment sector for exposure to the retail sector.

As part of a tactical strategy, a hypothetical diversified private equity real estate fund (the Fund) is weighted above the target allocation range for the apartment sector and at the minimum target range for the retail sector (Exhibit 12.11). If the portfolio manager of the Fund decided to re-turn allocations to midtarget levels, a total return swap could accomplish the rebalancing quickly. Disposition of assets may not be ideal, due to mar-ket conditions (e.g., low liquidity, unable to sell for an acceptable price), contractual obligations with deal partners, and the disposition/acquisition transaction costs.

To overcome these practical difficulties in the direct investment mar-ket, a property derivatives strategy could be formulated to quickly execute

EXHIBIT 12.10 Quarterly Cash Flow for Short Position

Notional amount:	$ 10,000,000								
Margin	$ 300,000								
Fixed spread:	2.50%								
Term:	2 years		Starting 9/30/07 ending 6/30/09						

Quarter ending:	9/30/2007	12/31/2007	3/31/2008	6/30/2008	9/30/2008	12/31/2008	3/31/2009	6/30/2009
NPI Capital Return:	2.25%	1.86%	0.34%	-3.07%	-3.07%	-3.07%	-2.16%	-2.16%
Fixed Spread:	0.63%	0.63%	0.63%	0.63%	0.63%	0.63%	0.63%	0.63%

Short side cash flows (receives fixed spread, pays NPI Capital Return)

	9/30/2007	12/31/2007	3/31/2008	6/30/2008	9/30/2008	12/31/2008	3/31/2009	6/30/2009
Fixed spread:	$ 62,500	$ 62,500	$ 62,500	$ 62,500	$ 62,500	$ 62,500	$ 62,500	$ 62,500
NPI CR:	$ (225,000)	$ (186,000)	$ (34,000)	$ 307,167	$ 307,167	$ 307,167	$ 215,625	$ 215,625
Net cashflow:	$ (162,500)	$ (123,500)	$ 28,500	$ 369,667	$ 369,667	$ 369,667	$ 278,125	$ 278,125

Sum of past cashflows:	$ (257,500)
NPV of future cashflows:	$ 1,577,406

Reported NPI returns shaded; implied NPI returns unshaded.
Source: ING Clarion Research & Investment Strategy.

EXHIBIT 12.11 Hypothetical Fund Allocation

Sector	Current Allocation	Target Ranges
Apartment	22%	15%–20%
Industrial	18%	15%–20%
Office	31%	30%–40%
Retail	20%	20%–25%
Hotel	9%	5%–10%

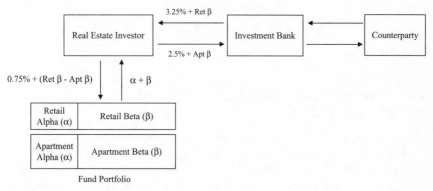

EXHIBIT 12.12 Total Return Swap, Apartment for Retail
Source: ING Clarion Research & Investment Strategy.

portfolio recommendations. A total return swap of the NPI Apartment subindex for the NPI Retail subindex would return the hypothetical portfolio weights to their target ranges (Exhibit 12.12).

Exhibit 12.13 shows the current pricing in the NPI swap market. Because the quoted rates for the swaps are negative, the Fund would pay 2.5% plus the apartment total return, represented in the exhibit as β (beta), while receiving 3.25% plus the retail total return.

The net effect would be for the investor to receive 0.75% plus the percentage difference between the retail total return and the apartment total

EXHIBIT 12.13 NPI Swap Market Pricing

Sector	Expiration	Midpoint
Apartment	Dec 09	−2.50%
Retail	Dec 09	−3.25%

Source: Merrill Lynch, July 2008.

EXHIBIT 12.14 Hypothetical Portfolio Rebalanced with Swap

Sector	Previous Allocation	Revised Allocation
Apartment	22%	20%
Industrial	18%	18%
Office	31%	31%
Retail	20%	20%
Hotel	9%	9%
Swap	—	2%

return. The hypothetical portfolio's allocation to the apartment sector would be reduced to 20% and the retail allocation would be increased to 22% (Exhibit 12.14).

Case Study 3: Hedging Land Using Residential Property Derivatives

Home price risk is often one of the largest risk components of a land investment or condominium development and should be hedged if possible. This is traditionally done through the use of option contracts on land. That strategy is preferred, but in the absence of option contracts, property derivatives may offer an alternate solution.

The value of residential land is derived from home prices. Real estate investors commonly value land using the residual valuation method. Under this method, the price a developer is willing to pay for land is equal to the selling price of the developed property minus the construction and financing costs associated with it (Exhibit 12.15).

The revenue of the project directly depends on home prices through the residual valuation methodology and, therefore, it is clear that home prices constitute a major risk factor for the profitability of the investment.

Home price risk can be mitigated through options. This risk is often mitigated by purchasing call options on land instead of purchasing the land outright. Exhibit 12.16(A) shows the payoff of a call option on land as it

EXHIBIT 12.15 Residual Valuation Calculation

(+) Avg. home price
(−) Direct construction cost
(−) Builder indirect costs
(−) Builder paid − Additional fees
(+) Amenity premiums
(=) Residual lot value

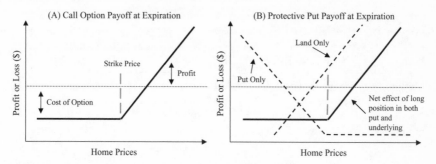

EXHIBIT 12.16 Option Strategies Payoff at Expiration
Source: ING Clarion Research & Investment Strategy and Smithson.

relates to home prices. If declining home prices drive down the value of the land, the holder of the call option can walk away from the deal, and his loss is limited to the cost of the option contract. If home (and land) prices increase, the holder of the call option can decide to exercise the contract, and a profit is made from the spread between the price agreed to in the option contract and the current market pricing.

This technique is effective at mitigating home price risk on land values as well as other site-specific variables such as zoning, environmental, entitlements, and so on. As long as options on a site are available, this strategy may be useful for land investment.

By using residential property derivatives, it may be possible to re-create the home price risk mitigation benefits of a call option on land. A protective put is an option strategy where an investor holds a long position in an underlying asset and purchases a put on the same asset to protect against price depreciation. This strategy affords an investor the same downside protection as the call option, while maintaining all of the upside. The payoff of this strategy is shown in Exhibit 12.16(B). The "Land Only" dotted line represents the revenue or profit on the land as a function of home prices. The "Put Only" dotted line represents the profit resulting from holding a put contract on a home price index. If home prices are below the strike price at the contract expiration, then the put contract will make a profit, offsetting the loss taken on the residual value of the land due to the fall in home prices. The net effect of the strategy has a payoff structure of the call option outlined above.

There are several steps that are involved in the execution of this strategy:

- *Identify opportunities where this strategy may be useful.* Because this strategy only hedges home price risk, land parcels that are fully entitled and ready to build are the ideal fit. Infill locations are preferred, because they minimize the basis risk of the index.

EXHIBIT 12.17   Residential Indexes

Feature	S&P Case-Shiller	RPX	Implications for Hedging Use
Methodology	Repeat sales regression methodology	$/sf average daily spot prices of 7-, 14-, or 28-day periods	RPX is more volatile due to index construction.
Frequency	Monthly	Daily	Derivative values fluctuate more with RPX.
Property type	Existing single-family homes	New and existing SFH, new and existing condos	Property type covered by index should match your land use.
Geography covered	Boston, Chicago, Denver, Las Vegas, Los Angeles, Miami, New York, San Diego, San Francisco, Washington, DC, and 10-city composite	New York, Los Angeles, Miami, Phoenix, and 25 MSA Composite	Geographies listed are available for derivatives trading.
Derivatives availability	Listed on Chicago Mercantile Exchange and through brokers: forward contracts, options on forwards	Available through interdealer brokers: OTC Swaps, forwards	S&P not available as a swap.

Source: ING Clarion Research & Investment Strategy, Standard & Poor's, and RadarLogic.com.

- *Select index/financial product to use for the hedge.* There are currently two residential housing indexes available as financial products: the Residential Property Index (RPX) and the S&P Case-Shiller Home Price Index (Exhibit 12.17). It is important to consider the characteristics of each index to minimize the basis risk of a hedge.
- *Observe pricing in the market for index futures.* An example of futures market pricing on the S&P/Case-Shiller index for the Los Angeles MSA is shown in Exhibit 12.18. The "Spot Index" column indicates the latest reported index value. In this case, it is the May 2008 value, which represents a trailing three-month average of real estate price movements ending three months prior (March 2008). The "Futures Settlements" columns indicate the futures market price for the index value in November of each future year for five years. For example,

EXHIBIT 12.18 S&P/Case-Shiller Futures Pricing

S&P/Case-Shiller	Spot Index Published May-08	Futures Settlements				
		1 Year Nov-08	2 Year Nov-09	3 Year Nov-10	4 Year Nov-11	5 Year Nov-12
Los Angeles	207.11	175.00	157.00	152.20	189.60	158.40
	Δ to Spot	−15.5%	−24.2%	−26.5%	−8.5%	−23.5%
	Annual HPA	−28.7%	−16.9%	−11.5%	−2.5%	−5.8%

Source: ING Clarion Research & Investment Strategy and Tradition Financial Services.

purchasing the "Nov-10" futures contract would cost $147 today, and at expiration would be worth the value of the November 2010 index level. Profit or loss is determined by the difference between the price paid and the final index level at expiration. The rows beneath the prices show the cumulative and annualized change from the Spot Index that each Futures Settlement price implies.

In a liquid and properly functioning futures market, these prices would accurately summarize market opinion of likely future price movements. A study by the Office of Federal Housing Enterprise Oversight (OFHEO) found that Case-Shiller futures prices on distant contracts (expiring in over six months) generally predict larger home price declines than ultimately occurred.[6]

■ *Calculate the cost of the hedge.* Purchasing options on the futures contracts limits the downside risk but carries a premium. This premium is determined by the difference between the spot index value and the strike price, the length of time until the option expires, and the volatility of the underlying index. The size of the option premium may make the hedging strategy unfeasible.

ADDITIONAL CONSIDERATIONS

In order to execute any of the aforementioned strategies, the mechanics of the process as well as the legal and accounting issues must be addressed. Consultation with legal and accounting professionals is necessary to fully evaluate

---

[6]Andrew Leventis, "Real Estate Futures Prices as Predictors of Price Trends," OFHEO Working Paper 08-01, January 2008, http://www.ofheo.gov/media/WorkingPapers/WorkingPaper081.pdf.

these considerations. Additional considerations concerning the practical execution of the strategies may include without limitation:

- Confirm that executing derivatives trades are legal and in compliance with corporate policy.
- Determine whether funds can execute derivates trades based on Investment Management Agreements. For example, by law some private equity real estate funds are defined as "pension fund advisors" and cannot trade derivatives. They may be able to buy bonds or structured notes instead.
- Determine how derivatives gains and losses are to be reported within a fund's structure. From preliminary analysis, we would report gains and losses from their derivatives positions below the Net Operating Income line as extraordinary income. Legal and accounting counsel should be engaged in order to determine the appropriate procedures.
- Enter into negotiated International Swaps and Derivatives Association (ISDA) agreements with investment banks, brokers, and dealers within the marketplace. In order to enter into a single trade with a broker, a fund could execute a contract that includes ISDA language which sets up the legal framework. The ISDA covers timeliness of cash flows, settlement, and what happens if one of the parties defaults on the contract. ISDA documents that are received from banks tend to favor the banks and may require negotiation in order to get the best terms. While permanent agreements are being negotiated, trades could be executed on an ad hoc basis.
- Determine appropriate level of employee resources to source, monitor, and execute derivatives strategies.

CHAPTER 13

Opportunities in Infrastructure Investment

David Lynn and Matson Holbrook
Summer 2008[1,2]

The infrastructure sector has become increasingly popular as an alternative investment in recent years. While countries such as Australia, Canada, and the United Kingdom have already established infrastructure platforms to facilitate private capital flows, investing in U.S. infrastructure remains relatively limited in scope. However, opportunities are becoming more abundant as public funding for maintaining, constructing, and repairing these assets today is in short supply. Population and economic growth will likely continue to overburden existing capacity, making the need for capital even more pressing. With characteristics, risks, and returns similar to those of investment real estate, we believe that infrastructure has the potential to attract a larger share of U.S. institutional investors' portfolios.

BACKGROUND

Infrastructure systems are key elements in the economic and social development of a community. These systems serve the public good by helping

---

[1]This paper was originally produced in summer 2008. The data, opinions, and forecasts have not been updated for book publication.

[2]A version of this chapter was published by the CCIM Institute in *Commercial Investment Real Estate* 28, no. 2 (March–April 2009): 39–41. Reprinted with permission of *Commercial Investment Real Estate*.

EXHIBIT 13.1   Infrastructure Investment Categories[a]

Transportation	Utilities	Communications	Social Facilities	Specialty
Toll roads	Gas	Cable and satellite networks	Health care	Forestry
Bridges	Electricity		Recreational	Car parks
Tunnels	Water treatment/ distribution	Transmission/ broadcast towers	Educational	Storage
Airports			Correctional	
Seaports	Renewable energy			
Rail networks				

[a]Ernst & Young, Overview, in *Investing in Global Infrastructure 2007: An Emerging Asset Class.* (2007), 5.
Source: ING Clarion Research & Investment Strategy.

to "sustain community life, safeguard the environment, protect community health, support the economy, and allow people and goods to move safely and efficiently."[3] Infrastructure investments can typically be divided into five categories: transportation, utilities, communications, social facilities, and specialty (Exhibit 13.1).

As evidenced by the numerous signs of distress that have materialized in recent years, the existing state of U.S. infrastructure is grim. Failures include the collapse of the I-35W bridge in Minneapolis and the steam pipe explosion in New York City in 2007, the levee breaches in New Orleans in 2005, and the power grid blackout in the Northeast in 2003.[4] Coupled with increasing usage and congestion across much of the infrastructure stock in the United States, we believe that these events underscore the need for improved maintenance and system upgrades.

Years of underinvestment and insufficient government funding have led to the deteriorated state of U.S. infrastructure, and we anticipate that population and economic growth will continue to overburden existing capacity. Government leaders, preoccupied with closing budget gaps and staying in office, have been reluctant to raise taxes or pursue alternative sources of

---

[3]American Public Works Association (APWA), "Infrastructure Facts: Facts about America's Public Infrastructure," http://www.apwa.net/Advocacy/Infrastructure/ (accessed April 17, 2008).

[4]Building America's Future, "Resources—U.S. Infrastructure Investment: America's Infrastructure Needs," http://investininfrastructure.org/resources/index.html (accessed April 17, 2008).

revenue to repair and maintain the various infrastructure categories. Consequently, repair and maintenance fees will be costly—the American Society of Civil Engineers estimated that $1.6 trillion would be needed to fund domestic infrastructure investment over the five-year period from 2006–2011.[5] Since public funding may not sufficiently cover current and future needs, private investment is viewed by both the public and private sectors as an increasingly viable option to fill the gap.

Opportunities

Institutional investors, including investment banks, private equity funds, infrastructure funds, insurance companies, and endowment funds have shown increased interest in infrastructure over the past several years. Not only has this interest been driven by the excess amounts of private capital in the marketplace, but also by the appealing characteristics of infrastructure as an investment. While the nature of the various infrastructure categories can be quite diverse, the performance attributes of the underlying assets share many similarities:[6]

- *Monopolistic* market positions are often held by infrastructure investors due to high initial fixed costs, resulting in substantial barriers to entry for potential competitors.
- *Stable and predictable* cash flows are only minimally impacted by changes in the overall economy, thereby reducing volatility; this bond-like quality is comparable to a fixed-income investment.
- Rent escalations are typically CPI-linked, acting as a *hedge against inflation.*
- The lifetime of infrastructure assets often spans decades, providing a *long-term* investment horizon that is appealing to many institutional investors, specifically pension funds, which need to match assets with liabilities.
- *Demand is somewhat inelastic,* as infrastructure assets, with little or no risk of technological obsolescence, provide essential services to consumers.
- A *low correlation* to equity and fixed-income securities benefits portfolio diversification.

---

[5]American Society of Civil Engineers, *2005 Report Card for America's Infrastructure*, 3. http://www.asce.org/reportcard/2005/index.cfm (accessed April 17, 2008).

[6]Mark Weisdorf, "Asset Class Advocate," *The 2008 PERE Special Report on Infrastructure* (March 2008): 8.

EXHIBIT 13.2 U.S. Transportation Infrastructure Transactions[a]

Asset	Cost	Year	Buyer	Description	Details
Chicago Skyway	$1.83 bln	2005	Macquarie/ Cintra	7.8-mile connector between the Indiana Tollway and the Dan Ryan Expressway in Chicago	99-year lease; buyer has right to all toll revenue
Indiana Tollway	$3.85 bln	2006	Macquarie/ Cintra	157-mile east-west portion of I-90 from Ohio border to Illinois border	75-year lease; buyer has right to all toll revenue

[a]Ernst & Young, Overview, in *Investing in Global Infrastructure 2007: An Emerging Asset Class.* (2007), 5
Source: ING Clarion Research & Investment Strategy.

Private equity investments in infrastructure are typically made in three ways. Privatization allows private investors to acquire public infrastructure assets or invest in state-owned companies. Public-private partnerships (PPP) enable private companies to build or operate new infrastructure developments or existing assets under concession agreements with the government. Finally, private-to-private transactions facilitate the transfer of interests between two private parties.[7] The PPP model has recently been the method of choice for private investors looking to add infrastructure assets to their portfolios.

The area of greatest infrastructure investment activity in the United States has involved the transportation sector (Exhibit 13.2). In both transactions listed next, a joint venture between Macquarie Infrastructure Group (Australia) and Cintra Concesiones de Infraestructuras de Transporte SA (Spain) purchased concession rights to the revenue generated by the toll operations of two roads. Under the agreements, Macquarie/Cintra is allowed to raise tolls by a fixed percentage above the higher of either gross domestic product (GDP) or the Consumer Price Index (CPI). In return, they are responsible for the upkeep and maintenance of the toll roads over the lifetime of the leases.

---

[7]Jonathan D. Miller, *Infrastructure 2007: A Global Perspective* (Washington, DC: Urban Land Institute, 2007), 55.

In addition to the previously mentioned transactions, PPPs have recently been used in 16 states to address 24 transportation projects.[8] Looking forward, numerous other projects are currently in discussion, including the privatizations of Chicago's Midway Airport and the Pennsylvania Turnpike.

RETURNS

What kind of returns can institutional investors expect when investing in infrastructure assets? The answer to this question typically depends on the stage of the developmental or operational life cycle of the asset. Existing, or mature, infrastructure assets can be considered similar to core real estate assets in that they have long lease terms and stable cash flows. Alternatively, investments in infrastructure development are comparable to opportunistic real estate on the risk-return spectrum. Falling between these two categories is a third subset that focuses on operational enhancements of existing assets. While investments in mature infrastructure assets can offer annualized returns in the mid to high single digits, investments in infrastructure development can produce annualized gains in the high teens or above in some cases.[9]

RISKS

Although there are numerous benefits associated with infrastructure, institutional investors should be aware of the inherent risks associated with the sector. Proper evaluation of risk is particularly important when investing as a PPP, especially in relation to the following key elements:[10]

- *Long-term uncertainty.* With concession contracts stretching for as long as 99 years, the accuracy of forecasting decreases as political, economic, and other future events deviate from initial assumptions.
- *Revenue risk.* Revenues could fall short of projections if public demand and willingness to pay do not meet expectations.

---

[8]Ibid., 53.
[9]Ibid.
[10]Ernst & Young, Overview, in *Investing in Global Infrastructure 2007: An Emerging Asset Class,* (2007), 9–10.

- *Operational risk*. It is essential that the private partner in a PPP has the requisite competence, experience, resources, and skills to effectively operate the infrastructure asset.
- *Political risk*. Governments, in some cases, may not hold up their end of the contract for reasons that range from corruption to a change in administrations or internal political pressures.
- *Environmental risk*. Environmental reviews and approvals can increase the project budget while delaying start dates for new developments; significant capital expenditures may be incurred if unforeseen environmental hazards arise.
- *Community acceptance risk*. High usage fees for infrastructure assets may generate community opposition, especially if the operator's profits are perceived to be excessive.
- *Refinancing risk*. As many infrastructure projects are leveraged in excess of 50 percent, refinancing at higher interest rates could increase risk exposure.

EXPANDING INVESTMENT UNIVERSE

Despite the risks associated with infrastructure as a real estate sector, the global infrastructure investment universe is expanding. In addition to the reasons cited above, this expansion is being driven by global economic macro trends. These trends include legislation encouraging private participation in infrastructure, the extension of successful private equity and real estate funds into alternative investments and the substitution of infrastructure for long-term bonds by pension funds.

The growth in number of global infrastructure funds illustrates this expansion. Between early 2006 and mid-2007, 72 new infrastructure funds were launched; they raised an estimated $120 billion (with an additional $40 billion raised by existing funds during that period).[11] Approximately half of these new funds followed the private equity model by raising capital from large institutional investors.[12] The remaining funds were raised from other sources including insurance companies or pension funds investing their own capital, IPOs on major stock exchanges or specialist teams within larger commercial banks, asset management companies or family offices.[13]

---

[11] Ryan J. Orr, "Global Infrastructure Report 2007: The Rise of Infra Funds," *Project Finance International* (June 2007): 2.

[12] Ibid, 3.

[13] Ibid.

Fifty-six of the 72 funds focus on four main world regions—the United States, Europe, MENA (Middle East and Northern Africa) countries, and India—while 18 of the 20 largest funds focus primarily on the U.S. or European markets.[14]

Additionally, based on global GDP as well as trends in government and private spending on infrastructure, it is estimated that the potential for new private investment in infrastructure ranges from $240 billion to $360 billion annually worldwide.[15] If the approximate $600 million in private-to-private utilities and telecom transactions from 2006 is included, the annual private infrastructure investment universe could approach $1 trillion globally.[16]

CONCLUSION

What are the implications for investors? The United States, unlike other countries with developed infrastructure investment platforms, is still considered an emerging market, where recent infrastructure failures have resulted from a combination of increased infrastructure usage and lack of funding. Foreign companies with long-term track records have begun to take advantage of existing opportunities. We anticipate that the need for private funding to assist federal, state, and local governments in meeting the infrastructure demands of the expanding U.S. population base should continue to increase. With characteristics, risks, and returns similar to those of institutional real estate, we believe that infrastructure should be considered as an increasingly attractive option for investors' portfolios.

---

[14] Ibid.

[15] This estimate is based on global GDP of $48 trillion, governments spending on average 5%, or $2.4 trillion, of GDP on infrastructure, and private investment equaling 10% to 15% of government spending.

[16] Ernst & Young, 8.

Typical Land Development
Pro Forma Analysis—
Three Scenarios

EXHIBIT A.1 Base Case Scenario

Plans Offered	Sq. Ft.	Unit Mix	Total Revenue	Price Per Unit	Price/Sq. Ft.
Plan 1	1,952	45	13,725,000	305,000	156.25
Plan 2	2,147	45	14,400,000	320,000	149.05
Plan 3	2,376	45	15,075,000	335,000	140.99
Plan 4	0	0	0	0	0.00
Plan 5	0	0	0	0	0.00
Plan 6	0	0	0	0	0.00
Plan 7	0	0	0	0	0.00
Plan 8	0	0	0	0	0.00
Plan 9	0	0	0	0	0.00
Plan 10	0	0	0	0	0.00
Plan 11	0	0	0	0	0.00
Plan 12	0	0	0	0	0.00
Plan 13	0	0	0	0	0.00
Plan 14	0	0	0	0	0.00
Total:	291,375	135	43,200,000	NA	NA

	Percent of Revenue	Total Expense	Cost Per Unit	Cost/Sq. Ft.
Other Revenue:				
Lot Premiums		540,000	4,000	1.85
Net of Cost Upgrades/Options		518,400	3,840	1.78
TOTAL REVENUE		44,258,400	327,840	151.89

(*continued*)

EXHIBIT A.1 (*Continued*)

	Percent of Revenue	Total Expense	Cost Per Unit	Cost/ Sq. Ft.
Less Development Costs:				
Land Value at Sale	14.91%	6,600,000	48,889	22.65
Land Development	9.62%	4,256,884	31,532	14.61
Fees, Permits, and Bonds	5.35%	2,368,755	17,546	8.13
Land Development Contingency	1.09%	482,636	3,575	1.66
Legal, Broker, Misc.	0.95%	422,600	3,130	1.45
TOTAL LOT COSTS	31.93%	14,130,875	104,673	48.50
Less House Costs:				
Direct Construction Costs	34.12%	15,103,138	111,875	51.83
Direct Construction Contingency	1.02%	453,094	3,356	1.56
Indirect Costs—Capitalized	2.18%	964,500	7,144	3.31
Indirect Expenses	1.58%	697,500	5,167	2.39
Customer Service	0.37%	162,000	1,200	0.56
TOTAL HOUSE COSTS	39.27%	17,380,232	128,742	59.65
TOTAL COSTS	71.20%	31,511,106	233,416	108.15
HOUSING GROSS MARGIN	**28.80%**	12,747,294	94,424	43.75
OTHER COSTS				
Sales Concessions & O/S Broker	1.10%	486,000	3,600	
Closing Costs	0.03%	13,500	100	
Marketing Costs—Cap	0.61%	270,000	2,000	
Marketing Expense	1.27%	560,000	4,148	
Inside Commission	0.98%	432,000	3,200	
HOA/Soft Costs	0.00%	—	—	
Overhead	2.44%	1,080,000	8,000	
Insurance	2.54%	1,123,200	8,320	
Loan Fees	0.88%	390,000	2,889	
Interest	6.86%	3,037,508	22,500	
TOTAL OTHER COSTS	16.70%	7,392,208	54,757	
Net Profit	**12.10%**	5,355,086	39,667	

Source: ING Clarion Research & Investment Strategy.

EXHIBIT A.2 20% Reduction in Home Prices/No Change in Land Price

Plans Offered	Sq. Ft.	Unit Mix	Total Revenue	Price Per Unit	Price/ Sq. Ft.	
Plan 1	1,952	45	10,980,000	244,000	125.00	20%
Plan 2	2,147	45	11,520,000	256,000	119.24	Reduction
Plan 3	2,376	45	12,060,000	268,000	112.79	in Prices
Plan 4	0	0	0	0	0.00	
Plan 5	0	0	0	0	0.00	
Plan 6	0	0	0	0	0.00	
Plan 7	0	0	0	0	0.00	
Plan 8	0	0	0	0	0.00	
Plan 9	0	0	0	0	0.00	
Plan 10	0	0	0	0	0.00	
Plan 11	0	0	0	0	0.00	
Plan 12	0	0	0	0	0.00	
Plan 13	0	0	0	0	0.00	
Plan 14	0	0	0	0	0.00	
Total:	291,375	135	34,560,000	NA	NA	

	Percent of Revenue	Total Expense	Cost Per Unit	Cost/ Sq. Ft.	
Other Revenue:					
Lot Premiums		540,000	4,000	1.85	
Net of Cost Upgrades/ Options		414,720	3,072	1.42	
TOTAL REVENUE		35,514,720	263,072	121.89	
Less Development Costs:					
Land Value at Sale	18.58%	6,600,000	48,889	22.65	Land Value
Land Development	11.99%	4,256,884	31,532	14.61	Unchanged
Fees, Permits, and Bonds	6.67%	2,368,755	17,546	8.13	from Base
Land Development Contingency	1.36%	482,636	3,575	1.66	Case
Legal, Broker, Misc.	1.19%	422,600	3,130	1.45	
TOTAL LOT COSTS	39.79%	14,130,875	104,673	48.50	

(continued)

EXHIBIT A.2 *(Continued)*

	Percent of Revenue	Total Expense	Cost Per Unit	Cost/ Sq. Ft.
Less House Costs:				
Direct Construction Costs	42.53%	15,103,138	111,875	51.83
Direct Construction Contingency	1.28%	453,094	3,356	1.56
Indirect Costs—Capitalized	2.72%	964,500	7,144	3.31
Indirect Expenses	1.96%	697,500	5,167	2.39
Customer Service	0.46%	162,000	1,200	0.56
TOTAL HOUSE COSTS	48.94%	17,380,232	128,742	59.65
TOTAL COSTS	88.73%	31,511,106	233,416	108.15
HOUSING GROSS MARGIN	**11.27%**	4,003,614	29,656	13.74
OTHER COSTS				
Sales Concessions & O/S Broker	1.25%	442,800	3,280	
Closing Costs	0.04%	13,500	100	
Marketing Costs—Cap	0.76%	270,000	2,000	
Marketing Expense	1.58%	560,000	4,148	
Inside Commission	0.97%	345,600	2,560	
HOA/Soft Costs	0.00%	-	-	
Overhead	2.43%	864,000	6,400	
Insurance	2.53%	898,560	6,656	
Loan Fees	1.10%	390,000	2,889	
Interest	14.67%	5,211,383	38,603	
TOTAL OTHER COSTS	25.33%	8,995,843	66,636	
Net Profit	**-14.06%**	(4,992,230)	(36,979)	

Net Loss vs. 12.1% Profit in Base Case

Source: ING Clarion Research & Investment Strategy.

EXHIBIT A.3 20% Reduction in Home Prices/Reduction in Land Price to Maintain Base Case Return

Plans Offered	Sq. Ft.	Unit Mix	Total Revenue	Price Per Unit	Price/ Sq. Ft.	
Plan 1	1,952	45	10,980,000	244,000	125.00	20%
Plan 2	2,147	45	11,520,000	256,000	119.24	Reduction
Plan 3	2,376	45	12,060,000	268,000	112.79	in prices
Plan 4	0	0	0	0	0.00	
Plan 5	0	0	0	0	0.00	
Plan 6	0	0	0	0	0.00	
Plan 7	0	0	0	0	0.00	
Plan 8	0	0	0	0	0.00	
Plan 9	0	0	0	0	0.00	
Plan 10	0	0	0	0	0.00	
Plan 11	0	0	0	0	0.00	
Plan 12	0	0	0	0	0.00	
Plan 13	0	0	0	0	0.00	
Plan 14	0	0	0	0	0.00	
Total:	291,375	135	34,560,000	NA	NA	

	Percent of Revenue	Total Expense	Cost Per Unit	Cost/ Sq. Ft.	
Other Revenue:					
Lot Premiums		540,000	4,000	1.85	
Net of Cost Upgrades/ Options		414,720	3,072	1.42	
TOTAL REVENUE		35,514,720	263,072	121.89	
Less Development Costs:					
Land Value at Sale	2.37%	840,722	6,228	2.89	Land Value
Land Development	11.99%	4,256,884	31,532	14.61	Reduced
Fees, Permits, and Bonds	6.67%	2,368,755	17,546	8.13	by 87%
Land Development Contingency	1.36%	482,636	3,575	1.66	
Legal, Broker, Misc.	0.53%	186,470	1,381	0.64	
TOTAL LOT COSTS	22.91%	8,135,466	60,263	27.92	

(continued)

EXHIBIT A.3 (*Continued*)

	Percent of Revenue	Total Expense	Cost Per Unit	Cost/ Sq. Ft.
Less House Costs:				
Direct Construction Costs	42.53%	15,103,138	111,875	51.83
Direct Construction Contingency	1.28%	453,094	3,356	1.56
Indirect Costs—Capitalized	2.72%	964,500	7,144	3.31
Indirect Expenses	1.96%	697,500	5,167	2.39
Customer Service	0.46%	162,000	1,200	0.56
TOTAL HOUSE COSTS	48.94%	17,380,232	128,742	59.65
TOTAL COSTS	71.85%	25,515,698	189,005	87.57
HOUSING GROSS MARGIN	28.15%	9,999,022	74,067	34.32
OTHER COSTS				
Sales Concessions & O/S Broker	1.25%	442,800	3,280	
Closing Costs	0.04%	13,500	100	
Marketing Costs—Cap	0.76%	270,000	2,000	
Marketing Expense	1.58%	560,000	4,148	
Inside Commission	0.97%	345,600	2,560	
HOA/Soft costs	0.00%	—	—	
Overhead	2.43%	864,000	6,400	
Insurance	2.53%	898,560	6,656	
Loan Fees	1.10%	390,000	2,889	
Interest	5.40%	1,917,281	14,202	
TOTAL OTHER COSTS	16.05%	5,701,741	42,235	
Net Profit	12.10%	4,297,281	31,832	

Same Profit as Base Case

Source: ING Clarion Research & Investment Strategy.

U.S. Hotel Chain Scales

EXHIBIT B.1 U.S. Hotel Chain Sales

Luxury	Upper Upscale	Upscale	Midscale W/O F&B	Midscale W/F&B	Economy	
Colony	Affinia Hospitality	Adam's Mark	Amerihost	Best Western	1st Interstate Inn	Microtel Inn
Conrad	Concorde Hotels	Aloft	Americinn	Clarion	Admiral Benbow	Motel 6
Fairmont Hotel	Doral	Amerisuites	Baymont Inns & Suites	Doubletree Club	America's Best Inns	National 9
Four Seasons	Doubletree Hotels	Aston	Bradford Homesuites	Golden Tulip	America's Best Suites	Park Inn
Hotel Sofitel	Embassy Suites	Ayres	Cabot Lodge	Harvey Hotel	America's Best Value	Passport Inn
Inter-Continental	Embassy Vacation Resorts	Cambria Suites	Candlewood Hotel	Hawthorn Inn & Suites	Budget Host Inn	Peartree Inn
Loews	Gaylord Entertainment	Chase Suites	Clubhouse Inns of America	Holiday Inn	Country Hearth Inn	Red Carpet Inn
Luxury Collection	Helmsley Hotel	Club Med	Comfort Inn	Holiday Inn Select	Crestwood Suites	Red Roof Inn
Mandarin Oriental	Hilton Hotels	Coast Hotels USA	Comfort Suites	Howard Johnson	Cross Country Inn	Roadstar Inn
Pan Pacific	Hilton Gaming	Courtyard	Country Inn & Suites	Jolly Hotels	Crossland Suites	Rodeway Inn
Preferred	Hyatt	Hilton Garden Inn	Drury Inn	Little America	Days Inn	Savannah Suites

The Peninsula Group	Jury's Hotels	Crowne Plaza	Drury Lodge	Marc	Downtowner Motor Inn	Scottish Inn
Prince Hotels	Langham Hotels	Four Points	Drury Plaza Hotel	Ohana Hotels	E-Z 8	Select Inn
St. Regis	Le Meridien	Harrah's	Extended Stay Deluxe	Park Plaza	Econo Lodge	Select Suites
Regent Hotels	Marriott	Hawthorn Suites	Fairfield Inn	Quality	Inns of America	Shoney's Inn
Ritz-Carlton	Marriott International	Hawthorn Suites Ltd	Hampton Inn	Quality Inn Suites	Exel Inn	Studio 6
Star Hotels	Marriott Conf. Center	Homewood Suites	Hampton Inn & Suites	Ramada	Extended Stay America	Studio Plus
W Hotels	Millennium Hotels	Hotel Indigo	Heartland Inn	Ramada Plaza	Family Inns of America	Suburban Extended Stay Hotels
	New Otani Hotels	Hotel Novotel	Holiday Inn Express	Red Lion	Good Nite Inn	Sun Suites Hotels
	Nikko	Hyatt Place	Innsuites Hotels	Romantik Hotel Westmark	Great Western Guesthouse Inns	Super 8
	Omni	Hyatt Summerfield Suites	La Quinta Inns			Thift Lodge
	Renaissance	Outrigger	La Quinta Inns & Suites	Sunspree Resorts	Homegate	Travelodge
	Sheraton Hotel	Radisson	Lees Inn Of America	Westcoast	Homestead Studio Suites	Vagabond

(Continued)

EXHIBIT B.1 (*Continued*)

Luxury	Upper Upscale	Upscale	Midscale W/O F&B	Midscale W/ F&B	Economy
	Sonesta Hotel	Residence Inn	Mainstay Suites	Wyndham Garden Hotel	Howard Johnson Exp. Inn
	Swissotel	Resortquest Hawaii	Phoenix Inn		Wandlyn Inn Innkeeper
	Westin	Sierra Suites	Ramada Limited		Inncall
		Springhill Suites	Shilo Inn		Intown Suites
		Staybridge Suites	Signature Inns		Jameson Inn
		Woodfield Suites	Silver Cloud		Key West Inn
		Woodfin Suites	Sleep Inn		Knights Inn
		Wyndham Hotels	Townplace Suites		Lexington Hotel Suites
		Xanterra Parks & Resorts	Wellesley Inn		Master Hosts Inn
			Wellesley Suites		Masters Inn
			Wingate Inn		Mcintosh Motor Inn

Source: ING Clarion Research & Investment Strategy and Smith Travel Research, 2007.

Modern Portfolio Theory in Real Estate Portfolio Analytics

Modern Portfolio Theory (MPT) has increasingly gained general acceptance as a preferred method for intelligently diversifying pools of real estate assets. Long and widely used in the creation of portfolios in and across the public markets, MPT did not find a room in private real estate investment until the late 1990s, once the NCRIEF Property Index (NPI) had been available for almost 20 years and covered two complete economic cycles. Since then, real estate investors have recognized the role of cycles in the performance of individual assets and portfolios of assets, and as a result, MPT has become a well-accepted framework to construct or rebalance real estate portfolios.

MPT assumes investors are risk-averse, meaning that given two assets that offer the same expected return, investors will prefer the less risky one. Thus, an investor will take on increased risk only if compensated by higher expected returns. It is possible to create a real estate portfolio that will generate a desired return at the least possible risk (Exhibit C.1). The "secret" is to understand each market's cycle and to combine offsetting markets into a "smart" portfolio that takes advantage of the differing behaviors, or diversification. Offsetting cycles are identified using correlations (the statistic that measures how coincidental—or not—two return series are).

The steps to conduct the portfolio analysis using MPT are:

1. Define relevant investment universe (quadrants, regions, sectors, markets, etc.).
2. Calculate each investment option's:
   - Expected return
   - Standard deviation
   - Cross-correlations

Combine 3 Assets (1, 2, and 3) into Portfolios
Portfolio Return = Weighted Sum of Each Asset's Return
Portfolio Risk < Weighted Sum of Each Asset's Risk

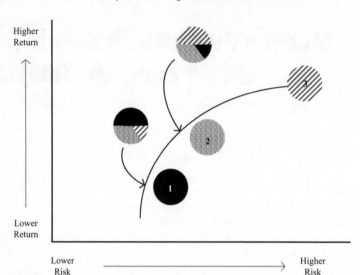

EXHIBIT C.1 Modern Portfolio Theory Overview
Source: ING Clarion Research & Investment Strategy.

3. Calculate the efficient frontier.
4. Locate an existing portfolio in risk/return space.
5. Evaluate strategy choices and implement most useful strategies.

The major limitation of applying MPT in private real estate portfolios is that it uses the returns of average assets in a market (e.g., quadrant, sector, region, or metro, etc.), not actual asset level returns. Actual returns on individual assets in a market may differ (for better or for worse) based on the occupancy, rollover schedule, quality of the tenants, location, etc. However, a large portion of an asset's performance is influenced by the market in which the building is located because of market pressures on rents, occupancy, and pricing ("a rising tide lifts all boats"). This way, the real estate cycles can be observed.

Commercial Real Estate Indexes

EXHIBIT D.1 Commerical Real Estate Indexes

Index	Primary Data Source	Type	Methodology	Frequency	Subindexes	Comments
NPI	NCREIF Members	Appraisal	Simple Δ psf	Quarterly	National, by Property Type, by region	The NPI has exhibited less volatility over time than transaction-based indexes.
S&P/GRA Commercial Real Estate Indices (SPCREX)	Multiple public sources; no primary data collection	Transaction	Simple 3-month moving average Δ psf	Monthly	10 indexes (national, regional, and by property type)	The Chicago Mercantile Exchange lists the index.
Moody's/REAL Commercial Property Price Indices (CPPI)	Transactions > $2.5 million (captured by Real Capital Analytics)	Transaction	Repeat-Sales Regression	Monthly, Quarterly, and Annual	29 indexes (by property type and composite) at the national, regional, and MSA levels	The repeat sales methodology is widely accepted in the residential market, and has much theoretical appeal.

Real Estate Property Index (REXX)	Cushman & Wakefield and Newmark/Knight Frank	Inferred	Δ Rent Model (utilizes current/historical real estate market and macroeconomic data)	Quarterly	16 office sector indexes at the national and MSA levels	REXX also tracks rent data, provided by Cushman Wakefield, Newmark/Knight Frank, and CBRE/Torto Wheaton in a number of key U.S. office markets.
HQuant Lodging Index (HLI)	Smith Travel Research	ADR	ADR	Daily	National, Regional, top 25 markets	Hotels only

Source: Morgan Stanley and ING Clarion Research & Strategy.

Example NPI Forecast Methodology

This model[1] takes advantage of the lag effect of the NPI in predicting the index, while incorporating forward-looking expectations about the underlying property market:

$$NPI_t = \alpha + \beta * NPI_{t-1} + \gamma * NPI_{t-2} + \delta \, TBI_t$$

NPI_t = NPI total return at time t

TBI_t = TBI total return at time t

Assumption:

TBI is used as a proxy for the underlying market. Forward looking expectations for underlying market are derived from our proprietary cap rate shift model.

---

[1] J. Y. Lim and Y. Zhang, A Study on Real Estate Derivatives, unpublished master's thesis, Massachusetts Institute of Technology, 2006.

Selected Bibliography

Admati, A., and M. Perry. 1987. Strategic Delay in Bargaining. *Review of Economic Studies* 54: 345–364.

American Public Works Association. 2008. "Infrastructure Facts: Facts about America's Public Infrastructure."

American Seniors Housing Association (ASHA). 2007. "ASHA 2007 survey: Largest 50 U.S. Managers/Largest 50 U.S. Owners."

American Seniors Housing Association (ASHA). 2007. *"The State of Seniors Housing."*

Ashar, A. 2004. "Long Term Development Trends of U.S. Ports." Transportation Research Board (December).

Ball, M., C., Lizieri, and B. MacGregor. 1998. *The Economics of Commercial Property Markets.* New York: Routledge.

Building Owners and Managers Association (BOMA) International. 2003. *Developing, Leasing and Managing Healthcare Real Estate.*

Davis, Morris A., and Michael G. Palumbo. 2007. "The Price of Residential Land in Large U.S. Cities." *Journal of Urban Economics* 63, no. 1 (February): 352–384.

Ernst & Young. 2007 "Overview." In *Investing in Global Infrastructure 2007: An Emerging Asset Class.*

Ernst & Young. 2008. *The 2008 U.S. Lodging Report.*

Ernst & Young. 2008. *Hospitality Top 10 Thoughts for 2008.*

Esaki, H., and J. Kotowsky. 2007. *Commercial Property Return Indices: Choosing from the Menu.* New York: Morgan Stanley Fixed Income Research (September).

Fisher, J., D. Gatzlaff, D. Geltner, and D. Haurin. 2003. "Controlling for the Impact of Variable Liquidity in Commercial Real Estate Price Indices." *Real Estate Economics* 31, no. 2: 245–267.

Geltner, D., and J. Fisher. 2007. "Pricing and Index Considerations in Commercial Real Estate Derivatives." *Journal of Portfolio Management*, Special Real Estate Issue, 99–118.

Gimmy, Arthur E., Susan B., Brecht, & Clifford J. Dowd. 2003. *Senior Housing, Looking Toward the Third Millennium.* Chicago: Appraisal Institute.

"Global Logistics: With West Coast Port Congestion Gone for Now, Many Shippers Continue to Migrate to East Coast Ports." 2008. *Supply Chain Logistics* (March 25).

Hull, John C. 2006. *Options, Futures and Other Derivatives.* Upper Saddle River, NJ: Prentice Hall.

Lecomte, Patrick. 2007. "Beyond Index-Based Hedging: Can Real Estate Trigger a New Breed of Derivatives Market?" *Journal of Real Estate Portfolio Management* 13, no. 4: 345–378.

Leventis, A. 2008. "Real Estate Futures Prices as Predictors of Price Trends." OFHEO Working Paper 08-01.

Lim, J. Y., and Y. Zhang. 2006. A Study on Real Estate Derivatives. Unpublished master's thesis, Massachusetts Institute of Technology.

Maekawa, S. 2008. Bargaining Model in the Property Market with Outside Option. Unpublished manuscript, Korea Real Estate Analyst Association.

Mayer, Christopher J. and C. Tsuriel Somerville. n.d. "Land Use Regulation and New Construction." *Regional and Urban Economics* 30, no. 6: 639–662.

Miller, Jonathan D. 2007. *Infrastructure 2007: A Global Perspective*. Washington, DC: Urban Land Institute.

Muthoo, A. 1999. *Bargaining Theory with Applications*. Cambridge: Cambridge University Press.

National Investment Center for the Seniors Housing & Care Industries. 2001. *The Case for Investing in Senior Housing and Long Term Care Properties*.

Naylor, S., and A. Mansour. 2007. *U.S. Private Equity Real Estate Derivatives: Is Now the Time?* San Francisco: RREEF Research (December).

Nelson, Arthur C. 2004. "Toward a New Metropolis: The Opportunity to Rebuild America." Brookings Institute (December).

Orr, Ryan J. 2007. "Global Infrastructure Report 2007: The Rise of Infra Funds." *Project Finance International* (June).

Osborne, M. J., and A. Rubinstein. 1990. *Bargaining and Markets*. New York: Academic Press.

Peiser, Richard B., and Anne B. Frej. 2004. *Professional Real Estate Development: The ULI Guide to the Business*, 2nd ed. Washington, DC: Urban Land Institute.

Porter, M. E. 1979. "How Competitive Forces Shape Strategy." *Harvard Business Review* 57, no. 2 (March–April): 135–145.

Shleifer, A. and R. Vishny. 1992. "Liquidation Values and Debt Capacity: A Market Equilibrium Approach." *Journal of Finance* 47, no. 4: 1343–1366.

Smithson, C. W. 1998. *Managing Financial Risk: A Guide to Derivative Products, Financial Engineering, and Value Maximization*. New York: McGraw-Hill.

United Nations Department of Economic and Social Affairs. 2006. *World Urbanization Prospects: The 2005 Revisions* (October).

Urban Land Institute (ULI). 2004. *Professional Real Estate Development: The ULI Guide to the Business*. Washington, DC.

Index